EARLY
PERENNIALS

Volume 1

THE RANDOM HOUSE BOOK OF
EARLY
PERENNIALS

ROGER PHILLIPS & MARTYN RIX

Assisted by Peter Barnes James Compton & Alison Rix
Layout Jill Bryan & Gill Stokoe

Random House New York

Acknowledgements

We would like to thank James Compton for his help with the *Labiatae* and *Kniphofia*, Peter Barnes for the ferns, Brian Mathew for photographs of *Iris* and *Acanthus*, Martin Gardiner for the photographs taken in Chile, and Jacqui Hurst for help with the studio photographs.

Most of the specimens photographed in the studio came from the following gardens, and we should like to acknowledge the help we had from them, and from their staff:

The Crown Estate Commissioners at the Savill Gardens, Windsor Great Park; The Royal Botanic Garden, Edinburgh; The Royal Botanic Gardens, Kew; The Royal Horticultural Society's Garden, Wisley; University Botanic Garden, Cambridge; The Chelsea Physic Garden; Eccleston Square, London SW1; Washfield Nurseries, Hawkhurst, Sussex; Beth Chatto Gardens, Elmstead Market, Essex; Middelton House, Enfield, Middlesex; David Austin Hardy Plants; Kelways, Langport, Somerset; Green Farm Plants, Bentley, Hants; Goldbrook Plants, Hoxne, Suffolk; Hopleys Plants, Much Hadham, Herts.; Sandling Park, Hythe, Kent.

We would also like to thank the following for their help, encouragement, and for growing the perennials we photographed: Crynan Alexander, John D'Arcy, Claire and David Austin, Bill Baker, David Barker, Igor Belolipov, Alan Bloom, John Bond, Sandra Bond, Roger Bowden, Chris Brickell, Patty Carr, Beth Chatto, Duncan Donald, John Drake, Alec Duguid, Pamela Egremont, Jack Elliott, George Fuller, Martin Furness, Jim Gardiner, Martin Gardiner, Geoffrey and Kathleen Goatcher, François Goffinet, Tony Hall, Brian Halliwell, Carolyn and Alan Hardy, Harry Hay, Diana Hewitt, Nigel Holman, Tinge Horsfall, Christopher Lloyd, John Lloyd, David McClintock, Keith MacDevette, Deborah Maclean, John and Marisa Main, Brian Mathew, Philip McMillan Browse, Michael Metianu, Bob Mitchell, Shirley Moorhead, Mikinori Ogisu, Andrew Paterson, Roger Poulett, Charles and Brigid Quest-Ritson, Richard Rix, Ted Rix, Tony Schilling, Bill Smalls, Gordon Smith, Geff Stebbings, Elizabeth Strangman, Greta Sturdza, Harriot Tennant, Ann Thatcher, Piers Trehane, Rosemary Verey, Peter Yeo.

We would also like to thank Brent Elliott and the staff of the Lindley Library for all their help and patience during the preparation of the text.

Published in the United States by Random House, Inc., New York
Originally published in Great Britain by Pan Books, a subsidiary of
Macmillan Publishers Ltd., London.
9 8 7 6 5 4 3 2
Text © 1991 by Roger Phillips and Martyn Rix
Illustrations © 1991 by Roger Phillips and Martyn Rix

Library of Congress Cataloging-in-Publication data
Phillips, Roger, 1932–
    The Random House book of perennials / Roger Phillips and Martyn
Rix. – 1st ed.
        p.   cm. – (The Pan garden plants series)
    Includes index.
    Contents: v. 1. Early perennials – v. 2. Late perennials.
    ISBN 0–679–73797–9 (v.1). – ISBN 0–679–73798–7 (v. 2)
    1. Perennials.   2. Perennials – Pictorial works.   I. Rix, Martyn.
II. Title. III. Series.
SB434.P5   1991
635.9'32—dc20

First U.S. edition
Manufactured in Singapore

91–18246

Contents

Candelabra primulas and *Iris laevigata* at Trebah, Cornwall

Introduction

In this book we illustrate over two thousand, five hundred herbaceous perennials; only a small sample of the many thousands grown in gardens, but sufficient, we hope, to show enough of those commonly cultivated, and a selection of rarities, to satisfy the beginner and excite the specialist. We have concentrated on plants which are hardy enough to tolerate at least −5°C of frost, and remain outside during the winter. We have not covered alpine and rock garden plants, nor desert plants and succulents, nor herbaceous perennials which require protection from frost, nor annuals and biennials. These will be the subjects of later volumes in this series.

The Photographs

When shooting flowers in the garden or in the field, it is preferable to work from a tripod so that you can take advantage of the opportunity to use a slow shutter speed and thus a smaller aperture, giving a greater depth of field. In practice the best speed to use is normally 1/15 sec., although if there is a strong wind you may have to go up to 1/30th or in extremes 1/60th.

The studio shots are taken on a Bronica 120, with a normal lens, with two Bowens quad units as a light source. The field shots are taken with a Nikon FM. The film in both cases is Ektachrome 64, that used for the field shots being pushed one stop in development.

The Order

The plants are arranged in four groups by flowering time; spring, early summer, mid-summer, and late summer and autumn. Within these seasons the plants are arranged by family in a botanical order, beginning with the buttercup family (*Ranunculaceae*), and ending with grasses and ferns. Where one or two species in a genus flower at a different season from the majority of the genus, they are put with their families, though out of season, so *Iris unguicularis* is put with the rest of the irises, though it flowers in early spring. Where there are distinct groups

in a genus flowering at different seasons, as in *Anemone*, the genus appears in two separate groups. The text gives the months of flowering in the wild, as the months of flowering in gardens differ greatly in different parts of the world. The text is arranged in alphabetical order on the page.

We have chosen a traditional family order, following P. H. Davis and J. Cullen, *The Identification of Flowering Plant Families*. This is roughly similar to the order found in Clapham, Tutin and Warburg, *Flora of the British Isles*, and P. A. Munz, *A California Flora*, and differs radically from the modified system of Engler and Prantl used in the *European Garden Flora*.

The Names

The plants are called by their Latin scientific names, and English names are used for only a few familiar plants. Taking *Primula florindae* Kingdon-Ward 'Rubra' (*Primulaceae*) as an example, the scientific name of a plant is made up as follows. The first name is that of the genus, i.e. *Primula*. This is followed by the specific name which is often descriptive, or refers to the plant's habitat or collector, i.e. *florindae*, which refers to Florinda, the first wife of the plant's discoverer and collector, Frank Kingdon-Ward. (His second wife, Jean, *née* Macklin, is remembered in *Lilium*

James Compton and John D'Arcy on Carlyle's Hoek, NE Cape Province

macklinae.) The specific name is followed by the name of the author of the species, called the authority, in this case also Kingdon-Ward. The authority is usually abbreviated: the common authority, L., refers to Linnaeus, whose *Species Plantarum* (1753) is used as the starting point of scientific naming. A garden plant can also have a cultivar name, which refers to a particular variety of the species, usually a clone, but also, as here, a colour variant which is reproduced by seed. The cultivar name is indicated by single inverted commas. 'Rubra', in this case, means red. More modern cultivar names must be in a modern language, not Latin, e.g. 'Festive Skirt' or 'Gei-sho-ui', both names of Irises. The name is often followed by the name of the family, in Latin, usually ending in -*ae*. Throughout this scheme, the Latin names are put in italics, the English or cultivar names in Roman.

The names used have mostly followed those found in Piers Trehane's *Index Hortensis Volume 1: Perennials*, an excellent and convenient source of the names of all perennials, including bulbs and alpines, which also contains, in its introduction, further details about plant naming. In some cases, familiar large genera, which have been split in the *Index*, are here retained in their familiar form, e.g. *Polygonum*. Trehane's name will always be found listed as an alternative. Some of the familiar names of small genera have also been used here, e.g. *Peltiphyllum* Engler is retained instead of *Darmera* Voss. We have however tried to use up-to-date specific names, but as long as a name is quoted with its authority, its modern equivalent is easy to find. In addition, it is often unwise to hasten to use the newest name for a well-known plant; they often soon revert to their more familiar names.

The Text

The text gives the country from which the species originated, its habitat, distribution and flowering time in the wild. This is intended to help the traveller who may wish to see the plant in the wild, and the gardener who can use the information to grow the plant better in his own climate and locality. We have in many cases added brief cultural notes, but these are meant only as a supplement to the descriptions of habitat, which have been made as detailed as possible, using our own experience of the plants in the wild, as well as accounts published in local floras.

The few words of description are intended to complement the photographs and help in the identification of the plant, by choosing the diagnostic characters of the species, and characters which can be seen in the photograph are usually omitted.

Measurements are given in metres and centimetres; as a guide 1m equals around 3 feet, and 2.5cm equals about 1 inch.

Hardiness

All the plants shown in this book will grow outside somewhere in the British Isles and in north-western North America. In colder climates, deciduous herbaceous plants can generally be protected with a very deep mulch. Plants of doubtful hardiness will usually survive better if grown in very well-drained soil and kept rather dry in winter. The figure given shows the degrees centigrade of frost which most can survive, but there are great variations of hardiness even within a single species. Again many plants are not tolerant of heat in summer, and the native habitat and locality of a species is an indication of its likely heat tolerance. Himalayan alpines and those from very wet summer climates such as New Zealand are generally least tolerant of summer heat or drought.

This table compares the minimum temperatures (in degrees Fahrenheit and Centigrade) of the hardiness zones published by the United States Department of Agriculture for North America with the European zones published in the *European Garden Flora*. The Californian system, used by the *New Western Garden Book* and in other Sunset books is more complex, but there heat and drought rather than frost are the likely problems for growers of perennials. The climatic notes given in the *New Western Garden Book* give minimum temperatures for inland areas. (The numbers given below are approximate, avoiding fractions.)

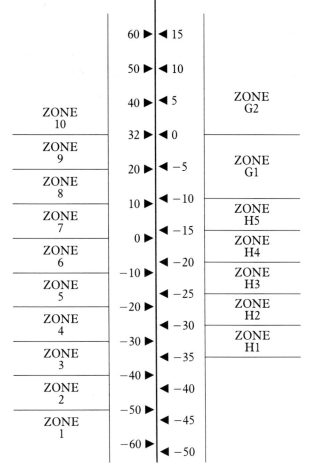

United States Department of Agriculture Zones (average annual minimum in degrees Fahrenheit)		European Garden Flora Zones (mean January minimum in degrees Centigrade)
	60 ▶ ◀ 15	
	50 ▶ ◀ 10	
ZONE 10	40 ▶ ◀ 5	ZONE G2
ZONE 9	32 ▶ ◀ 0	
ZONE 8	20 ▶ ◀ −5	ZONE G1
ZONE 7	10 ▶ ◀ −10	ZONE H5
	0 ▶ ◀ −15	ZONE H4
ZONE 6	◀ −20	ZONE H3
ZONE 5	−10 ▶ ◀ −25	ZONE H2
ZONE 4	−20 ▶ ◀ −30	ZONE H1
ZONE 3	−30 ▶ ◀ −35	
	−40 ▶ ◀ −40	
ZONE 2	−50 ▶ ◀ −45	
ZONE 1	−60 ▶ ◀ −50	

A lupin garden at Chatsworth

Rodgersia podophylla in autumn colour

The Wild Origins of Herbaceous Perennials

The hardy perennials grown in gardens originate in temperate climates in all parts of the world, but the majority are from areas with cold or dry winters and wet summers. A few, mainly from central Asia or the Mediterranean areas of Europe, western Asia or south-western North America, require moist winters and springs, and tolerate dry summers, but these Mediterranean climates are especially rich in bulbs and annuals. Those that do survive in these climates are very useful, however, for climates such as southern California and southern Europe in areas or dry parts of the garden where irrigation is restricted; many of these, such as bearded irises, paeonies and gypsophila have swollen roots to survive periods of drought.

The list below gives the original habitats of some large groups of common garden perennials, and gives an indication of the sort of conditions they need for optimum growth.

Anemones, Japanese   China, on rocks, cliffs in shade, wet in summer.

Astilbes   China and Japan, on damp rocks, by streams, wet in summer.

Carnations and pinks   Southern Europe, on rocks, cliffs and old walls, dry in summer.

Delphiniums   Central Europe, in subalpine woods and meadows, in rich but well-drained soil, moist in summer.

Day-lilies (*Hemerocallis*)   China and Japan, in marshy meadows and rocky slopes, wet in summer.

Hostas   Japan and China, in woods, shady rocks and cliffs, with cloudy, wet summers.

Irises, bearded   Eastern Europe and western Asia, on rocky slopes, moist in spring, dry in summer.

Kniphofias (Red-hot poker)   South Africa, on wet peaty and sandy soils, often in marshes, wet in summer, drier in winter.

Michaelmas daisies (*Aster*)   North America, in woods and meadows, moist in summer.

Paeonies (*P. lactiflora* cvs.)   Siberia and North China, in meadows and open scrub, on deep, rich soil, with summer rain and very cold winters.

Penstemons   Mexico and North America, in many different habitats, often dry and rocky.

Primroses   Europe and western Asia, in woods and on shady rocks, usually on heavy soil, moist in summer.

Water-lilies   Europe and North America, in still water.

In the wild, herbaceous plants have to compete with trees and shrubs for water and light. Many of the early spring-flowering ones grow in deciduous woods, and flower before the leaves come on the trees. They can survive during summer with very little light and in fact they are soon scorched and killed by sun and dry wind in summer; in many cases shelter from wind is as important as summer water. Others grow in places inhospitable to tree growth, such as in dry steppe climates; they require full sun and exposure throughout the summer, and are generally tolerant of summer drought. Small areas of herbaceous perennials may be found in forest areas in very wet places along streams, on wet or dry rocks, on avalanche tracks, or on screes where landslides are frequent. Those which grow in open meadows or in mountains above the tree line must tolerate grazing, and are often spiny, poisonous or otherwise unpalatable, e.g. delphiniums, primulas, sea holly, day-lilies, etc. Because mountains attract rain, most of them need summer moisture at the root, but sun and wind on the leaves. It is mainly those from very cloudy mountains, such as the Himalayas, which tolerate summer shade in gardens, though they are often unable to survive summer heat, and so are the most difficult to grow in lowland areas with hot summers.

Propagation

The majority of perennials, i.e. those which form multiple crowns, are easily propagated by division of the clumps. This is best done in spring in wet climates, or in autumn in climates where spring and summer are rather dry. Early planting gives the divisions (or newly acquired plants) more time to become established before they have to endure the heat of summer. In wet winter climates or where irrigation is possible, spring division is better because the young plants are less likely to rot over winter. Division is simple; the clumps are dug up, and either broken apart by hand, or, if they are tough, forced apart by inserting two forks back to back, and levering the clump apart.

Anemones and *Agapanthus* with *Sedum*

A wonderful range of foliage at Barnsley House

Many plants form clumps, but instead of branching rhizomes and fibrous roots they have deep, fleshy roots which end in a rosette of leaves; oriental poppies, acanthus and Japanese anemones have root systems of this kind, and the plants are hard to move and slow to establish thereafter. Root cuttings however, succeed very well; pieces of root a few inches long should be carefully inserted in sandy soil, with the upper end of the root near the soil surface. The upper end soon grows leaves, the lower end roots. The root cuttings may be taken in autumn, and planted out in spring when well rooted. Stem cuttings are useful for plants which either have many long-lived stems from a compact rootstock, or for those which are almost shrubby at the base, and are therefore unsuitable for division. Examples which are commonly raised by cuttings which root easily are carnations and pinks, wallflowers such as 'Bowles' Mauve', origanums and diascias. The cuttings are best taken in mid-summer, and kept well shaded and humid until they have rooted; then they will have time to make an established plant before winter. Cuttings taken later often root well, but may succumb in winter before they have become established.

Seed forms the best means of increase for species which are not easily raised from cuttings or division. Usually this is best sown as fresh as possible. Large seeds of woodland plants, such as epimediums and corydalis and many primulas lose viability very quickly and should be kept moist if possible between collection and sowing. Others need a cold period after sowing before they germinate, so if sown in summer or autumn will begin to grow in the spring. Others still need first a warm, wet period, then a cold period before they germinate, and a few even need scorching by fire. It may be difficult to discover the exact conditions required for a particular species, but seed catalogues often give some guidelines, and if in doubt it is safest to sow the seed as fresh as possible, and allow seeds that do not germinate immediately to be frosted for a couple of months during the winter. Germination is then likely in the spring, or as soon as the soil warms up.

Herbaceous Perennials in the garden

The traditional place to grow perennials in a garden is in herbaceous borders. These are long and rectangular, often in pairs with a grassy path between, and backed by yew hedges. The planting is confined to deciduous herbaceous perennials, for the very good reason that they may be dug up, divided and replanted in the spring while the beds are weeded and manured. The borders are totally brown through the winter, but make a fine and colourful show from early summer onwards, any bare patches which appear in late summer being filled with annuals which have been brought on in pots. These were the great borders of Edwardian England, filled with gorgeous imperial paeonies from Kelways, the tall spires of delphiniums and clouds of gypsophila.

A lavender edging at Mottisfont

A summer border at Crathes Castle, Aberdeenshire

Few private gardens still maintain them in the traditional manner, but there are fine examples at Newby Hall in Yorkshire, and around the parterre at Pitmedden near Aberdeen.

Perennials are now more often planted in different ways; they may be in mixed borders with shrubs, annuals and bulbs; they may be grown in a meadow garden, or planted in groups in mown grass, squeezed into crevices in walls, or pinned onto rocky slopes; they may be used as groundcover, or even planted as a hedge. They will tolerate the wettest and driest places, and many thrive in waterlogged soil.

Wherever they are planted their effect depends on their suitability for a particular position in the garden, and on the careful juxtaposition of different plants (now very much an 'in' subject, called plant associations).

Plant associations in the garden

The modern interest in perennials as garden plants can be traced back to the writings of William Robinson, an Irishman from Stradbally whose book *The Wild Garden* was first published in 1870, and was immediately influential. He championed both the use of wild flowers in the garden and the planting of large

Polemonium 'Lambrook Manor'

herbaceous perennials in grass or on the edges of shrubberies, e.g. the common double red paeony, *Paeonia officinalis* 'Rubra Plena', as well as the planting of large swathes of daffodils, anemones and other bulbs. Although many of these ideas proved failures when put into practice at Robinson's own garden at Gravetye Manor in Sussex on heavy Wealden clay, they were successful in other gardens; for instance, the paeony, pulmonarias and *Epimedium alpinum* still survive from the Robinsonian plantings at Mells Park in Somerset. Robinson combined these ideas on planting with a polemic against the tender bedding plants then widely used in Victorian gardens. One of the engravings in *The Wild Garden* entitled 'A beautiful Accident' shows a grouping of Sweet Cecily (*Myrrhis odorata*), white *Campanula persicifolia* and *Campanula alliarifolia*. In a later edition in 1894, a fascinating passage gives a list of the plants G. F. Wilson grew in the then newly established Wild Garden at Wisley; many of them such as *Lilium superbum*, *Galax aphylla*, and *Gentiana asclepiadea*, grow there today. When told that Wisley was 'fascinating, but no garden', Wilson is said to have replied, 'I think of it as a place where plants from all over the world grow wild.'

Robinson's ideas were developed further by Gertrude Jekyll, an artist before she began to design gardens in the 1880s, whose influence was spread both by her writings such as *Colour Schemes in the Flower Garden*, published in 1911, and by her association with Edwin Lutyens. Many of the gardens of Lutyens' fashionable houses were designed by Jekyll, and she summed up her intentions 'to devise living pictures with simple, well-known flowers'.

Jekyll was one of the first to propose borders or beds of one colour, but at the same time acknowledged the need for flexibility: 'A blue garden, for beauty's sake, may be hungry for a group of white lilies or something of palest lemon yellow.' Some of her ideas for plant associations are worth repeating in brief here. Her spring border consisted largely of ferns, such as *Dryopteris filix-mas* interspersed with hellebores, bulbs and *Bergenia*, with patches of *Valeriana phu* 'Aurea', the pinks and the yellows kept carefully separate. She made great use of grey foliage, and bold leaf shapes such as yuccas, *Acanthus*, *Bergenia*, seakale leaves and *Aesculus parviflora*. Her plan for a grey border included much *Eryngium*, *Echinops*, *Gypsophila*, pale heliotrope (would Robinson have approved of this!), and pale mauve delphiniums. Bearded irises were combined with catmint, lupins, old roses and pinks.

She does not seem to have liked hostas, then called *Funkia*, though several varieties were grown at that time, possibly because of their lack of subtlety. The other remarkable absentee from her lists is *Alchemilla mollis*, now universal in herbaceous gardens. It was introduced in 1874 to Austria from Ulu Dağ in Turkey, but it is not mentioned by Robinson, and is also absent from Gauntlett's *Hardy Plants Worth Growing*, a remarkable catalogue, extant in the 1930s. The alchemilla was brought to the notice of gardeners by W. T. Stearn in 1948, but did not achieve real popularity until the 1960s, after it received the Award of Merit of the Royal Horticultural Society when exhibited by Sunningdale Nurseries in 1958. However, a large planting may be seen in a photograph of Hidcote, dating from the 1920s.

E. A. Bowles is certainly one of the most important writers of the early twentieth century. He was more of a plantsman than Jekyll, loving rare and unusual species and mutations for their own sakes, and popularizing them through his books and his long association with the Royal Horticultural Society.

The present-day combination of an interest in rare, unusual or ancient garden plants, and artistic planting was stimulated by Vita Sackville-West and her writing about the garden at Sissinghurst Castle, still one of the best gardens for herbaceous plants in the world. Sissinghurst combines a formal layout with informal planting, the plants used for artistic effect but in many cases also rare and interesting. Vita Sackville-West's other interest was in old-fashioned varieties of roses, and these are used to good effect in many parts of the garden. The garden at Crathes Castle in north-east Scotland is similar in its basic formality, but here there is also an excellent collection of rare shrubs, in addition to a splendid display of perennials.

A third great garden, Hidcote, created from about 1903 by an American, Lawrence Johnston, has also been very influential, as the number of perennials named after the garden shows. Johnston also had a large garden in the south of France, at Serre de la Madone, which was important for the introduction of new plants into that part of France. Hidcote's greatness springs partly from its design, of a series of hedged-in 'garden rooms', but also from its reputation as a source and proving ground for new plants.

Both Sissinghurst and Hidcote are now in the care of the National Trust (and Crathes is run by the National Trust for Scotland), and it was through his position of Gardens Adviser to the National Trust as well as through his writings from 1940 onwards that Graham Thomas has had such an influence on gardening. His books on old roses, on perennials, on ground cover and on the art of planting are all classics, bringing the tradition of Robinson, Jekyll and Sackville-West up to the present day.

The vogue for cottage gardens, using simple plants in riotous profusion, was promoted by Margery Fish, a journalist before she and her husband began gardening in middle age at Lambrook Manor. She was a woman of great enthusiasms, and described many of her ideas for striking plant associations, using numerous variegated, purple, or silver leaves. The many cultivars named after her garden show what a good eye she had for an outstanding plant. *Polemonium* 'Lambrook Manor', shown here, is one of her selections, though it did not necessarily originate in her garden.

Many other gardens and nurseries still influence the availability and demand for perennials and their use in gardens. Christopher Lloyd at Great Dixter in Sussex has popularized many plants and scorned others. In his weekly articles in *Country Life* and through his own garden, he has long been a champion of meadow gardens, and those at Great Dixter are the best that can be seen today.

Alan Bloom and his son Adrian have what is probably the largest collection of perennials in their nursery at Bressingham in Norfolk. Alan Bloom has for many years been active in introducing new plants into general cultivation, and in creating new hybrids often of genera which have not been worked on before; *Aconitum* 'Ivorine', valuable for its early flowering and low, multi-stemmed habit, was one of his raising. He was one of the first to propose informal 'Island Beds' of perennials, surrounded by grass, the heights carefully graduated so that little staking was needed. These have tall plants, chosen for their sturdiness, in the middle, and low ones around all the edges. Good examples of these beds can be seen at Bressingham Gardens.

The long border at Great Dixter, Sussex

Through her nursery, aptly called Unusual Plants, and through her garden there, her writings and lectures, Beth Chatto has a devoted following, combining plants with horizontal and vertical shapes, different foliage types and colours to excellent effect. She regularly popularizes new plants through her nursery.

In America a rather similar function is played by the White Flower Farm in Litchfield, Connecticut. Its beautiful, twice-yearly catalogues are full of interesting perennials and have careful cultivation notes for American gardens.

Americans have also been the great plant breeders of the late twentieth century, concentrating on genera such as *Hemerocallis*, *Hosta* and bearded and spuria irises. There has been an immense growth of interest in hardy perennials in North America and in Europe in the past ten years, and the people mentioned above have been only some of the most public influences on this growth.

Lysimachia ephemerum in a rose border

Trollius europaeus in Perthshire

Natural Plant Associations

The essence of a successful plant association is that the plants chosen should grow happily together, that there should be some contrasts in the textures of foliage, and that the colours of those flowers which are open at the same time should not clash. Furthermore the plants should be of similar robustness so that the weaker ones are not overwhelmed by those that are over-vigorous. Though a particular area of the garden may look best at one season, there is usually scope for many layers of planting, so that there is some interest from spring to autumn. Snowdrops, aconites and other early bulbs may be covered by summer-leafing and flowering herbaceous plants, and the spaces taken by early flowering perennials such as oriental poppies can be filled by late-flowering ones. Flower-colour schemes may be changed through the season, beginning with the bright acid yellow and blues common in spring, with cool pinks, greys and blues in summer, and finally with warm orange, reds and yellows in autumn.

Most modern suggestions for successful plant associations concentrate on producing such harmony of colour, combined with contrasting leaf textures. Those with a feeling for plant geography may like to emphasize an additional theme – to use in an area only those plants which might be found growing together in nature, or at least those which come from the same geographical area. The few examples set out below, which include bulbs and a few dwarf shrubs, could be easily reproduced in the garden.

1. **Caucasian hay meadow**   This association contains many familiar herbaceous plants and bulbs, and is found both in the Caucasus proper and in northern Turkey. For rich, but well-drained soil, moist in summer. Typical species: *Galanthus, Scilla sibirica, Cyclamen coum, Iris histrioides, Omphalodes cappadocica, Helleborus orientalis, Brunnera macrophylla, Hesperis matronalis, Lilium monadelphum, Campanula lactiflora, Campanula alliarifolia, Geranium psilostemon, Geranium platypetalum,* (and other species), *Salvia forskahlii, Paeonia mlokesewitschii, Cephalaria gigantea, Telekia speciosa, Gentiana asclepiadea, Colchicum speciosum, Crocus speciosus.*

2. **North European subalpine meadow**   This association is found in the foothills of the Alps, and in a depauperate form on limestone hills in northern Britain. For rich soil, moist in summer. Typical species: *Leucojum vernum, Crocus vernus,*
Erythronium dens-canis, Narcissus poeticus, Narcissus pseudo-narcissus, Geranium pratense, sylvaticum and *pheum, Aquilegia alpina, Aquilegia atrata, Salvia glutinosa, Ranunculus aconitifolius, Trollius europaeus, Lunaria rediviva, Pulmonaria* (several species), *Campanula latifolia, Colchicum autumnale.*

3. **North American moist deciduous woodland**   This association is found from southern Canada, along the Appalachian mountains south to Georgia. Mostly spring-flowering. For acid, leafy soil, moist in summer. Typical species: *Erythronium americanum, Trillium grandiflorum, Trillium erectum, Dicentra eximea* and *canadensis, Adiantum pedatum, Clintonia umbellulata, Mertensia virginica, Tierella cordifolia, Podophyllum peltatum, Phlox ovata, Vertatrum viride* (in wet places), *Lilium canadense* (wet), *Smilacina racemosa, Geranium maculatum, Actaea rubra* and *alba, Cimicifuga racemosa, Aquilegia canadensis* (in dry places), *Monarda didyma, Gillenia trifoliata, Helianthus decapetalus, Matteuccia pensylvanica.*

4. **Himalayan wet meadow**   This association is found in forest clearings or above the tree line in the central and eastern Himalayas, and into western China. Summers are cool, with very heavy rainfall; winters are cold and dry. For peaty, acid or neutral soil. Typical species: *Primula* (many species), *Meconopsis* (many species), *Thalictrum chelidonii, Ligularia* species, *Polygonum macrophyllum, Euphorbia griffithii, E. shillingii* and *E. wallichiana, Rodgersia* species, *Iris clarkei* and *delavayi, Aconitum* species, *Codonopsis species, Allium wallichii, Hemerocallis forrestii, Nomocharis* species, *Rheum alexandrae.*

5. **Mediterranean dry hillside**   In this habitat summers are hot and dry, winters and springs cool and wet. Dwarf shrubs such as lavenders and Cistus are common, as are annuals and bulbs of many genera. Herbaceous plants include the following: *Iris* (bearded types), *Paeonia rhodia* and *arietina, Stipa gigantea, Asphodeline lutea, Echinops ritro, Centranthus ruber, Origanum* species, *Convolvulus althaeoides, Euphorbia characias, rigida* and *myrsinites, Erysimum* and *Cheiranthus* species, *Acanthus spinosus, Phlomis lychnitis, Anchusa azurea, Dictamnus albus.*

6. **European dry woodland**   This type of habitat is found in Italy and other parts of southern Europe which are dry in summer, and often have deep shade. These are difficult conditions in a garden. Plants such as the following are found naturally in these places: *Geranium macrorrhizum* and *nodosum, Lithospermum purpureocaeruleum, Epimedium alpinum, Doronicum orientale, Vinca difformis* and *V. minor, Acanthus mollis, Iris graminea, Ranunculus creticus, Cyclamen* species, *Anemone blanda, Digitalis laevigata.*

7. **Californian dry woodland**   The conditions here are similar to European dry woodlands, but bulbs, especially *Erythronium* species, are common. The large proportion of bright red species in

Athyrium niponicum 'Pictum' a good form!

A valley of *Geranium clarkei*, *Nepeta* and *Pedicularis* in Kashmir

this area is a response to the importance of hummingbirds as pollinators. Herbaceous species include the following: *Aquilegia formosa*, *Dicentra formosa*, *Delphinium cardinale*, *Ipomopsis aggregata*, *Vancouveria chrysantha*, *Heuchera* species, *Iris innominata* and the *Californicae* section, *Geranium richardsoni*.

8. Central Asian steppe This type of habitat extends from central Turkey eastwards across Asia to north-west China and Mongolia. Summers are hot and dry, winters cold and frozen, and so the growing season is restricted to a few weeks in autumn and a short spring. The flora is, however, very rich and includes numerous bulbs and the following drought-resistant perennials: *Paeonia anomala*, *Tulipa fosteriana* and other species, *Iris albertii* and *I. scariosa*, and *Iris spuria* in wet places, *Gypsophila paniculata*, *Eremostachys* species, *Salvia* species, *Eremurus* species (see *Bulbs*), *Limonium platyphyllum*, *Perovskia atriplicifolia*, *Althaea rugosa*, *Achillea filipendulina*, *Ligularia macrophylla*.

9. North American prairie and grassland This type of habitat is found on very shallow soils and in grassy or boggy clearings east of the Appalachians, where most of the natural vegetation was forest, but more commonly in the drier Midwest. Familiar species include the following: *Phlox maculata*, *Aster novae-angliae*, *Coreopsis verticillata*, *Asclepias tuberosa* (in dry places), *Solidago* species, *Echinacea purpurea*, *Lobelia cardinalis* (by streams), *Oenothera speciosa*, *Veronicastrum virginicum*, *Helianthus* species, especially *Helianthus salicifolius*, *Lupinus perennis*.

10. New Zealand tussock grassland This type of habitat is found mainly in the mountains, and particularly in South Island. It is dominated by clump forming grasses and sedges, with peaty soils, moist in the summer. The following flowering plants are found in this habitat: *Ranunculus lyallii*, *Astelia nervosa*, *Celmisia* species, especially *Celmisia spectabilis* at high altitudes, *Aciphylla* species, *Phormium cookianum*, *Acaena microphylla*, *Carex flabellata*.

11. Western Chinese woodland The ancient forests of Mount Omei and other parts of western Sichuan contain numerous endemic plants as well as animals such as the Giant Panda. The woods are very dense, hot and wet in summer, drier and sunnier in winter, with several species of *Acer*, *Corylopsis*, *Styrax* and numerous other beautiful trees and shrubs. Soils are very leafy, though the underlying rock is often limestone. Some notable species are: *Epimedium acuminatum* and *E. davidii*, *Corydalis flexuosa* and other species, *Adiantum venustum*, *Anemone flaccida*, *A. davidii* and *A. tomentosa*, *Cardiocrinum yunnanense*, *Paris polyphylla*, *Meehania fargesii*, *Sanicula* species, *Paeonia mairei*, *Primula* species, *Tiarella polyphylla*, *Iris japonica* (in more open places), *Hosta* species, *Rodgersia aesculifolia*.

12. Drakensberg grassland The higher parts of the Drakensberg mountains in Natal are preserved as species-rich grassland by regular careful burning in late winter. Soils are often peaty over a gravelly subsoil and afternoon thunderstorms are frequent in summer. Many of the most familiar species from this area grow along streams or in marshy places. Bulbous plants such as *Cyrtanthus*, *Dierama*, *Gladiolus*, *Moraea* and *Watsonia* are frequent. *Rhodohypoxis* are found in wet, shallow peaty soils. Herbaceous perennials include the following: *Kniphofia*, *Agapanthus*, *Diascia*, *Phygelius*, *Leonotis* (in drier places), *Glumicalyx gosoleoides*.

Colour in an early summer border

Helleborus foetidus

Helleborus foetidus
'Wester Flisk'

Helleborus vesicarius

Helleborus × nigercors

Helleborus lividus

Helleborus purpurascens

Helleborus niger

Helleborus argutifolius

Photographed 10 February. ½ life size

Helleborus niger in the University Botanic Garden, Cambridge

Helleborus × *nigercors* 'Alabaster'

Helleborus × *nigristern*

Helleborus lividus 'Boughton Beauty'

Helleborus argutifolius Viv. syns. *H. corsicus* Willd., *H. lividus* subsp. *corsicus* (Willd.) Tutin (*Ranunculaceae*)   Native of Corsica and Sardinia, in maquis scrub, in dry grassy glades among bracken, by streams and roadsides, flowering in January–June. Stems to 75cm, and more across in large specimens. Flowers 2.5–5cm across. Leaf segments green, with coarse spiny teeth. For well-drained soil; hardy to −10°C with shelter. Short-lived, but usually self-seeding.

Helleborus foetidus L. **Stinking Hellebore** Native of SW Europe, from England and Portugal to Germany and Italy, growing on rocky slopes, roadside banks and open woods, usually on limestone, flowering in January–April. Stems to 80cm, with leaves in a rosette around the inflorescence, usually glossy, very dark green; hardy to −20°C, with shelter from wind. The variety 'Wester Flisk' has greyish-green leaves with narrower segments and the flower stalks are tinged with red; it comes true from seed. For well-drained soil in sun or part shade, and especially tolerant of dry shade.

Helleborus lividus Ait.   Native of Majorca, growing on limestone rocks and in woods and scrub, flowering in February–April. Stems to 45cm. Leaf segments marked greyish, toothless or with fine small teeth. Flowers and stems often pinkish. Hardy only to −5°C.
'Boughton Beauty'   A robust form of *H.* × *sternii* Turrill, a hybrid combining the greater size and hardiness of *H. argutifolius* with the colour of *H. lividus*. Hardy to around −10°C.

Helleborus niger L. **Christmas Rose**   Native of mountain woods, usually on limestone in the E Alps and N Apennines, from S Germany and Switzerland (Ticino) to Italy and Yugoslavia, growing in conifer woods up to the *Pinus mugo* zone, and sometimes in open grassland, flowering in January–April. Flowers 4–8cm across; stems to 30cm in the tallest forms, when the flowers are fading. Many garden forms have been selected, mainly for their tall stems and large flowers. Subsp. *macranthus* (Freyn) Schiffner, from N Italy and Yugoslavia, in spite of claims made for it, is distinguished by its leaves, with spiny teeth on broadly lanceolate, greyish leaflets, and white not pink-tinged flowers, with narrower petals. Cultivation is not always easy, but a rich, limy soil, in partial shade, deeply cultivated, and protection for the buds, young leaves and roots from slugs will give a good chance of success.

Helleborus × **nigercors** J. T. Wall   This is the usual name for hybrids between *H. niger* and *H. argutifolius*, which combine the large white flowers of the former with the profusion of the latter. Unfortunately, these hybrids are sterile, and very hard to propagate vegetatively, so they are usually raised from seed by hand-pollinating *H. niger* with *H. argutifolius* pollen. The resulting seedlings, like that shown here, are closer to *H. niger*; one was named 'Alabaster' in 1967. Other forms I have seen, closer to *H. argutifolius* with a taller stem, may have been the reciprocal cross. The cross between *H.* × *sternii* and *H. niger* is called *H.* × *nigristern*, and may be expected to have a pinkish tinge.

Helleborus argutifolius

Helleborus purpurascens Waldst. & Kit. Native of SE Poland, Hungary and Czechoslovakia to Romania and the W Ukraine, growing in open woods and scrub, flowering in March–April, earlier in gardens in S England. Leaves deciduous, usually with 5 segments, divided to the middle into 2–5 lobes. Stems 5–20cm at flowering. Flowers greenish or purplish, sometimes glaucous outside, 5–7cm across. For a warm position in partial shade in humus-rich, but not acid, soil. Probably the hardiest species.

Helleborus vesicarius Auch.   For fruit and text see page 16.

Helleborus cyclophyllus in N Greece

Helleborus multifidus subsp. *bocconei* near Florence

Helleborus purpurascens

Helleborus atrorubens

Helleborus atrorubens Waldst. & Kit. syn. *H. dumetorum* Waldst. & Kit. subsp. *atrorubens* (Waldst. & Kit.) Merxm. & Podlech (*Ranunculaceae*)   Native of NW Yugoslavia, growing in grassy places and scrub, flowering in February–April. Leaves deciduous to 45cm, with 7–11 undivided segments. Flowers 4–5.5cm across, brownish to deep purplish, inside and out. For a warm, sheltered position. Hardy to –15°C.

Helleborus cyclophyllus Boiss.   Native of Albania, Bulgaria, S Yugoslavia and Greece, growing in woods, scrub and on grassy hillsides, flowering in February–April. Stems to 60cm; leaves deciduous, with 5–9 usually undivided ovate-lanceolate segments, hairy beneath. Flowers *c*. 6cm across, usually yellowish green, but not whitish as in *H. orientalis*. Easily grown in sun or partial shade.

Helleborus multifidus Vis. subsp. **bocconei** (Ten.) B. Mathew syn. *H. siculus* Schiffner Native of C & S Italy, and Sicily, growing in open woods and scrub in the hills, flowering in February–March. Stems to 20cm; leaves evergreen, to 42cm across, with 5–7 leaflets, hairy beneath, each divided to halfway into 3 or 5 segments. Flowers 4.5–6cm across, sweetly scented with a hint of cat, in gardens sometimes opening in late November, as in the form shown here from the hills above Florence. Easily grown in heavy limy soil in partial shade.

Helleborus multifidus Vis. subsp. **multifidus** Native of Albania and W Yugoslavia especially Dalmatia, in scrub and grassy rocky hillsides flowering in March–April. Stems to 50cm; leaves finely divided, with 9–15 segments, each divided into 3–12 lobes. Flowers 3–4 cm across, green. It is the deeply dissected leaves which are the interesting feature of this species, not the rather small flowers. It requires a warm sheltered position in the garden.

Helleborus purpurascens Waldst. & Kit. Native of Romania, Hungary, E Czechoslovakia, SE Poland and W Russia, growing on the edges of woods and scrub, often on sandy soils, flowering in March–April, earlier in gardens in S England. Plant forming eventually low mats. Stems 5–20cm at flowering; leaves deciduous, with 2–6 leaflets, hairy beneath. Flowers appearing before the leaves, 5–7cm across, purplish, reddish or greenish inside, glaucous outside. For a humus-rich, but not acid soil in partial shade.

Helleborus vesicarius Auch.   Native of N Syria and S Turkey, from SW Adiyaman, west to the Amanus and south to Mt Cassius (today Akra Dağ), on limestone rocks and in oak scrub at 550–1300m, flowering in March–May, often earlier in gardens in S England, fruiting in May–June. Plant with a long, swollen rootstock. Stems to 45cm, much branched. Flowers 16–18mm long; capsules inflated, 5–7cm long, with 1–6 large spherical seeds 5–6mm across. Deciduous in summer; leaves appearing in autumn. Easy to grow in a bulb frame, or in some other hot position, kept dry in summer. The plant is liable to die if transplanted, so is best established from pot-grown seedlings. In cultivation the unusual fruits are produced only after cross-pollination. Hardy to –10°C.

Helleborus vesicarius in fruit, near Maraş, S Turkey

Helleborus vesicarius

Helleborus viridis subsp. *occidentalis* with *Anemone nemorosa* at Postling, Kent

Helleborus viridis L. subsp. **occidentalis** (Reuter) Schiffner   Native of NW Europe, from N England (N Yorkshire and Westmorland) south to France, Spain and W Germany (with the larger-flowered and hairy-leaved subsp. *viridis* from C France and Austria to NW Italy), growing in woods and sunny banks on chalk and limestone, flowering in February–April. Stems 20–40cm; leaves deciduous, with 7–11 leaflets, glabrous beneath, narrowly elliptical, serrate. Flowers 3–5cm across, often with purple markings inside, glaucous green. A small-flowered but graceful plant, easily grown in heavy moist soil in partial shade.

Helleborus multifidus subsp. *multifidus*

Helleborus viridis subsp. *occidentalis*

Helleborus orientalis
(white seedling)

'Sirius'

Seedling

Seedling

Seedling

'Celadon'

Helleborus orientalis
wild form from
Turkey

'Aeneas'

'Dido'

Helleborus orientalis
wild form from
Turkey

Helleborus orientalis
wild form from
Turkey

Helleborus orientalis
(double seedling)

'Zodiac'

Seedling

'Atrorubens'

Helleborus orientalis subsp.
guttatus

Seedling

'Queen of the Night'

'Philip Ballard'

Helleborus atrorubens
hybrid

'Cosmos'

A selection of *Helleborus orientalis* seedlings and named cultivars from Washfield Nurseries, 14 February. ⅔ life size

Helleborus orientalis Lam. (*Ranunculaceae*)
Lenten Rose   Native of NE Greece and
European Turkey, eastwards along the Black
Sea coast to the S Caucasus, in Soviet Georgia,
at up to 2200m in Turkey, growing in scrub and
on the edges of woods, usually in grassy places
in heavy soil where it thrives because it is not
grazed. Flowering stems to 60cm; leaves to
60cm, evergreen except in exceptionally cold
winters, with 7–10 usually undivided or forked
segments, up to 45cm across.

Flowers in Turkey or Greece, usually whitish
or greenish, rarely with pinkish edges. In the
Caucasus two other subspecies occur as well:
subsp. *abchasicus* (A. Br.) B. Mathew has deep
purple or pinkish-grey flowers, often heavily
spotted with minute spots; it is found mainly in
Abchasia in the W Caucasus, and hybridizes in
the wild with subsp. *orientalis*. The second
subspecies, subsp. *guttatus* (A. Br. & Saur) B.
Mathew has white flowers with larger reddish
spots, and is found near Tblisi in the C
Caucasus, and further east.

All forms are easily grown in rich, heavy soil
in sun or partial shade, in a warm and sheltered
position, kept moist in summer. Hardy below
−15°C, though the leaves are killed by cold
winds around −10°C. The greenish wild-
collected forms from W Turkey may start
flowering as early as November in gardens.

Numerous cultivars have been selected and
named, concentrating on features such as
blackish-purple, white or yellow flowers,
contrasting nectaries, different degrees of
spotting, and flowers which do not hang down.
Unfortunately, the named varieties are slow to
increase and regularly cross- and self-seed in
most gardens. Some nurseries therefore
concentrate on producing good seedling strains.
A selection of such seedlings, from Washfield
Nurseries in Hawkhurst, Sussex, is shown here,
together with some named ones.
'Aeneas'   A double-flowered form of *H.
torquatus*, found by Elizabeth Strangman in
Crna Gora (Montenegro), Yugoslavia, in 1971.
'Atrorubens' syn. 'Early Purple'   This is not
the same as *H. atrorubens* Waldst. & Kit. but is
an old *H. orientalis* subsp. *abchasicus* form,
known since 1843, with deciduous leaves, and
reddish-purple flowers, appearing earlier than
most other cultivars.
'Celadon'   Probably a hybrid with *H. odorus*,
raised by Elizabeth Strangman.
'Cosmos'   Raised by Eric Smith in *c.* 1973.
'Dido'   A double *H. torquatus* found by
Elizabeth Strangman in Crna Gora
(Montenegro), Yugoslavia, in 1971.
'Old Ugly'   Raised by Elizabeth Strangman in
the 1960s. A *Helleborus viridis* hybrid.
'Philip Ballard'   Raised in 1986 by Mrs Ballard
of Malvern, Worcs, who has specialized in
breeding blacks and yellows with large
horizontal blooms.
'Pluto'   Raised by Eric Smith of the Plantsmen
in 1960. A *Helleborus torquatus* hybrid, with
purple nectaris.
'Queen of the Night'   Raised by Elizabeth
Strangman in the 1970s. Note the dark
nectaries.
'Sirius'   Scented; possibly a hybrid of *H.
odorus*, raised by Eric Smith in *c.* 1974.
'Zodiac'   A strain, raised by Eric Smith in
c. 1974.

Helleborus orientalis (double seedling)

Helleborus 'Cosmos'

'Old Ugly'

A white *orientalis* seedling from Boughton

A red *orientalis* seedling

A yellow seedling

Helleborus orientalis is easily raised from seed,
and often self-sows around the parent plants, so
that there is a danger that these seedlings may
grow up and overwhelm the parents if they are
named cultivars. Old plants are best moved or
divided in winter or early spring while in flower,
before root growth begins; thereafter they
should not be allowed to dry out until
established.

'Pluto'

Caltha howellii in NE California

Caltha howellii

Hylomecon japonicum

Chelidonium majus var. *grandiflorum* near Yumin, Sinjiang

Caltha howellii (Huth) Greene
(*Ranunculaceae*)   Native of S Oregon and
California, from Tulare Co. northwards, and in
the northern coast ranges at 1500–3000m,
growing in bogs and wet ground by streams,
flowering in May–July according to altitude.
Plants tufted, to 30cm. Leaves 3–10cm across.
Petals 12–16mm long; seed pods stalked.
Flowers solitary, on a leafless and unbranched
stem. *C. leptosepala* DC. from W North
America, from Alaska to Washington, Montana
and New Mexico, differs in having the seed
pods on very short stalks, and leaves longer than
broad. Both require damp peaty soil, preferably
by running water. Hardy to –20°C.

Caltha palustris L. **King Cup, Marsh
Marigold** or **Cowslip** (in America)   Native of
most of the Northern Hemisphere from Ireland
southwards to Spain, and east to Siberia and
Japan; and in North America from
Newfoundland to South Carolina, and west to
Saskatchewan, growing in marshes, wet alder
woods, or by streams, flowering in March–June,
according to latitude. Plant with several hollow
spreading stems from a central rootstock, to
60cm high. Leaves 5–20mm across. Flowers up
to 5cm, usually yellow, or white in var. *alba*,
the white form which possibly belongs to var.
himalayensis (D. Don) Mukerjee. In the
Himalayas, where it is very common at 2400–
4000m, from Kashmir east to Bhutan, it is
commonly white-flowered; flowering in May–
August, according to altitude. Easily grown in
moist soil, preferably at the edge of water.
'Plena' has double flowers on a rather small
plant.

Caltha polypetala Hochst. ex Lorent   Native
of Bulgaria, the Caucasus, N & NW Iran and
NE Turkey, growing by streams in alpine
meadows at 1700–3600m, flowering April–July,
usually by melting snow. Differs from *C.
palustris* in having 7–10 petals, but is otherwise
similar, and probably requires the same
treatment in cultivation.

Caltha polypetala of gardens   This large
Kingcup is frequent in gardens, and usually
called *polypetala*. It is, however, quite different
to the wild *C. polypetala* Hochstt. (q.v.) It has 5
or occasionally 6 petals, not 7–9 which is the
distinguishing feature of true *C. polypetala*. The
large Kingcup can be recognized by its great
size, to 80cm, its creeping and rooting stems, its
leaves which are 10–25cm across and its rather
sparse but large flowers, 5cm or more across. It
is quite different from the creeping subsp. *minor*
(Mill.) Clapham from mountains in N England
& Ireland, which is always smaller in leaf and
flower. In its creeping stems it is also similar to
var. *flabellifolia* (Pursh.) Torrey & Gray, but
that does not necessarily have large flowers.
Var. *barthei* Hance, from Japan, is large in size
of leaf and flower, but not creeping. 'Polypetala'
grows easily in wet ground or shallow water and
is hardy to −20°C, probably lower.

Chelidonium majus L. (*Papaveraceae*) **Greater
Celandine**   Native of much of S & E Europe,
NW Africa, Turkey and Asia east to Japan, and
naturalized in E North America, growing on
rocky slopes, in woods and scrub, flowering in
April–August. A short-lived perennial with a
fleshy rootstock and stems to 90cm. Flowers
normally 2–2.5cm, but in the plants shown

Caltha polypetala

Caltha polypetala in the Caucasus

Caltha palustris var. *alba*

Caltha palustris 'Flore Pleno'

Caltha palustris near Sellindge, Kent

here, growing in Sinjiang, 3.5cm across. This is var. *grandiflorum* (DC.) Fedde, from C Asia and NW China. A double-flowered variety is also common in cultivation, and a cut-leaved variety, var. *laciniatum* (Mill.) Syme, has deeply cut leaves. Easily grown in any garden soil, and commonly found as a weed in old gardens. Hardy. The plant contains a yellow juice, a traditional remedy for warts.

Hylomecon japonicum (Thunb.) Prantl & Kuen. (*Papaveraceae*)   Native of Honshu, Korea and NE China west to Hubei, growing in woods in valleys and on hills, flowering in April–June. Plant rather like a refined form of poppy, forming small patches, having short rhizomes, and flowering stems to 30–40cm. Flowers with petals 2–2.5cm long. Does well in leafy soil, in semi-shade or shade. Another species, *H. vernalis* Maxim., comes from E Siberia.

Stylophorum diphyllum (Mich.) Nutt. (*Papaveraceae*)   Native of E North America, from W Pennsylvania and Ohio south to Tennessee, and west to Wisconsin and Missouri, growing in damp woods, flowering in March–May. Plant with few, rather delicate stems 30–45cm tall, from a stout root. Leaves deeply and irregularly lobed, the terminal lobe not much larger than the laterals. Flowers *c.*5cm across. Capsule ovoid, with a pointed beak. Easily grown in moist, leafy soil. Hardy to −20°C.

Stylophorum lasiocarpum (Oliv.) Fedde Native of C & E China, in Hubei and Sichuan, growing in woods and scrub, flowering in May. Plant forming dense leafy clumps about 30cm high, 45cm across. Leaves dandelion-like, with a large ovate, toothed terminal segment. Flowers *c.*5cm across. Capsule narrow, cylindrical, 5–8cm long. For leafy soil, in a cool sheltered position; hardy to −15°C perhaps. This plant is cultivated in China for the medicinal properties of its thick root, which contains a red juice.

Stylophorum lasiocarpum

Stylophorum diphyllum

Trollius
'Feuertroll'

Ranunculus acris
'Flore Pleno'

Trollius
'Alabaster'

Trollius 'Helios'

Trollius europaeus

Trollius 'Superbus'

Specimens from Beth Chatto, 20 May. ⅗ life size

Trollius acaulis in Kashmir

Trollius chinensis

Trollius ranunculinus in Turkey

Trollius pumilus

Trollius yunnanensis

Ranunculus baurii from Bustervoedpad

Ranunculus acris L. **'Flore Pleno'**
(*Ranunculaceae*) This is a double-flowered
form of the common Meadow Buttercup which
is such a feature of moist cow pastures in
England and western France, flowering in May–
July. It is also found wild all across Eurasia from
Greenland to Japan. Stems to 100cm. Lowest
leaves with 3 more or less equal, deeply cut
lobes. Not producing runners like *R. repens*, so
unlikely to become a nuisance in gardens. The
double-flowered form, shown here, has been
known since 1580, and is said to have been
found wild in Lancashire. Hardy to −25°C or
less.

Ranunculus baurii MacOwan syn. *R. cooperi*
Oliv. Native of South Africa, in the
Drakensberg, and nearby mountains in
Transvaal, and NE Cape Province, at 1900–
3000m, growing in marshy peaty places,
seasonal pools, bogs and by streams; flowering
in October–November, or April–May in
gardens in the north. Plant forming clumps of
fleshy deciduous leaves. Petiole to 25cm; blade
peltate, *c*.8cm across with short, blunt teeth.
Flowers *c*.4cm across, shining yellow, with
many petals. For moist, peaty soil in full sun.
Hardy to −15°C perhaps.

Trollius acaulis D. Don (*Ranunculaceae*)
Native of N Pakistan to W Nepal and especially
common in Kashmir, growing on moist grassy
slopes at 3000–4300m, flowering by melting
snow in May–June. Plant forming small
clumps. Stems *c*.10cm at flowering time in the
wild, soon elongating. Flowers 5cm across. For
moist, peaty soil in sun or partial shade,
preferably by running water. Hardy to −20°C.

Trollius chinensis Pritz. syn. *T. ledebourii*
hort. Native of N China, growing in wet
meadows and by streams, flowering in June–
July. Plant forming substantial clumps, with
stems to 1m. Leaves deeply divided into narrow
lobes. Flowers to 3.5cm across, orange-yellow,
the upright narrow petals conspicuous and
longer than the stamens. For rich, wet soil by
streams or ponds. Hardy to −20°C or below.

Trollius × cultorum A group of hybrids
between *T. asiaticus*, *T. chinensis* and *T.
europaeus*, about thirty of which are in
cultivation at present. They flower from April to
June according to variety. Shown here are:
'Alabaster' A beautiful very pale greenish
yellow.
'Feuertroll' ('Fire Globe') Rich orange
yellow.
'Helios' An early-flowering variety. 'Earliest
of All' is another early one.
 Globeflowers require moist, rich soil in sun or
partial shade to thrive and flower well. They
detest drought. All are hardy to −20°C or less.

Trollius europaeus L. **Globeflower** Native of
Europe from Scotland and NE Ireland to
Finland and N Russia, south to the Alps,
Yugoslavia and Romania in the mountains; also
in the Caucasus and NE North America,
growing in moist or shady meadows, by rocks in
streams and in open woods, flowering May–
August. Stems 30–70cm, not elongating greatly
during flowering. Flowers to 3cm across;
nectaries yellow, as long as the stamens.
'Superbus' is a tall form, though not with
exceptionally large flowers. For moist, rich soil
in sun or partial shade. Hardy to −20°C or less.

Trollius pumilus D. Don Native of the
Himalayas from Nepal and Bhutan eastwards to
Gansu and Shaanxi, growing in alpine meadows
and by streams, flowering in June–August.
Plant forming small clumps with stems to 30cm,
but usually *c*.15cm. Leaves 5cm across. Flowers
c.3cm across, opening flat, yellow or orange-
yellow. A small plant for a moist position in sun
or partial shade. Hardy to −20°C.

Trollius ranunculinus (Smith) Stearn syns. *T.
caucasicus* Stev., *T. patulus* Salisb. Native of
the Caucasus, NW Iran and NE & E Turkey, by
streams in alpine meadows at 2000–3000m,
usually flowering near melting snow in May–
June. Stem 9–70cm; at first short, elongating
during flowering. Petals 5–7; flowers 2.5–3.5cm
across, open, with the stamens exposed. For
moist soil in full sun by running water. Hardy to
−20°C.

Trollius yunnanensis (Franch.) Ulbr. Native
of NE Burma and SW China, in the Dali and
Lijiang mountains, in Yunnan, Sichuan and
Shaanxi, growing in mountain pastures at 3000–
3500m, flowering June–August. Height to
75cm but usually *c*.30cm, with a branched and
sparsely leafy flowering stem. Leaves with 3–5
broad overlapping lobes. Flowers open, *c*.4cm
across, usually without narrow, elongated
petals. For moist, peaty, but well-drained soil in
sun or partial shade. Hardy to −20°C. *T.
stenopetalus* Stapf. is very similar and possibly
only a variety of *T. yunnanensis*, but is said to
differ in its 'more boldly divided leaves and
narrower petals'.

Ranunculus aconitifolius beside a stream in the Valais, Switzerland

Ranunculus aconitifolius 'Flore Pleno'

Ranunculus lingua

Ranunculus aconitifolius L. (*Ranunculaceae*)
Native of Europe in the Alps, Jura and S
Carpathians south to C Italy and C Yugoslavia,
growing in subalpine meadows and by streams at
up to 2500m, flowering in June–August. Stems
to 50cm, forming a handsome clump. Leaves 3–5
lobed, the middle lobe fully divided from the
others; pedicels 1–3 times as long as its
subtending leaf, pubescent near the top. Flowers
10–20mm across. *R. acris* 'Flore Pleno', 'Fair
Maids of France' or 'Fair Maids of Kent' has
been known in gardens since the 16th century. It
has stems up to 60cm and tight double flowers.
Both require rich moist soil in partial shade. *R.
platanifolius* L. is larger, to 130cm, with
straighter stems; leaves 5–7 lobed, the middle
lobe not fully divided from the others. Pedicels
4–5 times as long as the subtending leaves,
usually glabrous near the apex. Common in
Europe, north to Belgium, Norway and Sweden
and extending to Spain, Corsica, Sardinia,
Greece and south-western Russia, in similar
habitats. Both are hardy to −20°C, perhaps less.

Ranunculus bulbosus L. '**F. M. Burton**'   The
species is native of Europe, Turkey (very rare),
the Caucasus and North Africa, growing in
rather dry grassy places, meadows and
particularly on chalk downs, flowering in April–
June. A variable species divided into several
subspecies. Plant tufted with a swollen base,
sometimes also with fleshy roots. Leaves 3-
partite, the middle segment usually stalked.
Flowers with reflexed sepals, and petals 7–15mm
long. 'F. M. Burton', shown here, has pale-
yellow flowers.

Ranunculus constantinopolitanus (DC.)
d'Urv. '**Flore Pleno**' syn. *R. bulbosus*
'Speciosus Plenus'   Native of SE Europe, from
Romania and Bulgaria to Greece and Turkey,
south to Syria and east to the Crimea, the
Caucasus and Iran, growing in damp meadows,
flowering in April–June. Plant forming dense
clumps. Flowering stems 20–75cm. Basal leaves
cordate at the base with 3 deep lobes, each
deeply toothed. Petals 8–15mm long. The
double-flowered form, shown here, has been
cultivated since the 18th century, often under
the name *R. bulbosus* 'Speciosus Plenus' or
'Flore Pleno'. *R. bulbosus*, however, has a
grooved not smooth pedicel, and a pubescent
not glabrous receptacle. Easily grown in any
moist, good soil. Hardy to −20°C.

Ranunculus cortusifolius Willd.   Native of
the Azores, Madeira and the Canaries, growing
in damp, shady places and roadsides in heather
and laurel forest, flowering in March–April.
Plant with few stems to 100cm, from a group of
several long fleshy roots. Basal leaves up to
30cm wide. Flowers to 50mm across. For rich
soil in sun or partial shade, moist in spring, dry
but shaded in summer. Hardy to −5°C perhaps.

Ranunculus creticus L.   Native of Crete,
Karpathos and Rhodes, growing on limestone
rocks under trees, at up to 400m, flowering in
March–May. A compact perennial, with few
stems to 60cm from a cluster of fleshy roots.
Basal leaves 8–15cm across. Petals 1.5–2.5cm
long. Sepals not reflexed. Easily grown in well-
drained soil in a hot, dry position, dry in

Ranunculus lyallii

Ranunculus penicillatus

Ranunculus creticus from Rhodes

summer. Hardy to −10°C perhaps. *R. cortusifolius* differs in its larger size and thick, leathery leaves.

Ranunculus lingua L. **Greater Spearwort**
Native of most of Europe from Scotland eastwards to the Caucasus, N Turkey, and Siberia, growing in reed swamps and by ponds and canals in shallow water, flowering in June–September. Stems 50–120cm, upright from a creeping rhizome. Basal leaves ovate, or ovate-oblong, cordate, produced in autumn, absent at flowering. Stem leaves oblong-lanceolate. Flowers 2–5cm across. A handsome plant for the margins of ponds and slow streams, with a succession of flowers throughout the summer.

Ranunculus lyallii Hook. fil. **Giant Buttercup** Native of New Zealand, in South Island from Marlborough southwards, in subalpine meadows and by mountain streams at 450–1500m, flowering in October–January. Stems to 1.5m, though rarely more than 1m in gardens. Leaves peltate, shallowly bowl-shaped, 12–30cm across. Flowers 5–7.5cm across. *R. insignis* Hook. fil. is smaller, with slightly lobed leaves and yellow waxy flowers 2–5cm across. It grows in alpine grassland, wet cliffs and rock crevices at 1000–2000m in both islands, from East Cape to Kaikoura. Both these species need a cool position and moist peaty soil. They grow best in cool moist climates, such as Scotland. Hybrids have been made between the two species, with cream-coloured flowers, but I have never seen them.

Ranunculus penicillatus (Dumort.) Bab. syn. *R. pseudo-fluitans* (Syme) Newbould Native of N & W Europe as far south as Hungary and the Crimea, growing in fast-flowing streams, flowering in May–August. Plant often without floating leaves, with hair-like leaves longer than the internodes forming bright-green mats which are usually all submerged. Flowers with petals 10–15mm long. This species is valued in fast flowing streams because it provides cover for fish without causing silting. As can be seen here, it is also very showy when in flower, usually in May.

Ranunculus constantinopolitanus 'Flore Pleno'

Ranunculus bulbosus 'F. M. Burton'

Ranunculus cortusifolius

Pulsatilla alpina subsp. *apiifolia* above St Luc, Valais

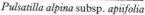

Pulsatilla alpina subsp. *apiifolia*

Pulsatilla alpina near Crans, Valais

Pulsatilla alpina (L.) Delarbre syn. *Anemone alpina* L. (*Ranunculaceae*)   Native of the Pyrenees and the Alps east to Austria and Yugoslavia and of the Caucasus, growing in alpine and subalpine meadows, flowering in May–August, according to altitude, soon after the snow melts. Plant forming clumps, often with many stems up to 45cm. Flowers 4–6cm across. A plant for well-drained, rich, deep, sandy and peaty soil in full sun: seed is reported to take two years to germinate, even when sown fresh. Two subspecies are recognized: subsp. *apiifolia* (syn. *Anemone sulphurea* L.) with pale yellow flowers, usually found on acid soil, and subsp. *alpina*, with white flowers, usually found on calcareous soil. Hybrids between the two are not uncommon. The closely related *P. alba* Rchb. has smaller flowers 2.5–4.3cm across, and usually glabrous leaves with terminal segments divided to the midrib. It is found from C France east to Romania and W Russia on acid soils.

Pulsatilla armena (Boiss.) Rupr. syns. *P. violacea* Rupr., *Anemone albana* Stev. subsp. *armena* (Boiss.) Smirn.   Native of N & E Turkey from Amasya and Erciyes Dağ near Kayseri eastwards to Soviet Armenia, at up to 4200m, in Turkey, flowering in May–June, often growing on volcanic soil. Flowers always nodding, 2–3.5cm long. Stems 3–20cm. Leaves finely divided, silky. Hardy to −25°C.

Pulsatilla chinensis (Bunge) Regel   Native of N China and E Siberia, growing in dry grassy places and rocky hillsides, flowering in April–May. It is common north of Beijing, near the Great Wall, and among the ruins of the Ming Tombs. Plant forming small tufts of few rosettes. Leaves expanding during flowering, finally to 15cm or more long, with flat segments up to 1cm wide. Stems 10–15cm at flowering, elongating to 30cm in fruit. Hardy to −20°C, but reported to be difficult to grow in England, possibly easier in E North America, as it needs a dry winter and spring, and a warm, humid summer.

Pulsatilla halleri (All.) Willd. syn. *Anemone halleri* All.   Native in scattered localities across Europe; five subspecies, differing mainly in their leaves, are recognized from five areas: the SW and C Alps; the Rhodope mountains; the Crimea; the W Carpathians in Poland and Czechoslovakia; SE Austria; they grow in rocky, sunny subalpine meadows at *c.*1500m. Whole plant very silky, even after flowering. Leaves simply pinnate, with 3–5 segments, the terminal segment long-stalked; flowers dark to pale violet; very silky outside. In a sixth, subsp. *grandis* (Wenderoth) Meikle, from S Germany, Austria, Czechoslovakia, and Hungary south to the Crimea, the hairs on the stem and leaves are exceptionally dense, and either silvery or brownish. 'Budapest' is (or was?) a colour form of this subspecies, with pale-blue flowers, originally collected in the Budapest area. For well-drained soil in full sun, with protection from wet in winter; hardy to −20°C or lower.

Pulsatilla chinensis at the Ming Tombs   *Pulsatilla vulgaris* on Royston Heath   *Pulsatilla vulgaris* f. *rubra*

Pulsatilla occidentalis on Carson Pass, E California   *Pulsatilla vulgaris* f. *alba*

Pulsatilla occidentalis Freyn. syn. *Anemone occidentalis* Wats.   Native of C California to British Columbia and Montana, growing on steep rocky slopes at 1700–3000m, flowering June–August, according to altitude; often in north-facing gullies, flowering close to melting snow. Plant tufted, with stems to 60cm, elongating during flowering. Leaves 4–8cm wide, ternate, silky, finely bipinnate into linear segments. Petals 5–8, white, bluish outside, or purplish, 2–3cm long. For well-drained, peaty soil. Hardy to −20°C.

Pulsatilla vulgaris Mill. syn. *Anemone pulsatilla* L. **Pasque Flower**   Native of England, especially East Anglia, and of S Sweden, east to Finland and the Ukraine, growing in dry grassland, often on chalk soils. Plant with many stems to 15cm, from a tufted rootstock, elongating during flowering to 30cm. Flowers purple, 5.5–8.5cm across, appearing with the leaves. Leaves with *c*.40 lobes. Several colour forms of *P. vulgaris* are cultivated, the commonest being f. *alba* (white) and f. *rubra* (red-flowered). Another (not shown) is 'Barton's Pink'; 'Mrs van der Elst' is also pink, but I have seen neither of them. *Pulsatilla rubra* (Lam.) Delerbre is a distinct species from C & S France and Spain, with nodding reddish-brown or blackish flowers. All require well-drained, chalky soil. Hardy to −20°C.

Pulsatilla halleri at the Col de Glaize, France

Pulsatilla armena   *Pulsatilla halleri* subsp. *grandis*

Anemone demissa at Lijiang

Anemone trifolia

Anemone rivularis

Anemone flaccida at Baoxing, Sichuan, with *Corydalis flexuosa*

Anemone davidii at Baoxing

Anemone sylvestris

Anemone rupicola in Kashmir

Anemone narcissiflora (yellow form)

Anemone narcissiflora (pink form)

Anemone narcissiflora near Mount Elbrus, Caucasus

Anemone tetrasepala above Lake Vishensar, Kashmir

Anemone davidii Franch. (*Ranunculaceae*)
Native of W China, in Sichuan, growing in
grassy places by streams at *c.*2000m, flowering in
May–June. Plants with creeping underground
rhizomes, forming loose colonies. Very variable
in size. Flowers up to 7cm across, but only 4cm
in the form shown here. Easily grown in moist,
peaty soil, and well established on the peat banks
at Kew. Photographed near Baoxing in late May.

Anemone demissa Hook. & Thoms.   Native of
W Nepal, Sikkim and Bhutan to SW China
(Yunnan), growing in alpine meadows, grassy
clearings in forest and scrub, and on screes and
rock ledges, at 3000–4750m, flowering in May–
July, according to altitude. Plant with few silky
hairy stems from a stout rootstock, surrounded
by the remains of last year's leaf bases. Stems
10–30cm, with 3–6 flowers on short 2–4cm
pedicels. Petals 7–15mm long, white, yellow or
purple or blue! For well-drained, peaty soil in
full sun, kept moist in summer, dry in winter and
spring. Hardy to −20°C.

Anemone flaccida Schmidt.   Native of E Siberia,
Sakhalin, N & W China, and Japan, growing in
shady places in ravines in loose peaty soil, and
along streams in woods, flowering in April–June.
Plant forming clumps of several stems from
short, black, creeping rhizome. Leaves rather
fleshy, divided to the base into 3 or 5 deeply
toothed lobes. Stems 15–30cm, with a pair of
sessile leaves and 1–3 flowers, 1.6–3.5cm across.
Seeds with a very short style, ripening green
while the petals are still fresh. For moist peaty
soil in shade. Hardy to −20°C or less. A modest
but attractive plant for the woodland garden.

Anemone narcissiflora L.   Native of NE
Spain, the Pyrenees, the Alps, N Turkey, the
Caucasus, the Urals and mountains across

Siberia to N Japan and in W North America,
growing in grassy, peaty but well-drained
meadows, occasionally in partial shade. Flowers
produced from May (April in gardens in
England) to August according to altitude and
latitude. Very variable; flowers in umbels usually
white, pink-flushed outside, and aptly compared
by Reginald Farrer to apple blossom, but
sometimes pink or pale yellow in the Caucasus.
Stems to 40cm; seeds flattened. Easily grown in
sun or part shade, in moist soil, but rare in
gardens as it is slow to raise from seed and not
easily divided.

Anemone rivularis Buch.- Ham, ex DC.
Native of Kashmir and N India to Tibet and SW
China (Yunnan), at 1800–3060m, in meadows, in
clearings in forest, on bunds between rice fields,
by streams and in hedges, flowering from April–
August. Plant with several arching stems to 1m,
from a tufted rootstock. Flowers rather small,
1.5–3cm across, with 5–8 narrow petals often
blue outside. Clearly distinct from *A. narcissiflora*
and its relatives, by having the flowers on long
stalks of different lengths, not in an umbel.
Easily grown in moist but well-drained soil in sun
or part shade, flowering in late spring. Hardy to
−20°C perhaps.

Anemone rupicola Cambess.   Native of
Afghanistan to W China (Yunnan, and more
rarely in Sichuan), growing at 2700–4800m, on
rocky slopes, screes and alpine meadows, usually
steep and north-facing, with little other
vegetation, flowering from May–August, often
near melting snow. Plant with a tufted rootstock,
and stems to 20cm. Flowers 5–8cm across. Basal
leaves 3-lobed. It is related to *A. sylvestris* and has
woolly seeds like *A. vitifolia*. A plant for moist,
well-drained soil, in a cool position, preferably
north-facing but not shaded. Hardy to −20°C.

Anemone sylvestris L.   Native of Europe
from S Sweden and NE France eastwards to the
Caucasus but not in the Alps, growing in open
woods and on rocky hills, flowering in May–
June. Plant spreading by root-buds to form
dense colonies, with stems 15–50cm. Flowers
solitary, 4–7cm across, with 5–8 petals. Easily
grown in moist, leafy soil in semi-shade. Hardy
to −20°C or less.

Anemone tetrasepala Royle   Native of
Afghanistan to N India, frequent in Kashmir,
growing in meadows, often among large
boulders, at 2100–3600m, flowering from June–
August. Very similar to *A. narcissiflora*, but
basal leaves deeply divided into 5 rather broad,
shallowly incised lobes. Flowers white, often
with 4 petals, but may have up to 7. Stem
30–75cm. For well-drained peaty soil,
preferably moist in summer, with a cool root-
run. Hardy to −20°C.

Anemone trifolia L.   Native of N Portugal,
N & E Spain, on acid soils (subsp. *albida*
(Moriz)Tutin), and from Italy and C Austria to
Hungary and N Yugoslavia on limestone
(subsp. *trifolia*), growing in fields, wet
meadows, and open woods, flowering in April–
May, to July in the mountains.
   Plant similar to *Anemone nemorosa*, but
rhizomes less far-creeping, so forming denser
clumps. Leaves 3, each with 3 toothed but not
lobed leaflets. Flowers white, *c.*2cm across.
Anthers white and petals elliptical in subsp.
albida; anthers blue and petals ovate in subsp.
trifolia. For a moist position in leafy soil, or
partial shade. The subsp. *trifolia* is usually
found on limestone; subsp. *albida* on acid soil.
Hardy to −15°C.

Adonis chrysocyathus in Kashmir

Adonis vernalis at Wisley

Adonis volgensis in Turkey

Adonis brevistyla near Lijiang

Actaea alba (L.) Mill. syn. *A. pachypoda* Elliot (*Ranunculaceae*)   Native of E North America, from Nova Scotia south to Georgia, west to Minnesota and Missouri, growing in woods, flowering in April–June, according to latitude. Plant with few stems to 90cm from a stout rootstock, elongating to 120cm in fruit. Flowers to 10mm long, with 4–10 narrow petals, and numerous longer stamens. Fruits white, on thickened, fleshy red stalks. Easily grown in leafy soil, in shade or partial shade. Hardy to −20°C and below. Forma *rubrocarpa* (Killip) Fernald has red fruit on thickened pedicels, in contrast to *A. rubra* in which the berries are also red, but on slender stalks, in a dense inflorescence.

Actaea spicata L. **Baneberry** from mountain woods in Europe from N England eastwards, and in N Turkey; has black berries.

Actaea rubra (Ait.) Willd. f. **neglecta** (Gillman) Robinson   Native of North America, from Nova Scotia south to New Jersey, and west to South Dakota and Nebraska, with subsp. *arguta* (Nutt.) Hulton from there westwards to California and Alaska, growing in woods, flowering in April–June. Plant with several stems to 80cm from a stout rootstock. Flowers similar to *A. alba*. Fruits red, on slender green stalks, or white in f. *neglecta*. For leafy soil in shade or partial shade. Hardy to −20°C and lower.

Adonis brevistyla Franch. (*Ranunculaceae*) Native of Bhutan and W China, e.g. in Lijiang in Yunnan, growing in wet *Tsuga* forest, damp scrub, open mountainsides, and wet ravines at 2500–4110m, flowering in April–June. Plant with few stems from a stout branching root; flowering stems 20–40cm. Leaves 5–10 × 3–8cm long, much divided into flat, acuminate lobes. Petals 1.2–2.5cm × 0.5–1cm, obovate to oblanceolate, white or yellow, often bluish beneath. For moist peaty soil, sheltered from wind in shade or partial shade. Hardy to −20°C or so.

Glaucidium palmatum at the Savill Gardens, Windsor

Glaucidium palmatum var. *leucanthum* in the Cruickshank Botanic Garden, Aberdeen

Adonis chrysocyathus Hook. fil. & Thoms. Native of N Pakistan to W Nepal and Tibet; common in Kashmir, growing on damp grassy slopes and among rocks, often near melting snow, flowering in June–September. Plant 15–23cm in flower; taller, to 40cm, in late flower. Flowers 3–5cm across, with 16–24 petals. For well-drained, moist, sandy, peaty soil. Not common in cultivation. Photographed in Kashmir above Lake Vishensar.

Adonis vernalis L.   Native of E, C & S Europe, from France to Spain to Italy, and north to Russia and Finland, in dry stony grassland and scrub, often on limestone, flowering from April–May. Several stems from a stout, branched rootstock, to 40cm high. Flowers 4–8cm across, with 10–20 petals. Differs from *A. volgensis* in its narrower leaf lobes, fewer petals and often larger flowers. Easily grown in very well-drained, rather dry soil, in sun or part shade, but much loved by slugs, and therefore almost useless in the open garden where slugs are common. Hardy to −20°C.

Adonis volgensis Stev.   Native of Russia, SE Hungary, Romania and the Caucasus, south to Soviet Armenia and NE Turkey, in steppes and dry subalpine meadows at *c.*1800m, flowering from March–May. Flowers 30–35mm across; stems to *c.*30cm. Lobes of leaves linear-lanceolate, dentate. For well-drained, sandy soil, and tolerant of summer drought. Hardy to −25°C. Photographed on Mount Ararat in May.

Anemonella thalictroides (L.) Spach. (*Ranunculaceae*)   Native of E North America, from New Hampshire and Massachusetts, south to Florida, and west to Ontario, Minnesota and Kansas, growing in damp deciduous and mixed woods, flowering in March–June. Plant with delicate stems to 20cm from a bunch of tuberous roots. Leaves appearing after the flowering stem, with 9 stalked leaflets. Flowers to 2.5cm across, with 5–10, white or pink (f. *rosea*), petal-like sepals. A delicate plant for a loose leafy soil, in shade or partial shade.

Glaucidium palmatum Sieb. & Zucc.   Native of Japan, in Hokkaido and N & C Honshu, in woods in the mountains, flowering from May–July according to altitude. Plant with few stems to 30cm, from a stout rootstock. Leaves 8–20cm long and wide, 7–11 lobed. Flowers 5–8cm across, pale mauve or rarely white in var. *leucanthum* Mak. Carpels 2, with flat, obovate winged seeds about 10mm long. For cool, moist leafy soil, in shade and shelter from drying wind. Hardy to −15°C. Similar in general appearance to *Podophyllum*, but in a different family, usually *Ranunculaceae*, often *Paeoniaceae*, and sometimes considered to be the sole representative of its own family, the *Glaucidiaceae*.

Hydrastis canadensis L. (*Ranunculaceae*) **Orange Root**   Native of E North America, from Connecticut to Minnesota, and in W Ontario, Georgia, Missouri and Kansas, growing in woods, especially in the mountains, flowering in April. Stems several to 30cm from a thick yellowish horizontal rootstock. Basal leaves palmate with 5–9 lobes, 12–20cm across. Flowering stem with 2 leaves, the upper subtending the large solitary flower up to 10mm across, without petals, but with numerous stamens. For leafly soil in shade or partial shade. Hardy to −15°C, or below.

Actaea rubra

Actaea alba f. *rubrocarpa*

Hydrastis canadensis

Anemonella thalictroides f. *rosea*

Anemonella thalictroides near Charlottesville, Virginia

31

Epimedium × versicolor
'Sulphureum'

Epimedium × versicolor
'Neosulphureum'

Epimedium alpinum

Epimedium pubigerum
(from E Turkey)

Epimedium pubigerum

Epimedium × cantabrigiense

Specimens from Washfield Nurseries, Kent, 17 April. ½ life size

Epimedium alpinum L. (*Berberidaceae*)
Native of SE Europe from N & C Italy to
Austria and south to Albania, and naturalized
elsewhere in N Europe including England;
growing in shady, rocky places in the foothills
and low mountains, flowering in April–May.
Plant forming loose patches by a creeping
rhizome. Stems 15–30cm, with a single leaf
longer than the inflorescence. Leaflets 5–10,
deciduous, pubescent beneath when young,
later glabrous. Flowers 9–13mm across. Inner
sepals dark red; petals bright yellow. Easily
grown in well-drained soil in shade. Hardy to
−20°C.

Epimedium × cantabrigiense Stearn   A
hybrid between *E. pubigerum* and *E. alpinum*
which arose in the 1940s in the Wilderness
Garden at St John's College, Cambridge, among
W. T. Stearn's collection of *Epimedium* species,
planted out there during the war. Plant forming
a mound of firm leaves, 30–60cm tall. Leaves
evergreen, usually with 9 leaflets, to 10 × 7cm.
Flowers *c.*1cm across. Inner sepals red; petals
pale yellow, reduced to nectaries. Easily grown
in well-drained soil in partial shade. Hardy to
−20°C perhaps.

Epimedium dolichostemon Stearn   Native of
China, in W Sichuan, but exact locality not
known at present: newly described from an
introduction by Mikinori Ogisu. Plant forming
small clumps of evergreen leaves. Leaflets 3,
sagittate, acuminate, with spines on edges and
tip, *c.*10cm long, 3cm wide. Inflorescence with
2 leaflets, the main branch overtopping the
leaves, *c.*35cm high. Flowers whitish; inner
sepals 8–9mm long, slightly reflexed. Stamens
8–9mm long, the filaments longer than the
anthers. Nectaries small and strongly curved. A
very graceful species, for moist woodland
conditions. Hardy to −15°C perhaps. *E.
sagittatum* (Sieb. & Zucc.) Maxim. is similar in
habit, but has smaller flowers *c.*6mm across,
inner sepals 3–4.5mm long, and stamens
4–5mm long, the filaments shorter than the
anthers. It is native of China, in NW Hubei,
growing on shady rocks in the mountains.
Hardy to −20°C or so.

Epimedium pubigerum (DC.) Morr. &
Decne.   Native of SE Bulgaria and Turkey,
from near Istanbul eastwards along the Black
Sea coast to W Georgia, growing in woods,
scrub and hedges, flowering in April–May.
Plant forming evergreen clumps, with short
rhizomes. Stems 20–70cm, with 1–2 leaves,
shorter than the much-branched inflorescence.
Leaflets usually 9, to 8cm long, pubescent
beneath. Flowers *c.*1cm across; inner sepals
pink or white; petals yellow. Easily grown in
leafy soil in partial shade, but often damaged, as
are most *Epimediums*, by late frosts. Hardy to
−15°C.

Epimedium × versicolor Morr.   A hybrid
between *E. grandiflorum* and *E. pinnatum* subsp.
colchicum, known since 1854. Plant forming a
mound of leaves to 30cm high and across.
Flowering stem leafy or leafless. Flowers 2cm
across. Petals about equal to inner sepals; spurs
6–9mm. 'Sulphureum' and 'Neosulphureum'
are two clones of this cross. 'Sulphureum'
usually has 5 leaflets, or up to 9, and a leafy
flowering stem. 'Neosulphureum' usually has 3
leaflets, brownish when young, and slightly
shorter spurs. Other hybrids of this parentage,
such as 'Versicolor' and 'Cuprea', have pinkish
or reddish sepals. All are easily grown in partial
shade and leafy soil. Hardy to −20°C.

Epimedium × youngianum Fisch. & Mey.   A
hybrid between *E. diphyllum* and *E.
grandiflorum*, possibly of wild origin in Japan.
Plant forming small clumps of leaves, with 2–6
or 9 leaflets 2–8cm long, 1–5cm across, to 15cm
tall. Flowering stem 10–30cm. Petals obovate,
with or without spurs, which vary in size and
shape. Selected forms include 'Roseum' syn.
'Lilacinum'?; 'Violaceum' (pinkish mauve);
'Niveum' (flowers small, white); 'Yenomoto
Form' (a good white, larger than 'Niveum').
For moist leafy soil in a partially shaded
position, moist in summer. Hardy to −20°C or
less. The easiest of the smaller species.

Epimedium dolichostemon   *Epimedium pubigerum*

Epimedium × versicolor 'Neosulphureum'

Epimedium × youngianum 'Yenomoto Form'   *Epimedium × youngianum* 'Niveum'

Epimedium × youngianum 'Violaceum'

Epimedium × *rubrum*

Epimedium × *warleyense*

Epimedium perralderianum

Epimedium
× *perralchicum* 'Wisley'

Epimedium davidii
(p. 36)

Epimedium × *perralchicum*
'Fröhnleiten'

Specimens from Washfield Nurseries, Kent, 17 April. ⅔ life size

Epimedium × perralchicum Stearn **'Wisley'**
(*Berberidaceae*)   A hybrid between *E. pinnatum*
subsp. *colchicum* and *E. perralderianum* which
appeared at Wisley where the parents were
growing together. 'Fröhnleiten' is a German
hybrid of similar parentage. Both clones are
robust plants with good yellow flowers and
evergreen leaves; leaflets spiny at the margin,
the spines up to 2.5mm long. The flowering
stems are leafless, and the spurs slightly
upcurved. Hardy to −15°C or lower if protected
by dry leaves or snow.

Epimedium perralderianum Cosson   Native of
Algeria, growing in oak woods and scrub and
under cedars, on the north side of the Babor
mountains, at 1300–1500m, flowering in March.
Plant forming clumps of shining evergreen
leaves, with 3 spiny-edged leaflets, up to 30cm
tall. Flowering stem without leaves, *c.*20cm.
Flowers 15–25mm across; inner sepals
8–11mm, obovate. Petals with small brown
spurs 1–2mm long. For sun or partial shade,
with shelter from cold winds. Hardy to −15°C.

Epimedium pinnatum Fisch. subsp. **colchicum**
(Boiss.) Busch   Native of NE Turkey from
Trabzon eastwards to the W Caucasus, growing
in pine woods and azalea and oak scrub, at up to
50m in Turkey, flowering in April. Plant
forming dense clumps with short rhizomes.
Leaves with 3 or 5 leaflets, broadly ovate, to
15cm long, glaucescent beneath, sparsely
toothed or smooth on the margin. Inflorescence
leafless, 20–40cm, glandular or glabrous.
Flowers *c.*18mm across. Petals small with a
dentate lamina, and a brown or yellow spur,
2mm long. Easily grown in leafy, heavy soil in
semi-shade, but slow-growing. Hardy to
−15°C. Subsp. *pinnatum* differs in having more,
smaller and spinier leaflets, and brownish-
purple spurs, *c.*1mm long. It is found in
Parrottia and hazel scrub in the Talysh
mountains in Soviet Azerbaijan, and in N Iran,
both in the Talysh and the Caspian forest.

Epimedium × rubrum C. Morren   A hybrid
between *E. grandiflorum* and *E. alpinum* known
since 1854. Plant with long, thin rhizomes,
forming spreading clumps. Leaves red when
young and when old. Flower stem to 20cm, with
leaves. Inflorescence sparsely hairy or hairless.
Flowers 1.8–2.5cm across. Inner sepals
crimson; petals pale yellow, with short spurs.
For leafy or peaty soil in partial shade; one of
the most beautiful of all foliage plants for
ground cover. Hardy to −15°C.

Epimedium × warleyense Stearn   A hybrid
between *E. alpinum* and *E. pinnatum* subsp.
colchicum raised in Miss Willmott's garden at
Warley Place in Essex in around 1909. Plant
with a shortly creeping rhizome, forming large
clumps of evergreen leaves. Flowering stems to
50cm, leafless or with 1 leaf, in April–May.
Flowers 15mm across; inner sepals coppery red,
petals yellow, anthers green. For any good soil
in partial shade. Hardy to −15°C.

Vancouveria chrysantha Greene
(*Berberidaceae*)   Native of SW Oregon in
Josephine Co. and N California, growing on
open rocky hillsides in *Ceanothus* and
Arctostaphylos scrub, among *Berberis* or
bracken, at up to 1200m, flowering in June.
Plant creeping to form open patches. Stems
*c.*20–40cm. Leaflets *c.*4cm, dark green and stiff
in texture, evergreen. Flowers 1–1.3cm across,

on very glandular stalks. Suitable for a warm,
sheltered, and partly shaded position in sandy
soil. Hardy to −10°C.

Vancouveria hexandra (Hook.) Morr. &
Decne.   Native of N Washington and Oregon
south to C California (Mendocino Co.), growing
in shady woods (usually pine or Redwood), at
below 1500m, flowering in May–June. Plant
creeping to form large, loose patches. Stem 10–
40cm, without leaves. Leaflets up to 7.5 × 7cm,
thin, not leathery, deciduous. Flowers 1–1.3cm
long, to 18mm across, white; sepals, stamens
and ovary glandular, but pedicels glabrous. For
leafy soil in sun or partial shade. Hardy to
−15°C.

Vancouveria planipetala Calloni **Redwood
Ivy**   Native of California, from Montery Co.
northwards to SW Oregon, growing in
Redwood forests near the coast at up to 600m,
flowering in May–June. Plant with creeping
rootstock and evergreen leaves, with thick,
leathery leaflets, with a thickened and wavy
margin, to 4cm long. Flower stem leafless to
50cm. Flowers white or purplish, 6–8mm
across; sepals, stamens and ovary glabrous, but
pedicels glandular. For a sunny or partially
shaded, but warm, position, with shelter in
winter. Hardy to −10°C, perhaps.

Epimedium × rubrum (young leaves)

Epimedium × rubrum

Epimedium pinnatum subsp. *colchicum*

Vancouveria chrysantha at Washfield Nurseries

Vancouveria hexandra at Branklyn

Vancouveria planipetala

Epimedium davidii in mixed *Rhododendron* forest, south of Ya-an, Sichuan

Epimedium acuminatum Franch.
(*Berberidaceae*)   Native of Guizhou, Yunnan and Sichuan, especially on Emei Shan, growing in moist coniferous and deciduous woods and scrub in the mountains at 1400–4000m, flowering from April–June. Plant tufted, sometimes with a creeping rhizome. Stems 25–50cm; leaflets acuminate, *c.*8–18cm long, 1.5–7cm across, glabrous and reddish when young, but bristly below when mature. Inflorescence glabrous or sparsely glandular. Flowers 3–4cm across, yellow, white, purple or pinkish. Requires moist, leafy soil in a very sheltered position. This plant was collected by Roy Lancaster on Mount Omei.

Epimedium davidii Franch.   Native of W Sichuan, especially Baoxing and Emei Shan, in woods, scrub and shady leafy places in rocky gorges at 1600–2340m, flowering from April–June. Plant tufted, with a slowly creeping rhizome. Stems up to 30–50cm, with leaflets 6 × 4.5cm, glaucescent beneath and thinly pubescent, with short appressed hairs. Inflorescence very glandular. Flowers 2–3cm across, yellowish. Petals with curved spurs and a long blade forming a cup 7–13mm deep.

Epimedium diphyllum (Morr. & Decne.) Lodd.   Native of Japan, in Shikoku and Kyushu, growing in woods in the mountains, flowering in April–May. Plant forming small mounds of leaves to 30cm high and across, but usually lower. Leaves usually with only 2 leaflets, evergreen, often with few spines on the edge, 2.5–5cm long, obtuse, cordate. Flowering stem leafless. Flowers white, or rarely purplish, 10–12mm across; petals without spurs. For moist, leafy soil in a sheltered position. Hardy to −15°C. *E. setosum* Koidz. has similar flowers, but is deciduous, with longer, sagittate and acute leaflets.

Epimedium elongatum Komarov   Native of W Sichuan, near Tatsienlu, at 2800–4000m, growing in woodland and scrub, flowering in May–July. Plant forming a mound of evergreen leaves to 40cm. Leaves with 3 leaflets, *c.*8cm long, 4.5cm across, with spiny edges, glaucous beneath. Inflorescence with 2 leaves, a repeatedly branched irregular cyme, 15–20cm. longer than the leaves, with scattered hairs. Flowers with yellow spurs 2–7cm long, and almost no petal limb, on glandular pedicels. Easily grown in leafy or peaty soil in partial shade. Hardy to −15°C.

Epimedium grandiflorum C. Morren syn. *E. macranthum* Morr. & Decne.   Native of Honshu, Hokkaido and Kyushu, growing in moist woods in the hills, flowering in March–May. Plant forming small clumps 20–40cm high, and finally more across, from a short rhizome. Leaves deciduous, with leaflets, 3–6cm long. Flowers white or purple in f. *violaceum* (C. Morren) Stearn (syn. 'Lilacinum'). Petals with long, downward-curving spurs 1–2cm long and limb 5–8mm long. For leafy soil with shade and shelter. Hardy to −20°C. Several very attractive cultivars of this species are grown in Japan, Europe and North America. The commonest are: 'Rose Queen' (pinkish), 'White Queen' (white) and 'Nanum', a dwarf (with leaves) only 7.5cm tall. Var. *higoense* Shimizu grows on limestone rocks in Higo province, Kyushu, and has leaves minutely hairy above. *E. sempervirens* Nakai, from C Japan, is similar, but has evergreen leaves, very glaucous beneath, and white or purplish flowers.

Epimedium leptorrhizum Stearn   Native of C China, in Guizhou (Kweichow) province, near Guiyang, growing in woods, flowering in April. Rhizome thin, 1–2mm across, long-creeping. Basal and cauline leaves 3-foliolate; leaflets narrowly ovate, long acuminate, glaucous and pubescent beneath, 3–9.5cm long. Flowers 4cm across; petals without a lamina, with a 2cm-long spur. For moist, leafy soil in cool shade, and not tolerant of drought. Hardy to −10°C perhaps.

Epimedium setosum Koidz.   Native of SW Honshu, in Shigoku district, growing in woods, flowering from April–May. Plant forming small mounds of deciduous leaves, 25–40cm high. Leaflets 6–10cm long, 3–4cm wide, acute, with long brown hairs beneath when young. Inflorescence with one leaf. Flowers white, 10–12mm across, with short spurs. For leafy soil in a partially shaded and sheltered position. Hardy to −10°C, perhaps lower.

Epimedium grandiflorum 'Rose Queen'

Epimedium diphyllum

Epimedium grandiflorum f. *violaceum*

Epimedium grandiflorum

Epimedium elongatum

Epimedium acuminatum at Sandling Park, Kent

Epimedium setosum

Epimedium leptorrhizum at Washfield Nurseries, Kent

Achlys triphylla at the Royal Botanic Garden, Edinburgh

Caulophyllum thalictroides

Diphylleia cymosa at Sellindge, Kent

Jeffersonia dubia

Jeffersonia diphylla

Achlys triphylla (Sm.) DC. (*Berberidaceae*)
Deerfoot, Vanilla leaf   Native of N California,
in the Coast Ranges, north to British Columbia,
growing in moist forests in the mountains,
below 1500m, flowering in April–June. Plant
forming patches by scaly, creeping rhizomes.
Leaves trifoliate, with leaflets 5–10cm long.
Flowering stems 25–50cm. Flowers without
petals, but with 6–13 white stamens. A second
very similar species, *A. japonica* Maxim., is
found in N Japan, in Hokkaido and N Honshu.
It appears to have fewer flowers in the spike and
leaves with only 3 shallow lobes. For moist leafy
soil in partial shade. Hardy to −15°C.

Caulophyllum thalictroides (L.) Michx.
(*Berberidaceae*) **Blue Cohosh**   Native of New
Brunswick south to South Carolina and
Tennessee, growing in dry woods in the
mountains in the south, flowering in April–
May. Plant forming large patches which must
be of great age, since it is slow to increase in
gardens. Stem to 75cm, bearing leaflets to
7.5cm. Sepals 9, greenish-brown; petals 6,
reduced to nectaries; seeds blue, berry-like.
C. thalictroides var. *robustum* from Japan, E
Siberia and China, commonly has yellowish-
green flowers, but is otherwise little different.
Suitable for growing in dense shade of
deciduous trees. Hardy to −20°C or less.

Diphylleia cymosa Michx. (*Berberidaceae*)
Umbrella-leaf   Native from Virginia to
Georgia in the Appalachians, by mountain
streams, flowering from May–June. Plant with a
stout rootstock forming a dense clump of stems
to 1m: leaves 2, deeply 2-lobed, 10–40cm
across. Flowers *c*.10 in an umbel. Petals 6,
1–1.5cm long. Fruits 10mm long, with blue or
red pedicels. *D. grayi* Fr. Schm. from
mountains in Hokkaido, Honshu and also
reported from rain forest in Yunnan, has stems
30–70cm, smaller leaves, less deeply divided,
and fewer flowers often in a cyme, with fruits on
green pedicels. From photographs it would
appear to be less coarse as a garden plant. Easily
grown in shade or partial shade and shelter in
moist leafy soil. Hardy to −15°C or lower.

Jeffersonia diphylla (L.) Pers. (*Berberidaceae*)
Native of New York State and Ontario, south to
Alabama and west to Wisconsin, growing in rich
woods on limestone, flowering in May. Plant
forming a small clump of leaves, with stems up
to 20cm, lengthening in fruit. Flowers to 3.5cm
across, petals 8. Capsule splitting straight across
the top. Suitable for a choice position in cool
leafy soil. Hardy to −20°C or less.

Jeffersonia dubia (Maxim.) Benth. & Hook.
Native of Manchuria, and around Vladivostock,
growing in forest and scrub, flowering in April–
May. Plant forming small clumps with stems up
to 20cm, and leaves to 10cm across. Flowers
2.5cm across: petals 5 or 6, rarely white.
Capsule splitting obliquely. For moist peaty soil
in partial shade. Hardy to −20°C.

Podophyllum hexandrum Royle syn. *P. emodi*
Wall. (*Berberidaceae*)   Native of NE
Afghanistan, in Nuristan, east to C China, at
2000–3500m, growing in scrub, forest and
alpine meadows, flowering in May–August.
Plant forming a clump of stems from a thick
rhizome, with stems up to 30cm at flowering,

Podophyllum peltatum

Podophyllum hexandrum

Podophyllum peltatum in New York State, April

Podophyllum hexandrum at the Royal Botanic Gardens, Kew

later taller. Leaves unfurling after flowering, finally 12–25cm across, 3–5 lobed, variably marked with purple. Petals 6, 2.5–4cm long. Fruits reddish, 2–5cm long, edible but insipid. Var. *chinense* Wall. has larger pink flowers and more deeply divided leaves. For leafy soil in partial shade and a cool position. Hardy to −20°C.

Podophyllum peltatum L. **May Apple**, **American Mandrake** or **Wild Jalap**   Native of North America, from Quebec and Ontario south to Florida and Texas, growing in moist open woods, scrub and wet meadows, flowering in April–June. Plant forming large patches with a creeping rhizome. Leaves well developed at flowering; flowers *c*.5cm across, hidden beneath the leaves. Petals 9. Easily grown in moist shady position; this plant is interesting rather than showy. Hardy to −15°C or less.

Podophyllum pleianthum Hance   Native of Taiwan, C & SE China, growing in forests at 1000–2500m, flowering in March–April. Stems up to 80cm, from a short, thick rhizome. Leaves *c*.30cm across, peltate, with 6–9 shallow obtuse lobes. Flowers 5–8, with 6–9 petals up to 6cm long. Easily cultivated in leafy soil, but probably not very hardy – perhaps to −5°C. *P. versipelle* Hance, found on woods and shady rocks in Hubei, Sichuan, Yunnan and Xizang, is smaller than *P. pleianthum*, with leaves usually 15cm across, more deeply lobed, and petals 2–3.5cm long. Hardy at Kew to −10°C.

Podophyllum pleianthum at Sellindge, Kent

Dicentra spectabilis 'Alba'

Dicentra formosa 'Zestful'

Dicentra formosa

Dicentra formosa 'Langtrees'

Dicentra formosa 'Bountiful'

Dicentra spectabilis

Dicentra formosa 'Adrian Bloom'

Dicentra formosa 'Stuart Boothman'

Dicentra eximea

Specimens from Wisley, 14 April. ½ life size

Dicentra macrantha at the Royal Botanic Gardens, Kew

Dicentra formosa 'Langtrees'

Dicentra eximea 'Alba'

Dicentra cucullaria in the Blue Ridge Mountains, Virginia

Dicentra formosa in *Sequoiadendron* forest, Yosemite, California

Dicentra cucullaria (L.) Torr. (*Papaveraceae*) Native of E North America, from Nova Scotia south to North Carolina and west to Kansas, growing in cool places in mountain woods, flowering in May–September. Plant forming dense clumps from a tuberous rhizome. Leaves very finely divided. Stems 12–25cm, little longer than the leaves. Flowers 12–16mm long, the outer petals wide-spreading at the base. For cool leafy soil in shade. Hardy to −20°C and below.

Dicentra eximea (Ker-Gawl.) DC. Native of E North America, in New York south to Georgia and Tennessee, growing in rocky places in woods in the mountains, flowering in May–September. Plant forming compact patches, without a creeping rhizome. Stems to 60cm, little longer than the leaves. Flowers 16–20mm long, narrower than those of *D. formosa* and with more reflexed outer petals, pinkish, or white in 'Alba'. For moist but well-drained soil, growing well on rock outcrops in shade. Hardy to −20°C.

Dicentra formosa (Andr.) Walp. Native of W North America, in the Sierra Nevada in C California, and in the Coast Ranges, growing in Redwood and *Sequoiadendron* forest, and oak woodland, in dry or damp places in shade, at up to 2000m, flowering in March–July. Plant with fleshy creeping rootstock, forming small patches. Leaves to 50cm, usually *c*.25cm. Flower stems slightly longer than the leaves; flowers 14–18mm long.

Two subspecies are recognized in the wild:
Subsp. *nevadensis* (Eastw.) Munz from Tulare Co., at up to 3000m, has finely dissected leaves and usually pale outer and creamy inner petals, flowering in July.
Subsp. *oregona* (Eastw.) Munz from the inner coast ranges in Del Norte Co. and S Oregon, has shorter stems to 25cm, and yellowish outer petals and pink-tipped inner ones. It flowers in April–May. These have been selected and hybridized in cultivation to produce several cultivars:
'Adrian Bloom' Narrow greyish leaves and deep pink flowers.
'Alba' Flowers pure white; leaves green.
'Bountiful' Deep purplish-red flowers.
'Langtrees' syn. 'Pearl Drops' is a very attractive variety with broad silver-grey leaflets and cream and pink flowers.
'Stuart Boothman' Small, with very narrow leaflet and deep-pink flowers on shorter stems.
'Zestful' Paler pinkish flowers, close to the wild type of *D. formosa*.
All grow easily in partial shade in good soil and flower all summer if kept moist. The greyer, narrower-leaved forms do well in full sun also. Hardy to −20°C, perhaps.

Dicentra macrantha Oliver Native of E China, growing in wet woods, flowering in May. Plant with long-creeping, fleshy, brittle, thin rhizomes, forming spreading patches when growing happily! Leaves with yellowish stalks, to 45cm, with leaflets *c*.5cm long, coarsely toothed, but not lobed. Flowers *c*.7.5cm long. A beautiful and elegant plant, but difficult to grow. It needs shelter from any wind, and from late frost, and a moist leafy and sandy soil, with protection from slugs. Hardy to −15°C, perhaps. Another yellow-flowered species, *D. chrysantha* (Hook. & Arn.) Walp., is an upright plant to 1.5m, with masses of small, 1.3cm upward-facing flowers and finely divided, glaucous leaves. It is found in dry chaparral, especially after a burn, in S California.

Dicentra spectabilis (L.) Lemaire **Bleeding Heart** Native of N China, in Heilongiang (Manchuria) (very rare), and in Korea, growing in woods, and deep shady valleys, flowering in May–July, but in spring in gardens. Plant with fleshy arching stems to 60cm, from a thick root. Flowers *c*.2.5cm long, red or pure white in 'Alba'. Easily grown in moist sandy soil in partial shade. Hardy to −20°C and below.

Cardamine diphylla

Sanguinaria canadensis

Cardamine bulbifera

Cardamine enneaphyllos at Wisley

Cardamine laciniata in the Blue Ridge Mountains

Cardamine laciniata

Cardamine bulbifera (L.) Crantz syn. *Dentaria bulbifera* L. (*Cruciferae*) **Coral-root** Native of S Scotland and France eastwards to Turkey, the Caucasus, N Iran and C Russia, growing in wet woods of oak (in S England) or beech, flowering in April–June. Root fleshy, creeping underground. Stems to 70cm, with bulbils in leaf axils. Petals 12–16mm long, usually purplish. Easily grown, and interesting rather than showy. Propagates quickly from bulbils but requires moist soil to flower well. Hardy to −20°C and less.

Cardamine diphylla (Michx.) Wood syn. *Dentaria diphylla* Michx. Native of E North America from Nova Scotia and New Brunswick, south to Minnesota, Kentucky and South Carolina, growing in moist woods and meadows, flowering in April–May. Plant with creeping underground fleshy rhizome and upright stems to 35cm. Stem-leaves 2, opposite, with 3 ovate, shallowly crenate lobes. Basal leaves 3-foliolate. Flowers white, 12–16mm across. *C. maxima* (Nutt.) Wood is similar but has usually 3 alternate leaves and larger purplish flowers. For moist leafy soil in deciduous shade. Hardy to −20°C and less.

Cardamine enneaphyllos (L.) Crantz syn. *Dentaria enneaphyllos* L. Native of the E Alps and Carpathians to Albania and Yugoslavia, growing in subalpine woods. Rhizome swollen, to 6mm in diameter. Stems 20–30cm. Leaves ternate or digitate. Petals 12–16mm, pale yellow or white, almost equalling the stamens. For sandy leafy soil in partial shade, moist in summer. Hardy to −20°C.

Cardamine heptaphylla (Vill.) O.E. Schulz syn. *Dentaria pinnata* Lam. Native of Spain in the Pyrenees, and France to SW Germany, W Switzerland and NE Italy (Monte Baldo) and in the Apennines in Italy, growing in woods in the mountains, flowering in April–May. Rhizome scaly, 4–10mm thick. Stems 30–60cm, usually c.30cm. Leaves pinnate, leaflets varying from 3–5 pairs on lowest leaves, 2–3 pairs on upper leaves. Flowers usually white, rarely pink or purplish, petals 14–20mm long. For rich sandy and leafy soil in shade or partial shade, moist in summer. Hardy to −20°C or so.

Cardamine kitaibelii Becherer syn. *Dentaria polyphylla* Waldst. & Kit. Native of Switzerland, the Apennines and Yugoslavia, growing in scrub at up to 1700m, flowering in April–May. Rhizome scaly, 3–6mm thick; stem 20–30cm, elongating during flowering. Leaves pinnate with 2–6 pairs of coarsely-toothed

Cardamine kitaibelii

Cardamine pentaphyllos at Sellindge, Kent

leaflets. Petals 15–22cm. For moist, leafy soil. Hardy to −20°C.

Cardamine laciniata (Muhl.) Wood syn. *Dentaria laciniata* Muhl. **Cut-leaved Toothwort** Native of E North America, from Quebec south to Florida, west to Minnesota, Kansas and Louisiana, growing in moist woods, often in the mountains, flowering in April–June. Plant with short creeping underground fleshy but not scaly rhizome and upright stems to 35cm. Leaves 5–12.5cm across, 3-lobed with the lobes deeply cut and toothed. Flowers pale purplish or white, 14–18mm across. For moist leafy soil, in deciduous shade. Hardy to −20°C or less.

Cardamine microphylla (Willd.) O.E. Schulz syn. *Dentaria microphylla* Willd. Native of the Caucasus, and recorded from Mount Ararat (Ağri Dağ) in Turkey, growing on damp screes, in shady ravines, scrub, and by mountain streams at 2000–3000m, flowering in July–September. Rhizomes scaly and creeping, so the plant forms spreading mats. Stems to 15cm. *C. quinquefolia* (Bieb.) Schmalh is very similar but has biserrate leaflets in 2–3 pairs and purple petals 14–18mm long. From Bulgaria and Romania to Turkey and the Caucasus. Beautiful but has proved shy-flowering in cultivation and rather invasive. Hardy to −20°C or less.

Cardamine pentaphyllos (L.) Crantz syn. *Dentaria digitata* Lam. Native of Spain (in the Pyrenees) to S Germany, Austria and N Yugoslavia, growing in woods in the mountains, flowering in May–June. Rhizome scaly, 1.5–2.5mm wide. Stems 30–60cm, usually nearer 30cm. Leaves digitate or ternate, with 3–5 leaflets. Petals 18–22mm, white or pale purple. For sandy, leafy soil in partial shade, moist in summer. Hardy to −20°C or so.

Sanguinaria canadensis L. (*Papaveraceae*) **Bloodroot** Native of E North America, from Nova Scotia west to Nebraska, south to Arkansas and N Florida, growing in woods and shaded slopes, in the mountains in the south, flowering in April–May. Plant slow creeping from a thick rhizome with red juice. Leaves folded and vertical before they unfold, finally 15–30cm across, variably lobed. Flowering stem c.10cm at flowering, petals up to 2cm long, usually 8–16, but many in the double-flowered form which is commonly cultivated. For leafy soil in a cool position in deciduous shade. Hardy to −20°C or less. The single-flowered wild form, shown here, is more graceful than the double, but the flowers are very short-lived.

Cardamine heptaphylla at Sellindge, Kent

Cardamine microphylla near Kasbegi, C Caucasus

Cardamine pratensis in Kent

Cardamine pratensis 'Flore Pleno'

Cardamine rhaphanifolia in the Royal Botanic Garden, Edinburgh

Cardamine macrophylla at Baoxing, Sichuan

Cardamine amara by the River Don in Aberdeenshire

Cardamine amara L. (*Cruciferae*) **Large Bittercress** Native of most of Europe from Scotland and Ireland to Spain and Portugal eastwards to C Asia and Siberia, by rivers, streams and in wet woods usually in trickling water, flowering in April–June. Plant with creeping rhizome and stolons, so making large patches. Stems 10–60cm, usually *c.*30cm. Petals 7–9mm across, nearly always chalky white with dark anthers, but rarely pale purple. Basal leaves with 5–9 ovate or orbicular leaflets. Easily grown in moist soil in sun or partial shade. An invasive plant for the wild garden. Hardy to −20°C or less.

Cardamine macrophylla Franch. Native of China, in W Sichuan, growing by mountain streams and in damp woods at 2000–3000m, flowering in April–June. Rhizomes thin and fleshy, not far creeping. Stems upright, to 70cm. Basal leaves pinnate, with many pairs of leaflets. Flowers *c.*1cm across. For moist leafy soil in shade or by water. Hardy to −15°C.

Cardamine pratensis L. **Cuckoo flower, Lady's Smock** Native of most of Europe, to W Siberia and across northern North America, growing in damp meadows, by streams and in ditches, flowering from April–June. A variable plant of graceful habit, with stems 15–55cm, usually *c.*20cm, high. Roots fleshy, sometimes with stolons. Flowers pale pinkish purple, more rarely whitish, opening in the sun; petals 8–13mm. Very pretty, not invasive, and one of the best native species for damp gardens, but may require protection from wood pigeons, which eat the young buds in the spring. It is a host of the Orange Tip butterfly. The double form, 'Flore Pleno', has been grown in gardens since at least the mid-17th century.

Cardamine rhaphanifolia Pourr. syn. *C. latifolia* Vahl. Native of NW Spain, the Pyrenees and S Alps to Greece, Turkey and the Caucasus, growing in streams and springs in alpine meadows, and open woods, flowering in May–July. Stems 30–70cm, several from a creeping rhizome. Leaves with 1–5 pairs of leaflets, the terminal one large, 3–7cm wide. Petals 8–12mm, pinkish purple. For moist or wet soil in full sun. Hardy to −20°C.

Cardamine trifolia L. Native of C Europe, in the Alps and Carpathians, the Apennines and C Yugoslavia; rare in the west, growing in damp woods and shady places, flowering in April–June. Stem 20–30cm; rhizomes creeping, forming mats of leaves, simple or 3-fid. Petals 9–11mm, white or pink; anthers yellow. Fruit 20–25mm long, linear. For moist leafy soil in shade. Hardy to −20°C. Easily distinguished from the rather similar *Pachyphragma* by the fruit.

Hesperis matronalis naturalized in Aberdeenshire

Lunaria redidiva

Hesperis matronalis L. (*Cruciferae*) **Dame's Violet** Native of the Alps, Pyrenees and SE Europe, but commonly naturalized elsewhere, also in the Caucasus and N Turkey, Siberia and Soviet C Asia, growing in mountain woods, scrub and by streams, flowering in May–July. In the wild the white-and-purple-flowered subspecies are separate, whereas in cultivation they are mixed. Stems to 120cm, usually *c.*100cm. Petals 15–25mm, usually *c.*20mm; flowers scented. A short-lived perennial, suitable for growing in damp, shady or grassy places. Hardy to −20°C. Other closely related species, differing in leaf shape and hairs, are found in Turkey and SE Europe.

Lunaria redidiva L. (*Cruciferae*) **Perennial Honesty** Native of most of Europe east to Siberia, in moist, usually subalpine woods, and scrub in the mountains in the south, but not common, flowering in May–July. Stems 35–140cm, elongating during flowering. Leaves cordate. Petals 12–20mm, flowers scented. Seed pods 35–90mm long, elliptical. Hardy to −20°C. Honesty, *L. annua* L., is a biennial, with deep purple or white, unscented flowers and almost round seed pods, of which the shining septum is often dried and used for Christmas decoration.

Pachyphragma macrophyllum (Hoffm.) Busch (*Cruciferae*) Native of NE Turkey and the W Caucasus, usually growing in wet beech forests, at up to 1900m in Turkey, flowering in April–May. Plant with a creeping rhizome, with flowering stems up to *c.*10cm and inflorescence to 15cm, soon hidden by leaves. Basal leaves large, ovate cordate, with petioles up to 18cm long. Petals 8mm long. Fruit broadly obcordate, rounded at the base 12–17mm broad. For leafy soil, in damp shade. Hardy to −15°C?

Cardamine trifolia

Pachyphragma macrophyllum

Erysimum 'Jubilee Gold'

Erysimum 'Bredon'

Cheiranthus
'Harpur Crewe'

Erysimum concinnum

Erysimum 'Mrs L. K. Elmhirst'

Arabis caucasica 'Snowdrop'

Arabis blepharophylla

Specimens from Hopleys Nursery, 12 April. ⅓ life size

Alyssoides utriculata (L.) Medicus (*Cruciferae*)   Native of France, in SW Alps, east to Romania, Greece and N Turkey, growing on rock ledges at up to 1300m in Turkey, flowering in April–June. Stems to 40cm. Leaves variably hairy, petals 14–20mm long. Fruit inflated 10–15mm in diameter. Easily recognized by the inflated seed pods.

Arabis blepharophylla Hook. & Arn. (*Cruciferae*)   Native of California, around San Francisco, growing in rocky scrub below 300m, flowering in February–April. Plant with several stems to 20cm from a central rootstock, forming small tufts. Leaves in a basal rosette, obovate to oblanceolate, obtuse, 2–8cm long. Flowers pinkish purple; petals 12–18mm long. For well-drained soil in full sun, and tolerant of some drought in summer. Hardy to −15°C.

Arabis caucasica Schlecht. in Willd. syn. *A. albida* Stev.   Native of SE Europe from Italy eastwards to the Caucasus, N & E Turkey, W Syria and Iran and often naturalized elsewhere, growing on rocks and cliffs, flowering in March–August. Plant forming a mat of thin stems to 1m or more across. Flowering stems 15–35cm. Flowers white with petals 12–16mm long. 'Snowdrop' is a selected form, and a double 'Plena' is common. Pink forms are also in cultivation. Easily grown in well-drained, poor soil. Hardy to −20°C.

Cheiranthus cheiri L. syn. *Erysimum cheiri* (L.) Crantz (*Cruciferae*) **Wallflower**   Native of cliffs and rocks in Greece, Crete, W Turkey and W Syria, flowering in March–April. Plant subshrubby, with several stems to 50cm, usually *c*.30cm. Flowers in the wild deep yellow; petals 15–25mm long. Naturalized on walls in most of the rest of Europe; flower colour in cultivated wallflowers varies from red to pinkish or brown, yellow and cream. Although often grown as a biennial, it is a perennial, requiring very well-drained, dry soil to survive. 'Harpur Crewe' is a double-flowered form of the wild wallflower, known since the 17th century. It is a good perennial, compact and free flowering if grown in very poor limy soil. 'Bloody Warrior' is a dark-red double. Hardy to −15°C perhaps.

Erysimum 'Bowles' Mauve' (*Cruciferae*)   A hybrid between *E. scoparium* or possibly *E. linifolium* and *Cheiranthus* of as yet unknown origin. Plant subshrubby, forming a mound of greyish leaves to 1m in diameter. Flowers produced over a long period from April onwards, *c*.2cm across. 'Mrs L. K. Elmhirst' is very similar to 'Bowles' Mauve' but has dark-green not greyish leaves, with a sparser coating of longer hairs. Flowers paler, with dark veins, *c*.2.8cm across. Both grow well in very poor soil, and are hardy to *c*.−15°C.

Erysimum 'Bredon'   Probably a hybrid between *Cheiranthus cheiri* and an *Erysimum*, possibly *E. helveticum* (Jacq.) DC. or *E. grandiflorum* Desf. Stems to 20cm. Buds reddish; flowers April–July. 'Jubilee Gold', similar to Bredon, has toothed leaves.

Erysimum concinnum Eastw.   Native of W North America, from N California (Point Reyes) north to Oregon, growing on rocks and cliffs near the sea, flowering in March–May. Plant with a few stems to *c*.15cm from a central root. Leaves narrowly oblanceolate. Flowers pale yellow or creamy white, the petals 15–20mm long. A beautiful, short-lived plant for well-drained but rich soil. Hardy to −15°C perhaps.

Erysimum 'Constant Cheer'   Growth bushy, to 30cm, but usually *c*.20cm. Flowers opening brownish orange, turning purple, produced over a long season in spring and summer. 'Jacob's Jacket' has rather similar colouring. Hardy to −15°C, especially in poor, well-drained soil.

Erysimum semperflorens (Schousboe) Wettst.   Native of W Morocco, growing in dunes, scrub and rocky places, flowering in January–May. Plant with several upright stems to 40cm from a rather woody base. Leaves appressed-hairy; flowers *c*.18mm long, usually white or yellowish. For well-drained, poor soil in a warm position. *E. mutabile* Boiss. & Heldr., with which *E. semperflorens* has been confused, is endemic to Crete, growing on mountain cliffs and rocks. It has flowers which open yellow, changing to buff or purplish. Both are hardy to −15°C perhaps.

Erysimum semperflorens

Erysimum 'Bredon'

Erysimum 'Constant Cheer'

Wild Wallflower at Canterbury

Alyssoides utriculata

Erysimum 'Bowles' Mauve'

Euphorbia nicaeensis in S France

Euphorbia oblongifolia in C Caucasus

Euphorbia villosa

Euphorbia macrostegia from Iran, at Kew

Euphorbia myrsinites *Euphorbia hyberna* from Co. Cork *Euphorbia denticulata* near Lake Van,
SE Turkey

Euphorbia rigida near Mugla, SW Turkey

Euphorbia denticulata Lam. (*Euphorbiaceae*)
Native of E Turkey, N Iraq, NW & N Iran and
Soviet Armenia growing in open oak woods and
scrub, and on bare rocky slopes and steppes, at
800–3050m in Turkey, flowering in April–
August. Stems prostrate. Leaves glaucous,
fleshy, obovate to suborbicular, to 4cm broad.
Rays 5. Glands toothed like a comb, deep
crimson. Fruits 7–8mm across. This striking
plant proved hardy in a dry, well-drained
position in Cambridge, but is difficult to grow in
climates with wet, cool summers and warm, wet
winters.

Euphorbia hyberna L. subsp. **hyberna** Native
of SW Ireland, where it is common, and SW
England, where it is very rare, to N Italy, Spain
and Portugal, growing in open woods, on shady
and rocky banks and in hedges, flowering in
April–June. Stems 30–60cm, elongating during
flowering, from a stout rootstock. Leaves thin,
oblong, obtuse, glabrous above, pilose beneath,
sometimes becoming reddish. Rays 5. Glands
suborbicular. Capsule with short and long,
slender tubercles. Easily grown in a semi-
shaded position in moist soil. The Irish form
(illustrated here) does not turn red in summer,
so the reddening is not an invariable character of
the species. Some Spanish plants, however, do
have red stems. Subsp. *insularis* (Boiss.) Briq.,
with numerous axillary rays, nearly sessile
capsules and glands with thick margins, is
found in Corsica, Sardinia and NW Italy.

Euphorbia macrostegia Boiss. Native of S
Turkey, W Syria and Lebanon, and of W & S
Iran, growing in woods, Mediterranean scrub,
and in oak scrub on limestone in the Zagros in
Iran, at 650–2100m, flowering in April–July.
Stems to 60cm. Leaves green or glaucous, thin
but tough; stem leaves to 5cm across. Floral
cups nodding 2–4cm across, often purplish.
Glands short- or medium-horned. Capsule

glabrous. For well-drained soil in sun or partial
shade. Hardy to −15°C, perhaps.

Euphorbia myrsinites L. Native of S Europe
from the Balearic Islands, Corsica and North
Africa, eastwards to the Crimea, Turkey and C
Asia (Turkestan), growing on rocky slopes,
open pine forest, roadside banks and stony
mountain pastures, from 450–2200m in Turkey,
flowering from April–August. Stems prostrate,
to 30cm long. Leaves obovate-oblanceolate,
glaucous, fleshy. Rays 8–13. Glands 2-horned.
Capsule conical, with 3 rounded ridges. Easily
grown in well-drained soil or hanging over a
wall. Hardy to −15°C.

Euphorbia nicaeensis All. Native of Europe
from S France and Portugal eastwards to C
Russia, Turkey and the Caucasus, on open
slopes, roadsides, rocky places, scrub and open
forest at up to 1800m in Turkey, flowering in
May–August. Stems to 80cm, often reddish.
Leaves glabrous or minutely papillose,
glaucous, leathery, lanceolate to oblong, to
1.8cm wide, obtuse. Rays 5–18. Glands truncate
or emarginate, or with 2 short horns. Capsule
rugulose, sometimes pubescent. A variable
species, sometimes with few erect stems,
sometimes with stems numerous and
procumbent. Easily grown in dry, well-drained
soil. *E. niciciana* Borbas ex Novak is
confusingly similar, but usually has smaller
seeds and narrower, acute leaves to 8mm wide.
For a dry, sunny position. Hardy to −15°C.

Euphorbia oblongifolia (C. Koch) C. Koch
Native of N & E Turkey to the Caucasus, in
beech and spruce forests, rocky and grassy
slopes, screes, and alpine meadows at 1200–
2800m in Turkey, flowering in May–August.
Stem to 1m, pubescent or nearly glabrous.
Leaves often glaucous, to 4cm across, usually
obtuse, rather thin. Raylet cups 2–3cm across,

often purplish. Glands long-horned. Capsule
smooth or with granular surface. For good rich
but sandy soil in partial shade. Hardy to −20°C.

Euphorbia rigida M. Bieb. syn. *E.
biglandulosa* Native of S Europe from Portugal
(but not Spain!?) and North Africa to Italy,
Albania, the W Caucasus, Greece, Turkey, W
Syria and NE Iran. It grows on rocky limestone,
shale and schist slopes, open pine forest, scrub
and overgrazed hills, at up to 2000m in Turkey,
flowering in March–August. Stems semi-
prostrate or ascending, to 60cm. Leaves
lanceolate, very acute, stiff, fleshy, glaucous,
often reddish or orange. Rays 7–16. Glands 2-
horned. Fruit cylindrical, 6–7mm in diameter.
Hardy to c.−10°C or lower, but killed by cold
winds of c.−15°C when grown in the moist
climate of S England. In drier climates it should
be hardier, especially if introduced from a cold
locality. A most attractive species, for a dry
position such as a raised bed, or for growing
hanging over a wall.

Euphorbia villosa Waldst. & Kit. syn. *E. pilosa*
auct. non L. Native of S Europe from Spain,
France and North Africa, to Greece, the
Crimea, European Turkey, the Caucasus and W
Siberia, in damp meadows, open woods,
hedgerows and river banks, flowering in April–
June. Stems numerous, up to 120cm, scaly
below. Leaves rather thin, glabrous or
pubescent, oblong to elliptical. Rays 5 or more.
Glands suborbicular or ovate, without horns.
Capsule smooth or nearly smooth. Easily grown
in moist soil or partial shade. Hardy to −20°C,
perhaps. Formerly known, possibly not native,
from a wood near Bath, but not seen since the
1930s and probably extinct; often known as *E.
pilosa* L., which name correctly belongs to a
Himalayan species.

Euphorbia cyparissias

Euphorbia griffithii 'Dixter'

Euphorbia characias
subsp. *characias*

Euphorbia
polychroma

Euphorbia amygdaloides
var. *robbiae*

Euphorbia amygdaloides

Specimens from Wisley, 29 April. ²⁄₅ life size

Euphorbia amygdaloides L. (*Euphorbiaceae*)
Wood Spurge   Native of Europe from Ireland
and N England to Portugal and Algeria,
eastwards to Poland, Turkey and the Caucasus,
in woods, hedges and on grassy banks, usually
in rather moist soil, at up to 2000m in Turkey,
flowering in March–August. Stems tufted, more
or less upright to 80cm, leafy the first year,
usually flowering the second. Stems and leaves
often purplish, and deep purple in 'Rubra' (syn.
'Purpurea') which comes true from seed. Leaves
oblanceolate, usually less than 2cm wide,
2.5–7cm long. Rays 5–11. Glands with 2 long
horns. Capsule smooth. For moist soil in full
sun, or partial shade. Individual plants are not
long-lived, but seed easily. 'Variegata' has
yellow-edged leaves.

Euphorbia amygdaloides L. var. **robbiae**
(Turrill) Radcliffe-Smith   This variety differs
from ordinary *E. amygdaloides* in its creeping
underground rhizomes, forming spreading
patches, and its more leathery, oblanceolate
shining, nearly glabrous leaves, in a distinct
rosette on the non-flowering stems. It is native
of woods in NW Turkey, in the Belgrad forest
in European Turkey and as far east as Bolu in
Asia. Hardy to −15°C for short periods.

Euphorbia characias L.   Native of the
Mediterranean region from Portugal and
Morocco eastwards to S Turkey, growing on
rocky hills, in olive groves, in open forest and
on roadsides, at up to 1000m in Turkey,
flowering in January–May. Two subspecies are
recognized: subsp. *characias*, which is mainly
western, extends east to Yugoslavia and
Cyrenaica; it has stems usually up to 80cm, with
numerous softly hairy, greyish, usually
oblanceolate leaves 3–13cm long, to 1cm wide;
glands usually dark brown or reddish with short
horns or emarginate. Subsp. *wulfenii* (Hoppe ex
W. Koch) J. R.-Smith is taller, up to 1.8m, with
a larger flowering head, and yellowish glands
with long horns. It is commonest in Greece and
Turkey. A large and yellow form is in
cultivation as 'John Tomlinson', collected in
Greece. 'Lambrook Gold' is very similar. Both
subspecies are excellent garden plants, hardy to
−10°C or less if in very well-drained soil, but
killed by persistent lower temperatures,
especially when combined with damp.

Euphorbia cyparissias L.   Native of most of
Europe except the British Isles and Scandinavia,
where, however, it is often naturalized
especially on sand dunes; growing in dry rocky
meadows, at up to 2500m in the Alps, flowering
in May–September. Plant with a creeping
underground rhizome, forming large patches.
Stems to 50cm, but usually less than 30cm.
Leaves to 4cm long, linear. Rays 9–18. Glands
with 2 horns. Easily grown in dry soil, but likely
to become a nuisance with its fine, running
rhizomes. Often turning orange in poor soils in
summer.

Euphorbia griffithii Hook. fil.   Native of
Bhutan in clearings and in scrub in pine, oak
and *Rhododendron* forest at 2300–3500m,
flowering in May–August. Plant with shortly
creeping underground rhizome. Stems annual
40–80cm. Leaves linear or lanceolate, glabrous
or pubescent in var. *bhutanica* (Fischer) Long.
Bracts red or orange, glands semicircular,
capsule smooth. 'Dixter' has reddish-purple
leaves, dark-red bracts and is said to have
shorter stems. 'Fireglow' is the usual clone.
This is most beautiful when it is planted only
with greens for company, or with moisture-
loving ferns such as *Matteuccia struthiopteris*, and

Euphorbia × *martinii*

Euphorbia cyparissias

Euphorbia amygdaloides 'Rubra'

Euphorbia griffithii with *Matteuccia*

is wonderfully planted at the High Beeches where
it fills a marshy valley. Hardy to −20°C or less.

E. × martinii Rouy   A hybrid between *E.
amygdaloides* and *E. characias*, found in the wild
in S France and long cultivated. It makes a
clump of upright stems to *c.*60cm. A good plant
for a sunny border, larger and more impressive
than *E. amygdaloides* and neater and smaller
than *E. characias*. Hardy to −15°C.

Euphorbia polychroma Kerner syn. *E.
epithymoides* L.   Native of Europe from S
Germany to the Ukraine, Bulgaria and Greece,
in woods and scrub usually on limestone,
flowering in April–May. Stems many from a
large rootstock, 20–40cm tall. Leaves 3.0–
5.0cm long, 1.1–2.5cm wide, obovate-oblong or
elliptic-oblong, entire or toothed near apex,
softly hairy. Raylet leaves elliptical. Rays 4–5;
glands small, rounded; capsule with long,
slender tubercles. There is a very beautiful
purple-leaved and -stemmed form, 'Purpurea',
in cultivation, but it is rare. For good soil in
partial shade. Hardy to −25°C.

Euphorbia characias 'John Tomlinson'

VIOLA

Viola blanda in New York State

Viola canadensis

Viola elatior

Viola blanda Willd. (*Violaceae*) **Sweet White Violet**   Native of Quebec and New England, west to Minnesota, south to N Georgia in the mountains, in cool rocky woods, flowering in April–May. Plant stemless with a slender rootstock and thin, leafy runners. Leaves and flower stems from the base to *c*.5cm. Leaves ovate and cordate, with minute hairs only on the upper surface. Flowers white, slightly scented: upper petals reflexed and twisted. Seed capsules dark purple. For a cool shady position. Hardy to −20°C.

Viola canadensis L.   Native of New Brunswick, Saskatchewan, south to South Carolina, Nebraska and in the Rockies to New Mexico; growing in deciduous woods and forests in the mountains, flowering in May–July. Stems upright to 40cm, forming tufts. Leaves broadly ovate, acuminate or acute. Sepals very narrow, spreading petals white, yellow at base. Hardy to −25°C or less.

Viola elatior Fries   Native of C & E Europe, from N Italy and France east to Siberia and NW China, growing in damp meadows and scrub, flowering in April–June. Stems tufted to 50cm. Leaves lanceolate, subcordate; stipules equal to or longer than petiole. Flowers 2–2.5cm across; spur short, 2–4mm. *V. persicifolia* Schreber, the fen violet, is rather similar but is usually shorter, to 25cm at most, and has stipules shorter than the petiole. It is found in fens throughout Europe, including (but very rarely) England and Ireland. For good leafy or peaty soil in sun or partial shade. Hardy to −25°C.

Viola hirta L. **Hairy Violet**   Native of Europe except the extreme north, eastwards to the Caucasus, Siberia and C Asia, growing in woods, grassy banks and grassland, usually on limestone, flowering in March–June. Stems and leaves to 15cm, hairy, in a basal rosette, without creeping, stolons in summer. Flowers *c*.1.5cm across, bluish-violet, not scented. This species can be very showy in early spring, but lacks the scent of *V. odorata*. Hardy to −25°C.

Viola labradorica Schrank syn. *V. adunca* Sm. var. *minor* (Hook.) Fern.   Native of Arctic North America, south to New Hampshire, Colorado and California (a related var.) in the mountains, growing in woods and grassy places, flowering in May–August, though earlier in cultivation. Plants with short stems and stolons. Summer leaves sparsely hairy or smooth on the upper surface, ovate, obtuse. Stipules linear or with one or two narrow lobes at the base. Flowers pale to deep violet, to 10mm across. The

cultivated form of this species has deep-purple leaves. It is very similar to the European Wood Violet, *Viola reichenbachiana* Jord., but that has fimbriate stipules. Hardy to −25°C.

Viola obliqua Hill syn. *V. cucullata* Ait.   Native of E North America, from Quebec and Ontario, south to Georgia, growing in wet places, often in open woods, flowering in April–June. Plant spreading with a fleshy rhizome. Stems and leaves glabrous. Leaves *c*.8cm wide when full grown. Flowers violet or white with a darker throat, to 3.5cm across, not scented; hairs of the beard clavate. Cleistogamous flowers long and slender, on tall, erect peduncles, with green capsules. For good soil in a moist position in sun or partial shade. In spite of the fleshy rhizomes, this violet is easily killed by drought.

Viola odorata L. **Sweet Violet**   Native of most of Europe except the extreme north, from the Azores and North Africa east to the Caucasus, Turkey, Syria and N Iran, growing in woods, hedges and on sunny banks, flowering in February–May. Flower stems to 5cm; leaf stalks to 12cm; plant with leaves only from the base and with creeping stolons. Leaves more or less glabrous, ovate-orbicular, obtuse. Flowers heavily scented, *c*.1.5cm across, usually deep purple or white, but reddish, pink, pale-yellow and pale-blue forms are cultivated. All sweet violets, and especially the old cultivars respond to annual replanting in spring in rich, loose leafy soil, and much moisture in hot weather in summer. Hardy to −20°C. Numerous varieties have been cultivated in the past and some survive. 'Governor Herrick', shown here, has flowers 3–3.5cm across, from November to April.

Viola septentrionalis Greene   Native of E North America, from NE Canada to Ontario, and south to Connecticut and N Pennsylvania, growing in moist open woods, flowering in May. Plant with a spreading and creeping, thick rhizome. Stems and leaves finely hairy. Leaves to 7.5cm wide when fully grown. Flowers deep violet to white, to 2.5cm across. Cleistogamous flowers on short but ascending peduncles, with purple capsules. For moist, leafy soil in partial shade. Hardy to −20°C.

Viola sororia Willd. syn. *V. papilionacea* Pursh. **Confederate Violet**   Native of E North America, from Quebec west to Wyoming and south to Oklahoma and North Carolina, growing in moist meadows and shady banks, flowering in April–May. Young leaves glabrous or hairy. Leaf blades very blunt when mature. Flowers not scented, *c*.20mm across, normally violet-blue, but 'Freckles' has white flowers finely speckled with blue, and 'Albiflora' has pure white flowers. 'Priceana', syn. f. *albiflora* Grover, is the Confederate Violet, with greyish flowers, darker towards the middle, with green centres, heavily veined with blue. Hairs of the beard not clavate. Cleistogamous flowers on short, creeping peduncles. For moist soil in sun or partial shade. Hardy to −20°C or less.

Viola suavis M. Bieb.   Native of SE Europe, S Russia, Turkey, the Caucasus, C Asia, NW China and Kashmir, growing in scrub and on shady banks, often near streams, flowering in March–May. Very similar to *V. odorata* but with paler blue flowers with a white centre, more elongated leaves and underground stolons. For any good soil in sun or partial shade. Hardy to −20°C or less. This species is thought to have played a part in the breeding of some of the Sweet Violet cultivars.

Viola hirta

Viola labradorica

Viola odorata 'Governor Herrick'

Viola odorata in Kent

Viola odorata

Viola odorata (red form) in the Alhambra

Viola suavis in Xinjiang, NW China

Viola obliqua

Viola septentrionalis 'Alba'

Viola sororia 'Freckles'

Viola tricolor seedlings

'Jeannie'

'Martin'

'Joyce'

'Grace'

Viola gracilis 'Lutea'

Viola cornuta

'Penny Black'

'Chelsea Girl'

'Ardross Gem'

Viola corsica

'Little Liz'

'Huntercombe Purple'

'Blue Tit'

Specimens from the Savill Gardens, Windsor, 15 June. ½ life size

Viola tricolor seedling

Viola corsica

Viola cornuta 'Boughton Blue'

Viola 'Huntercombe Purple'

Viola 'Chelsea Girl'

Viola cornuta (a large form)

Viola cornuta L. (*Violaceae*)   Native of the Pyrenees in France and Spain, growing on rocky mountainsides and in alpine meadows, flowering in June–August. Sometimes naturalized from gardens elsewhere in the mountains of Europe. A long-lived perennial with numerous stolons from the base, forming a dense tuft. Stems to 30cm. Spur 10–15mm, longer than the petals, which usually do not overlap. Flowers 2–3cm across, scented; pale mauve is the commonest colour, but there are also whites and an unusual pinkish grey in gardens. 'Boughton Blue', raised by Sir David and Lady Scott at Boughton House, Northamptonshire, is one of the most beautiful of the forty or so cultivars which are at present in cultivation. Its flowers are a pure and rather pale sky-blue. Also shown is an extra large-flowered form. Hardy to −20°C.

Viola corsica Nyman syn. *V. bertolonii* Salisb. Native of Corsica and Sardinia, in rocky mountain pastures at 900–1300m, flowering in April–July. A long-lived perennial, with stems to 20cm. Flowers to 3.5cm from top to bottom: petals not overlapping, violet, rarely yellow. Spur 10–15mm. This is the plant often grown as *V. bertolonii* Salisb.; *V. bertolonii* Pio differs in having flowers more or less square in face view,

with overlapping petals. It is found throughout Italy, both in SW Alps and N Apennines and in S Italy and N Sicily.

Viola gracilis Sibth. & Sm.   Native of Yugoslavia, Bulgaria, Albania, Greece and W Turkey, growing in grassy mountain woods and alpine meadows, at 1250–2000m (in Turkey), flowering in May–August. Plant forming dense mats which last several years. Stems 5–30cm, usually *c.*15cm in gardens. Leaves orbicular-ovate or oblong, crenate, upper rounded. Flowers 2–3cm from top to bottom, either violet or yellow, not bicoloured. Spur 6–7mm, straight or slightly curved. Stipules with oblanceolate, spathulate lobes. Easily grown in ordinary garden soil in full sun. The commonest form in cultivation is yellow-flowered; it has produced purple-flowered branches in my garden.

Viola × wittrockiana Gams **Pansy**   This is the garden pansy, raised by crossing *Viola tricolor* with *Viola lutea* subsp. *sudetica* and *Viola altaica* Ker-Gawl. The large-flowered pansies, which are annuals, biennials or short-lived perennials, were bred from these species, the major development being in *c.*1800–1835, and by 1838 at least 400 show pansies had been named. The

formation of what are now called 'Violas' was started by James Grieve of Dickson's in Edinburgh in the 1860s by crossing the pansies with *V. lutea* and *V. cornuta* (q.q.v.) which are reliably perennial. In 1874, Dr Charles Stuart of Chirnside, Berwick, made hand pollinations and noted that the perennial suckering habit was produced only when *V. cornuta* was the seed parent. His perennial violas were called 'Violettas', and are similar to many of those grown today. *Viola* cultivars shown here are:
'Ardross Gem'
'Blue Tit'
'Chelsea Girl'
'Grace'
'Huntercombe Purple'
'Jeannie'
'Joyce'
'Little Liz'
'Martin'   Close to *V. gracilis* (q.v.) and with a very long flowering season. Raised by J. Elliott.
'Penny Black'   This black pansy is particularly short-lived, but comes true from seed. 'E. A. Bowles' syn. 'Bowles Black' has smaller flowers, shaped more like wild *V. tricolor*. 'Molly Sanderson' is a similar but neater plant, with rounded flowers above a low tuft of leaves.
Viola tricolor A striking group of seedlings, with spotted petals. (See p. 56.)

Viola lutea in Aberdeenshire, Scotland

Viola gracilis 'Lutea'

Viola 'Arkwright's Ruby'

Viola tricolor (wild form)

Viola 'Maggie Mott'

Viola gracilis Sibth. & Sm. 'Lutea' (*Violaceae*) see p. 55.

Viola lutea Hudson   Native of W Europe, from Scotland and Ireland to Spain, east to Switzerland, in grassy meadows, usually in the hills, flowering in May–June, and sparsely later. Plant with creeping underground stolons, forming loose patches in the grass; terminal segment of stipules not large and crenate, flowers usually yellow, rarely violet or particoloured, 1.5–2.5cm across, the lower petal to 1.5cm wide. Subsp. *sudetica* (Willd.) W. Becher has thicker stems and larger flowers *c*.2.3cm across. It is found from the Alps eastwards to Czechoslovakia, and it was this subspecies that was crossed with *V. tricolor* to produce the cultivated pansy (see p. 55).

Viola pedata L. **Bird's foot Violet**   Native of New York to Wisconsin, south to Florida and E Texas, growing on dry rocky banks, in open deciduous woods on well-drained soil, and on the edges of ditches in acid sandy soil, flowering April–June and again in late summer and autumn. Leaves deeply divided with a narrow central lobe and 2 sets of 4 lateral lobes. Flowers to 4cm across, usually all pale bluish-purple in var. *lineariloba* DC. syn. var. *concolor* Brainerd, but often the more striking deep-purple and pale bluish bicolour, var. *pedata* (syn. var. *bicolor* Pursh.). One of the most beautiful species but difficult to cultivate. Requires very well-drained soil and warmth and moisture in summer. Some have recommended that it be grown on clay soil, unpoisoned by humus, and, indeed, where these photographs were taken, it was growing on the shaley banks of a newly made road in full sun. Hardy to −20°C.

Viola tricolor L. **Heartsease**   Native of most of Europe and Asia, south to C Turkey and east to Siberia and the Himalayas, in grassy places and arable fields, flowering in April–September. Plant usually annual, but sometimes perennial. Stipules with the terminal segment lanceolate, leaf-like, larger than the others. Flowers variably coloured, often bicoloured. The wild type shown here, from NE Scotland, is a perennial, common in the north of England and Scotland, rare in the south, growing in pastures and disturbed grassland. It forms a mat of creeping stems. Subsp. *curtisii* (E. Forster) Syme is similar, but often has yellow flowers, and is usually found on sand dunes near the sea in W Europe and the Baltic. Other perennial subspecies are found in the mountains of the Balkan peninsula and southern and central Europe.

Cultivars of **Viola × wittrockiana**   (p. 55).
'Arkwright's Ruby'
'Irish Molly'   Flowers greenish bronze.
'Jackanapes'
'Maggie Mott'   An old variety, grown since before 1910. Flowers 4cm across.
'Rebecca'   Flowers white, with a purplish-blue, plicata-type margin.

Viola 'Jackanapes'

Viola pedata var. lineariloba in the Blue Ridge Mountains, Virginia

Viola pedata var. pedata in Virginia

Viola 'Rebecca'

Viola 'Irish Molly'

'Ballawley'

Bergenia × schmidtii

Bergenia cordifolia

'Britten'

'Admiral'

'Bach'

Bergenia purpurascens

'Brahms'

Specimens from Wisley, 28 April. ⅕ life size

Bergenia purpurascens

Bergenia (*Saxifragaceae*)   A genus of about 6 species, closely related to *Saxifraga*, with a thick fleshy creeping rhizome, forming spreading patches of large leathery leaves. All flower in early spring and require rich, moist but well-drained soil in shade or partial shade. Many hybrids have been raised in gardens in Europe, and a selection are given on the following page.

Bergenia ciliata (Haw.) Sternb.   Native of Afghanistan to SE Tibet, growing in woods and on shady rock ledges at 1800–4300m, flowering in March–July near melting snow. Basal leaves large, rounded, cordate at the base, entire but bristly 30cm or more across, reddish in autumn with long (*c*.15cm) bristly stalks. Flowers 1.5–2.5cm long, palest pink. Young leaves and flowers rather frost sensitive, doing well in cool shade. Hardy to −20°C.

Bergenia cordifolia (Haw.) Sternb.   Native of Siberia, in the Altai Mountains, flowering in February–March in gardens in western Europe. Leaves with blade to 30 × 20cm, obovate, bullate with wavy edges, not convex, remaining green in winter. Flowers *c*.2.2cm long, purplish pink. A widely grown species, introduced in the 17th century, and very tolerant of cold and heat, growing well in shady places in Mediterranean climates.

Bergenia crassifolia (L.) Fritsch   Native of Siberia, Mongolia and NW China in the Altai, east to the Pacific (var. *pacifica* (Kom.) Nekr. shown here), and naturalized in parts of Austria and France, growing on shady north-facing mountain rocks, and in subalpine woods, flowering in March–April. Leaves 15–30cm, elliptic, obovate with sparse, bristle-like teeth, reddish brown in winter. Inflorescence to 30cm; flowers drooping. Petals 10–12mm, bright purplish pink. Hardy to −20°C or less.

Bergenia purpurascens (Hook. fil. & Thoms.) Engler   Native of C Nepal, where it is common, to SW China (Yunnan), growing on rocks and open slopes at 3600–4700m. Leaves hairless, not toothed, striking deep purple in winter, blades 3–9cm long. Flowers in a dense nodding cluster 1.5–2.5cm long, on a tallish stalk to 30cm, deep pinkish purple. Hardy to −20°C, perhaps.

Bergenia stracheyi (Hook. fil. & Thoms.) Engler   Native of Afghanistan to N India (Uttar Pradesh) growing on rocky alpine slopes in full exposure at 3300–4500m. Common in W Himalayas, forming huge patches, excluding all other plants except sometimes *Codonopsis* (p. 354); flowering in June–August, but in early spring in gardens. Flowers pink, drooping in loose clusters, 2–2.5cm long. Leaves obovate, 5–10cm long. This species and its white form 'Alba' were the important parents of Eric Smith's hybrids which were named after composers. *Bergenia* hybrids are hardy, long-lived plants with evergreen leaves, many of which colour red or purple in winter. The flowers open in early spring and are often damaged by late frosts, so that some overhead protection will often prolong the flowering season. All are hardy to −25°C or less, and require a cool sheltered position in good soil.

Bergenia cultivars:
'**Abendglocken**' syn. 'Evening Bells'   Raised by G. Arends in *c*.1971.
'**Admiral**'   Raised by R. Eskuche.
'**Baby Doll**'   Raised by zur Linden.
'**Bach**'   Raised by Eric Smith of 'The Plantsman' in *c*.1972.
'**Ballawley**' syn. 'Delbees'   Raised at Ballawley Park, near Dublin, before 1950. Flowers April–May. Leaves, normally green, turn bronze-coloured in winter. Flower stalks bright red. Stems to 60cm. Leaves less tough and evergreen than many others, *c*.20cm across. Not as free-flowering as some other bergenias.
'**Beethoven**'   Raised by Eric Smith of 'The Plantsman' in *c*.1972.
'**Brahms**'   Raised by Eric Smith of 'The Plantsman' in *c*.1972.
'**Britten**'   Raised by Jim Archibald of 'The Plantsman' in *c*.1977.

Bergenia × schmidtii   A hybrid between *B. ciliata* and *B. crassifolia* raised in 1875. Plant vigorous and spreading, with leaves to 23cm long, 15cm wide. Early flowering, and often the first to flower, so that the flowers are often damaged by frost. Flowering stems to 30cm.

Bergenia 'Baby Doll'

Bergenia ciliata collected by Christopher Lloyd

Bergenia stracheyi 'Alba'

Bergenia stracheyi

Bergenia crassifolia var. *pacifica*

Bergenia 'Abendglocken'

Bergenia 'Beethoven'

Lathyrus roseus at Cambridge

Lathyrus venetus

Lathyrus aureus at Cruickshank Botanic Gardens, Aberdeen

Lathyrus aureus

Lathyrus vernus

Lathyrus vernus 'Roseus'

Lathyrus vernus 'Cyaneus'

Astragalus lusitanicus Lam. syn. *Phaca boetica* L. (*Leguminosae*)   Native of the Mediterranean region, growing in rocky scrub, pine woods and abandoned fields, at up to 800m in Turkey, flowering in March–June. Stems several, upright, to 70cm. Leaves 10–18cm long. Flowers 10–20 in an upright raceme, 20–25mm long, white with a blackish or reddish hairy calyx. Plants from Spain, Portugal and NW Africa, subsp. *lusitanicus*, have leaves glabrous above, and an often dark-reddish calyx: those from the E Mediterranean, with a blackish calyx and leaves silky above, have been called subsp. *orientalis* Chater & Meikle. Cultivated since the 17th century, but very rarely seen. For a rather dry sunny border. Hardy to −15°C, perhaps.

Lathyrus aureus (Stev.) Brandza syn. *Orobus aureus* Steven (*Leguminosae*)   Native of Bulgaria and Romania to N Turkey, the Caucasus and the Crimea, growing in woods and scrub, at up to 2000m, flowering in May–July. Stems 20–60cm; leaves without tendrils, with 3–6 pairs of leaflets with brownish glands beneath. Flowers 12–25, 17–22mm long, brownish orange. Seed pods 50–70mm long, densely glandular when young.
Lathyrus gmelinii Fritsch (syn. *L. luteus* (L.) Peterm.), from the Urals and C Asia, is similar, but has yellow flowers 25–30mm long, and 2–4 pairs of leaflets. Two other species in Europe have yellowish flowers; *L. laevigatus*, found from France and Spain east to Russia, and *L. transsilvanicus* from the Carpathians, but *L. aureus* is the only one with brown glands. As a further complication, *L. aureus* is very similar to *Vicia crocea* (Desf.) B. Fedtsch., from Turkey and the Caucasus, but that has leaves folded, not rolled in the bud, unequal stipules and shorter seed pods, 27–32mm long.

Lathyrus nervosus Lam. **Lord Anson's Blue Pea**   Native of Tierra del Fuego (very rare), Argentina north to 37°S, Chile north to 46°S, Uruguay and S Brazil, growing in scrub, flowering in December–January (May–July in the Northern Hemisphere). Plant with few climbing or creeping stems from a tufted rhizome, to 1.5m tall. Leaves sessile and stipules glabrous, glaucous, with a thickened margin. Inflorescence with 2–3 whorls of 3–4 flowers, each *c.*18mm across. For rich soil in a cool position in sun or partial shade, with water in summer. Hardy to −10°C. *L. magellanicus* Lam. is very similar, but has hairy, usually narrower, leaflets which often blacken when dried, and have a thin, membranous, not a thickened margin. It is found in W Argentina north to 40°S, in Chile north to 45°S, and in Tierra del Fuego, growing on sand dunes and shingle by the sea, and in grassland and scrub, flowering in December–February. It is possibly hardier than *L. nervosus* and is a stronger-growing plant, reaching 3m when growing well.

Lathyrus roseus Stev.   Native of the Crimea, the Caucasus, N & E Turkey and N Iran, growing in spruce and pine forest in oak and hazel scrub, flowering in May–July. Stems erect, to 60cm, from a large rootstock. Leaves without tendrils, with 1 pair of obovate leaflets, to 45mm long, 30mm across; stipules narrow, as broad as stem. Flowers 1–4 on a stalk, to 2cm across. For well-drained soil in sun or partial shade.

Lathyrus nervosus at Sissinghurst, Kent

Lathyrus nervosus at the Royal Botanic Gardens, Kew

Sophora alopecuroides in NW China

Astragalus lusitanicus near Marmaris, Turkey

Parochetus communis near Dali, Yunnan

Lathyrus venetus (Miller) Wohlf. syn. *L. variegatus* (Ten.) Gren. & Godr.   Native of S Europe, from Italy and Corsica east to C Russia and N Turkey, growing in forests, scrub and grassland, flowering in May–June. Plant tufted with numerous stems to *c.*40cm. Leaves with 2–4 pairs of acute leaflets. Flowers 10–30 in a dense raceme, 10–15mm long. Close to *L. vernus*, but usually larger, with more numerous smaller flowers and acute rather than acuminate leaflets. Easily grown in sun or partial shade in any soil. Hardy to −20°C.

Lathyrus vernus (L.) Bernh. syn. *Orobus vernus* L.   Native of most of Europe except the far south and west, from France east to the Caucasus and N Turkey and E Siberia, growing in woods and scrub, usually on limestone, flowering in April–June. Plant forming slowly spreading patches. Stems 20–40cm. Leaves 2–4 pairs, ovate, acuminate, 3.5–7cm long. Flowers 15–18mm long, usually reddish-purple, fading

to blue, but other colour forms are in cultivation, e.g. 'Albus' (white); 'Caeruleus' (pure blue); 'Roseus' (pink); 'Albo-roseus' (pink and white) is probably the same as 'Variegatus'. Also a blue unfortunately named 'Cyaneus', not to be confused with *Lathyrus cyaneus* (Stev.) C. Koch, which I have seen in alpine meadows in the Caucasus, and which has only 2 pairs of linear or narrowly linear-lanceolate leaflets, and semi-sagittate stipules, pale-blue flowers and stems which creep underground through the grass. Easily grown in shade or partial shade, in any soil. Hardy to −20°C.

Parochetus communis Buch.-Ham. ex. D. Don (*Leguminoseae*)   Native of the mountains of C Africa (Kenya, at about 3000m), India, the Himalayas to SW China and SE Asia, growing in ditches, on shady banks and damp forests in grassy places, at 100–4300m, flowering in May–November. Plant creeping, forming large

patches. Flower stems *c.*7.5cm tall, flowers 1.3–2.5cm long. Leaflets 8–20mm long. Suitable for growing under benches in a cold greenhouse, or in a sheltered position outside. Hardy to −5°C.

Sophora alopecuroides L. (*Leguminosae*) Native of Asia from Turkey (around Ankara) eastwards to N China, growing in sandy deserts and waste places especially by roadsides and irrigation channels, flowering in April–July. Plant spreading by creeping underground stems, with upright flowering stems to 1m or more. Leaves silky hairy. Flowers 18–20mm, whitish, in 60–80 flowered racemes. Pods 3–10 seeded, strongly contracted between the seeds. A common plant in heavily grazed desert areas of C Asia, protected from damage by the powerful heart poison it contains. Suitable for cultivation in dry or saline areas. Hardy to −25°C.

For late-flowering *Lathyrus* see vol. 2, pp. 58, 59.

Asarum caudatum at Santa Barbara Botanic Garden, California

Hacquetia epipactis at Sellindge, Kent

Oxalis oregana

Oxalis acetosella

Asarum hartwegii in N California

Asarum caudatum Lindl. (*Aristolochiaceae*)
Native of W North America, from California
north to British Columbia and Montana, in the
coast ranges, growing in deep shade in Redwood
forest and pine woods, flowering in May–July.
Rhizome far-creeping, so the plant forms wide-
spreading, rather open patches. Leaves 2–10cm
long, not veined above. Flowers hidden beneath
the leaves with petals 2.5–8.5cm long. Styles
fused. For loose, leafy soil in deep shade and
useful as ground cover in such a position. Hardy
to −15°C perhaps. There are thirty species of
Asarum in Japan, many very beautiful with
marbled leaves, but most require careful
cultivation in a shade house. The European
Asarabacca, *A. europaeum*, has smaller, usually
round leaves.

Asarum hartwegii S. Wats.   Native of
S Oregon, south to California and Tulare Co. in
the Sierra Nevada, growing in shady woods and
scrub at 700–2000m, flowering in May–June.
Plant with a thickish, shortly creeping rhizome.
Leaves cordate, ovate, 4–10cm long, with pale
veins. Flowers hidden beneath the leaves, with
brownish, hairy petals 2.5–6.5cm long. Styles
nearly separate. For leafy soil in shade, and
tolerant of drought. Hardy to −15°C.

Aristolochia hirta L. (*Aristolochiaceae*)   Native
of W and SW Turkey and on the islands of
Chios, Lesbos and Samos southwards, growing
in rocky places, on ruins, in vineyards and pine
woods at up to 1200m, flowering in March–
June. Plant with a swollen cylindrical rootstock.
Stems 15–50cm. Leaves 3–11cm long. Flowers
with a limb 1.5–8cm across, hairy outside and
inside. A strange plant, the inside of the flower
looking and smelling like mouldy meat, and
attracting flies. For well-drained, stony soil, dry
in summer. Hardy to −10°C, perhaps less.

Hacquetia epipactis (Scop.) DC. (*Umbelliferae*)
Native of E Alps, Italy, Austria and Poland,
eastwards to Czechoslovakia and Yugoslavia,
growing in rich woods usually on limestone at
up to 1500m, flowering in March–May. Stems
10–25cm, usually *c.*10cm, elongating during
flowering, ending in a rosette of green bracteoles
around a cluster of tiny yellow flowers. For
moist soil in shade or partial shade. Hardy to
−20°C or less.

Oxalis acetosella L. (*Oxalidaceae*) **Wood
Sorrel**   Native of Europe from Iceland east to
Japan and south to Spain, Italy and Greece, and
of North America east to Saskatchewan and
south to North Carolina in the mountains,
growing in moist woods, moorland and on

Aristolochia hirta in an ancient theatre in SW Turkey

Pachysandra procumbens

Pachysandra procumbens at Kew in early spring

shady rocks, flowering in April–June and
intermittently to September. Leaf stalks
5–15cm. Flowers 10–16mm long, usually white
with lilac veins, rarely pinkish. Needs moist
leafy soil and shade in summer. Hardy to
−25°C.

Oxalis oregana Nutt. **Redwood Sorrel**
Native of C California, north to Washington,
growing in Redwood forest, flowering in April–
September. Leaf stalks with rusty hairs,
5–17cm long. Flowers 8–20mm long, white or
pinkish veined purple with a pale centre, or
2–2.5cm long, deep-rose-purple in f. *smalliana*
(Knuth) Munz. Easily grown in moist, leafy soil
in shade. Hardy to −15°C.

Pachysandra procumbens Michx. (*Buxaceae*)
Native of E North America from West Virginia
to Kentucky, Florida and Louisiana, growing in
deciduous woods, flowering April–May. Plant
forming clumps or mats of creeping and
ascending pubescent stems to 30cm. Leaves
evergreen, though often damaged by cold
winters, ovate, oval or obovate, 5–10cm long,
untoothed or with few shallow teeth. Flowers in
the axils of the lower scale-like leaves, male
flowers on the upper part of the spike, with
conspicuous stamens and anthers; female
flowers few, below the male, with exposed
curved styles. Capsule with 3 carpels. Hardy to
−25°C.

Pachysandra terminalis Sieb. & Zucc. Native
of Japan in all the islands, and China, west to
Hubei and E Sichuan, growing in moist woods
in the valleys and low mountains up to 2000m,
flowering in April–May, fruiting in September–
October; commonly planted as ground cover.
Plant spreading by stolons to form a carpet of
tough, upright shoots sometimes to 30cm tall,
usually *c.*20cm. Leaves 5–10cm long,
evergreen, leathery. Male and female flowers on
separate parts of the plant, the male above, the
female below. Fruits white when mature, about
1.5cm long, rare in cultivation, or never
produced? 'Variegata' has leaves edged with
white. Easily grown in loose, leafy soil and
tolerant of dry shade. Hardy to −25°C.

Pachysandra terminalis in flower

in fruit with *Geastrum* and *Equisetum hyemale*

Pachysandra terminalis 'Variegata'

Vinca minor 'Flore Pleno'

Vinca minor 'Atropurpurea'

Vinca minor

Vinca minor 'Argenteo-variegata'

Vinca difformis

Vinca major 'Variegata'

Vinca major

Specimens from Wisley, 1 May. ⅖ life size

Vinca herbacea at the Royal Botanic Gardens, Kew

Vinca minor 'Argenteo-variegata'

Amsonia orientalis Decne. syn. *Rhazya orientalis* (Decne.) DC. (*Apocynaceae*)   Native of NE Greece and NW Turkey, where it is now almost extinct, growing in grassy places, wet during winter, flowering in May–June. Plant with many stems, to 60cm from a stout woody rootstock. Leaves 3–7cm long. Flowers glabrous outside, *c*.1.2cm across. Easily grown in good garden soil. Hardy to −20°C. This species is normally known by the name *Rhazya*, but is so similar to the American *Amsonia tabernaemontana* var. *salicifolia* (q.v.) that they would probably have been considered conspecific if they had grown in the same country.

Amsonia tabernaemontana Walter   Native of E North America, from New Jersey to Florida, west to Illinois, Kentucky, Missouri and Texas, growing in damp grassy places, flowering in April–July. Plant with many stems to *c*.50cm from a stout rootstock. Leaves variable in shape from ovate to lanceolate, 5–10cm long. Flowers with corolla tube pubescent outside, 1.2–1.8cm across. Hardy to −20°C or lower, and easy in good moist soil. Rarer in cultivation in Europe than *A. orientalis*.

Vinca difformis Pourret (*Apocynaceae*)   Native of SW Europe from Spain, Portugal and the Azores to C Italy, and of North Africa, growing on shady banks and streamsides in woods, flowering in March–April. Plant forming mounds of evergreen stems and leaves to 1m high and more across. Leaves 2.5–7cm, ovate to lanceolate, usually narrowly lanceolate, glabrous or minutely ciliate. Flowering stems to 30cm. Flowers 3–7cm across, pale blue to nearly white. Tolerant of sun or dry shade. Probably not very hardy except in S England, requiring protection from frosts below −10°C.

Vinca erecta Regel & Schmalh.   Native of of C Asia in the Tien Shan and Pamir Alai, growing on loose limestone screes at 1500–2000m, flowering in April–May. Plant with many upright deciduous stems to 30cm, elongating after flowering. Flowers *c*.2.5cm across, pale blue or white. For careful cultivation in well-drained soil, and full sun, kept rather dry in summer. Hardy to −15°C.

Vinca herbacea Waldst. & Kit.   Native of C Europe to Greece, SW Russia, the Caucasus, N Iran, Turkey, W Syria and N Iraq, growing in open woods, scrub, rocky slopes and screes, usually on limestone, up to 2000m in Turkey, flowering from March–May. Plant with deciduous stems to 60cm from a central rootstock. Flowering stems to 20cm upright. Leaves up to 5cm long. Flowers pale blue to purplish, 2.5–4.5cm across. One of the hardiest species, to −20°C, for dry, well-drained soil in sun or partial shade.

Vinca major L. **Greater Periwinkle**   Native of the N Mediterranean region from SW France to Italy and Yugoslavia, but widely naturalized

Vinca difformis

Vinca difformis near Malaga, Spain

Vinca erecta near Ferghana, C Asia

Vinca major f. *alba*

Vinca major subsp. *hirsuta*

elsewhere in Europe, flowering in February–
April. Stems trailing, to 2m or more, and
rooting. Leaves evergreen, 2.5–9cm long,
usually ovate. Flowering stems upright to 30cm.
Flowers 3–5cm across, bluish purple. *Vinca
major* f. *alba* has white flowers. Var. *oxyloba*
Stearn has narrower leaves and narrow, violet
corolla-lobes, but glabrous, or almost glabrous,
young shoots. Subsp. *hirsuta* (Boiss.) Stearn is
native of the S Caucasus in Georgia and along
the Turkish Black Sea coast, growing in scrub at
up to 200m, flowering in March–May. It has
hairy petioles and young shoots and long hairs
to 1mm long on the calyx lobes. Flowers violet,
to 4.5cm across, with narrow lobes.

Vinca minor L. **Lesser Periwinkle**   Native of
SW & C Europe, east to the Crimea and the
Caucasus, in woods or on rocky banks,
flowering in February–June. Probably not
native, but long grown and naturalized in the
British Isles, Scandinavia and Turkey. Stems
creeping and rooting to form mats. Leaves
evergreen, 1.5–4.5cm long. Flowering stems to
20cm. Flowers 2.5–3cm across. Easily grown in
sun or partial shade of deciduous trees. Hardy
to −20°C, with shade or snow cover. There are
numerous variants (*c*.17), differing in flower
colour, doubleness and leaf variegation:
'Albo-variegata' has white flowers and gold
variegated leaves;
'Argenteo-variegata' has silver-edged leaves;
'Atropurpurea' has deep-purplish-red flowers,
and
'Flore Pleno' has double purplish-blue flowers,
both with green leaves.

Vinca major var. *oxyloba* at the Royal Botanic Gardens, Kew

Amsonia tabernaemontana

Amsonia orientalis

Phlox pulchra 'Bill Baker' at Tidmarsh, Berks

Phlox maculata 'Alpha'

Phlox 'Chattahoochee'

Phlox maculata 'Omega'

Phlox 'Chattahoochee' (*Polemoniaceae*)   This striking clone is considered by Wherry to be a form of *P. divaricata* subsp. *laphamii* or a hybrid with *P. pilosa*. It was collected by Mrs J. Norman Henry in the Chattahoochee valley in N Florida and forms a spreading tuft of stems up to 20cm long. Leaves are hairy and ciliate with blades lanceolate to linear, and sessile, narrower than usual for *laphamii*; the plant generally does not produce rooting creeping shoots. *P.* 'Charles Ricardo' is similar but has a white, not red, eye.

Phlox divaricata L. syn. *P. canadensis* Sweet Native of Quebec to Ontario, south to Illinois, Arkansas and South Georgia, generally east of a line from Chicago to New Orleans; subsp. *laphamii* west of the line from South Dakota and Colorado to Louisiana and E Texas. Both grow on moist wooded hills and in river valleys on wooded river flats and up to 1000m; subsp. *divaricata* on acid or neutral soils, subsp. *laphamii* on limestone soils in drier areas. Plant spreading by creeping shoots which root at the nodes. Flowering shoots 25–45cm. Leaves on sterile shoots broadly elliptic, on flowering shoots lanceolate to ovate to 5 × 2.5cm. Flowers 2–3cm across; petals usually notched in subsp. *divaricata*, pale blue, lilac to nearly white, often with a paler eye, but rounded in subsp. *laphamii* with deeper coloured often bluish flowers. 'Dirigo Ice' is a cultivar with large, shallowly notched petals.

Phlox maculata L. **Meadow Phlox**   Native of North America, from Quebec and Vermont west to Minnesota, south to Missouri, Tennessee and North Carolina, growing in meadows, marshes and woods by streams, flowering in May–June. Stems several, often spotted and streaked with red, upright to 125cm from a shallow rootstock. Leaves dark, shining green, linear below, lanceolate above, the largest 6–13cm long, 10–25mm wide. Flowers in an elongated cylindric inflorescence, 18–25mm across. Easily grown in a normal moist herbaceous border, and should succeed also in a bog garden. Hardy to −20°C and below. A few varieties of this beautiful species are grown in gardens. Shown here are 'Alpha' mauve, and 'Omega' white with a pale-pink eye. 'Miss

Lingard', pure white, often listed under *P. suffruticosa*, and 'Rosalinde' pink, are grown in America. All these varieties are good in warm summers as they are not liable to mildew.

Phlox ovata L.   Native of SE Pennsylvania south to North Carolina, on the Piedmont, and in Indiana, growing in open woods, damp grassland or rocky slopes, flowering in May–July. Stems 25–50cm, from a creeping base; lower leaves stalked, ovate to elliptic. Flowers 16–30mm across, with a pale eye. For leafy soil in partial shade. Hardy to −25°C.

Phlox paniculata L. **Garden Phlox**   Native of North America, from New Jersey south to North Carolina, west to Ohio and south to Louisiana, growing in open woods, scrub, along streams and on hillsides, often on limestone, flowering in June–September. Plant with a short, thick rhizome and numerous, upright stems to 2m. Leaves opposite below, often subopposite above. Flowers 1.5–2.5cm across, dull to bright purple, pink or rarely white, with narrow or round, sometimes emarginate petals. Hardy to −20°C or lower; growing best in rich, moist soil with ample moisture in summer. The three varieties shown here are close to the wild type and distinct from the large-flowered garden forms shown on p. 308–9.

Phlox pilosa L.   Native of Ontario to Iowa, south to Texas and Florida, growing in grassland and scrub in rather dry soil, and formerly common on the northern prairies before they were ploughed for agriculture, flowering in April–June. Flowering stems 30–60cm, pubescent, with leaves linear below,

Phlox ovata at Wisley

Phlox divaricata in a garden in Texas

Phlox stolonifera 'Blue Ridge'

Phlox pilosa at Coldham, Kent

Phlox divaricata 'Dirigo Ice'

lanceolate above, to 8cm long, 6mm wide.
Flower purplish, pink or white, 2.2cm across.
For full sun and well-drained soil. Suitable for
the front of a summer border.

Phlox pulchra Wherry syn. *P. ovata* var.
pulchra Wherry Native of NW Alabama in a
small area west of Birmingham, in clearings and
on the edges of woods, flowering in April–May.
Stems 25–50cm with sterile shoots with
narrowly obovate leaves. Flowers pale purplish
to pink, 2.5cm across. Leaves on inflorescence
short-stemmed at base, sessile above. Close to
P. ovata, which differs in its long-stalked leaves
at the base of the flowering stem, brighter-
coloured flowers and clearly stalked leaves on
the sterile shoots. The clone shown here was
introduced to England and distributed by Bill
Baker. For clearings in woodland or partial
shade, making sure that the sterile creeping
stems are not swamped by stronger-growing
plants. Hardy to −20°C.

Phlox stolonifera Sims syn. *P. reptans* Michx.
Native of Pennsylvania to Georgia and
Kentucky, mainly in the Appalachian
mountains, growing in open deciduous woods,
flowering in April–June. Plant mat-forming
with creeping sterile shoots ending in a rosette
of spathulate leaves. Flowering stems 15–25cm.
Flowers *c.*3cm across, scented, with petals not
notched. 'Blue Ridge' is a good pale-blue form,
from Virginia. 'Pink Ridge' is pink-flowered.
Easily grown in semi-shade, forming very pretty
ground cover under deciduous trees. Best in
slightly acid, leafy but well-drained soil. Hardy
to −20°C or less.

Phlox paniculata (close to wild form) at Wallington, Northumberland

Phlox paniculata (white form)

Phlox paniculata (pink form)

Pulmonaria angustifolia (left), *P. longifolia* 'Bertram Anderson' (right)

Pulmonaria longifolia 'Bertram Anderson'

Pulmonaria angustifolia

Pulmonaria officinalis

Pulmonaria longifolia growing wild at Exbury, Hampshire

Nonea intermedia Ledeb. (*Boraginaceae*)
Native of the Caucasus and the extreme NE of
Turkey, growing in alpine meadows at *c*.2000m,
flowering in June–July. Plant forming small
tufts, without a creeping rhizome. Stems 30–
45cm. Leaves oblong, lanceolate, acuminate,
softly hairy. Flowers *c*.12mm long, 6–8mm
across, with scales and hairs in the throat of the
corolla. For moist peaty soil in sun or partial
shade. Hardy to −20°C or so. Several species of
Nonea are very similar in general appearance to
Pulmonaria, but differ in the absence of a
creeping rhizome, and in the presence of 5 hairy
scales in the throat of the corolla. *Nonea lutea*
(Desr.) DC. is a striking, *Pulmonaria*-like, pale-
yellow-flowered annual, and the perennial *N.
macrosperma* Boiss. & Held., from Turkey, also
has yellow flowers; *N. pulla* (L.) DC., from C
Europe, has blackish flowers.

Pulmonaria (*Boraginaceae*) **Lungwort**   These
are good garden plants for moist places between
shrubs, for the front of a border in partial shade,
for wooded gardens or for grassy banks partially
under trees. The flowers appear in spring, and
last until early summer. They are followed by
dense clumps of bold leaves, variably hairy and
often beautifully spotted with silver. In the
wild, the flowers have either long or short styles,
in the same way that primroses do; in gardens,
the species hybridize freely. Many are beautiful,
long-lived plants, which are easy to propagate,

and have been given cultivar names. As they are clones, their style length should be constant, and has therefore been noted here whenever possible. Most species, of which there are around fifteen, are mountain plants from eastern Europe. They differ in hair type as well as in leaf shape and spotting, and in flower colour. The distribution of hairs inside the corolla tube is also significant.

Pulmonaria angustifolia L. syn. *P. azurea* Besser   Native of France and Germany to Sweden and Baltic Russia, south to Italy and the northern steppes, growing in scrub and meadows, mainly in the mountains, at up to 2000m, flowering in March–May. Rhizome creeping, forming spreading mats. Stems to 30cm, usually *c*.20cm. Leaves unspotted, with equal setae, and without glands; inflorescence becoming very lax as flowering proceeds. Flowers bright blue; tube smooth inside below ring of hairs. Hardy to −20°C.

Pulmonaria longifolia (Bast.) Boreau   Native of W Europe, from Spain and Portugal to W France and S England, around the New Forest and on the Isle of Wight, growing in woods and hedges, and on grassy banks, flowering in February–May. Plant clump-forming. Leaves usually spotted, lanceolate or narrowly lanceolate, up to 50 × 6cm, with more or less equal setae and a few glands. Stems to 20cm; inflorescence remaining tight during flowering. Flowers usually blue; tube glabrous below ring of hairs. Shown here is the native form, growing wild in Exbury garden and in hedges and roadside banks nearby, and a striking tall form with longer, narrower leaves than the wild English form. This is 'Bertram Anderson', named after E. B. Anderson, a successful and influential grower of alpines, bulbs and other herbaceous plants in England. Hardy to −15°C perhaps.

Pulmonaria officinalis L.   Native of Holland and S Sweden south to N Italy and Bulgaria east to Romania; naturalized in places in England, growing in woods and hedges, flowering in March–May. Plant with short, creeping rhizome, finally forming patches. Leaves spotted, with lamina to 16 × 10cm, abruptly narrowed into stalk, with distinct spots and uniform setae and occasional glandular hairs. Flowers opening reddish, becoming bluish, glabrous inside below the ring of hairs. Inflorescence becoming laxer as flowering proceeds. Hardy to −20°C.

Pulmonaria rubra Schott   Native of the Carpathians in Hungary, south to Albania and Bulgaria, growing in rich, moist subalpine woods of beech and pine, usually on limestone, at 300–1600m, flowering in March–May. Plant clump-forming. Flowering stems to 30cm. Summer leaves usually unspotted; blade narrowed abruptly, to 15 × 7cm, with long and short setae and glandular hairs. Flowers red; tube hairy inside below the ring of hairs.

Pulmonaria saccharata Mill.   Native of SE France and N & C Italy in the Apennines, growing in woods and scrub, flowering from April–May. Plant clump-forming, without extending rhizome. Flowering stems to 30cm, with rather broad stem leaves. Summer leaves to 27 × 10cm, narrowed gradually into the stalk, often very heavily spotted, with more or less dense, unequal and rather fine short hairs, and long setae and glandular hairs. Flowers purplish to bluish purple, hairy inside below the ring of hairs. Hardy to −15°C, perhaps less.

Pulmonaria rubra at the Savill Gardens, Windsor

Pulmonaria saccharata from S France

Nonea intermedia in the N Caucasus

Pulmonaria officinalis
'Sissinghurst White'

'Margery Fish'

'Leopard'

Pulmonaria officinalis

'Blaues Meer'

Pulmonaria mollis

Pulmonaria angustifolia
'Azurea'

Pulmonaria officinalis 'Coral'

Pulmonaria rubra
'Bowles' Red'

Pulmonaria rubra 'Redstart'

Specimens from Wisley, 10 April. ⅔ life size

Pulmonaria officinalis 'Alba'

Pulmonaria 'Blaues Meer'

Pulmonaria 'Boughton Blue'

Pulmonaria 'Frühlingshimmel'

Pulmonaria vallarsae 'Margery Fish'

Pulmonaria 'Highdown'

Pulmonaria cultivars (*Boraginaceae*) Some of these may be selected forms of species, but often they are hybrids of unknown parentage. Other hybrids are likely to appear in gardens where more than one species is grown, and are usually sterile; for example, narrow-leaved plants with much spotting are probably *P. longifolia* × *P. saccharata* and a narrow white-leaved hybrid is most likely *P. longifolia* × *P. vallarsae*.
The following named clones are shown here:
'Azurea' A clone of *P. angustifolia* (short style). See p. 69.
'Blaues Meer' Possibly a form of *P. visianii* from the E Alps, or a hybrid of *P. angustifolia* (short style).
'Boughton Blue' Probably a hybrid between *P. officinalis* and *P. saccharata* (short style).
'Bowles' Red' A form of *P. rubra*. Slightly spotted leaf (short style).
'Coral' A pink-flowered clone, possibly a form of *P. officinalis*. The corolla is usually somewhat deformed and split, but very showy (long style).
'Frühlingshimmel' syn. 'Spring Beauty' Flowers pale blue. Possibly *P. officinalis* × *P. saccharata* (long style).
'Highdown' Probably *P. officinalis* × *P. saccharata* (short style). A good robust plant.
'Leopard' Probably *P. saccharata* or a hybrid. Leaves well spotted. Flowers red (long style).
'Margery Fish' Probably a form of *P. vallarsae* (q.v.).
'Mawson's Variety' A form of *P. angustifolia*.
'Redstart' A form of *P. rubra* (see previous page). Leaves not spotted (long style).

'Sissinghurst White' A white form of *P. officinalis*. Smaller and neater than 'Alba'.

Pulmonaria mollis Wulfen ex Hornem. Native of SE & C Europe, from Germany and Poland to Italy, Yugoslavia, Greece, Russia and Siberia, growing by streams, in woods and scrub at up to 1600m, flowering in April–May. Plant clump-forming, with flowering stems to 30cm. Summer leaves to 60 × 12cm; not spotted, with dense, soft, short hairs and scattered, slender, unequal setae and glandular hairs. Flowers bluish purple, very hairy below the ring of hairs. Recognized by its very soft, unspotted summer leaves. *P. vallarsae* from Italy is also softly hairy, but with shorter hairs and very spotted, sometimes almost entirely white leaves.

Pulmonaria officinalis (see previous page).

Pulmonaria vallarsae A. Kerner Native of Italy in the S Tirol and the Apennines, growing in scrub along rivers, among rocks and gravel, at 650–1500m, flowering in March–May. Plant clump-forming. Summer leaves very heavily spotted or even white all over; lamina up to 20 × 10cm, with wavy edge, with very dense, short fine hairs and a few long setae and glandular hairs. Flower stems to 45cm, densely glandular and sticky. Flowers reddish, becoming purplish, tube hairy inside, below the ring of hairs. 'Margery Fish', with pure silver leaves, probably belongs to this species.

Mertensia virginica

Mertensia ciliata with leaves of *Veratrum*

Mertensia simplicissima on a sandy shore in N Hokkaido, Japan

Brunnera macrophylla (Adams) Johnston syn. *Anchusa myosotodiflora* Lehm. (*Boraginaceae*) Native of the Caucasus, Georgia and NE Turkey, in spruce forest and on grassy slopes at 500–2000m in Turkey, flowering in March– May. Stems several, from a stout rootstock to 50cm, elongating during the flowering period. Leaves with long petioles to 20cm and ovate cordate blades 5–14cm long. Flowers 3.5–7mm across. *B. orientalis* (Schenk.) Johnston, from C Turkey to Lebanon, N Iraq and N Iran, is glandular, with leaf blades ovate-lanceolate or elliptic, tapering into a short stalk. It grows on moist shady banks in pine, fir and oak forest, flowering in April–July. The third species in the genus is *B. siberica* Stev. 'Hadspen Cream' is a form of *B. macrophylla* with an irregular creamy white margin to the leaf, raised by Eric Smith in the 1960s. 'Variegata' has a wider, paler margin to the leaf. 'Langtrees' (not illustrated) has silver-spotted leaves. Hardy to −15°C.

Caccinia macranthera (Banks & Sol.) Brand var. **crassifolia** (Vent.) Brand (*Boraginaceae*) Native of E Turkey, N Iraq and Iran, east to Pakistan and the Pamir Alai, growing on banks, dry hillsides and abandoned fields at up to 1900m in Turkey, flowering in April–July. Plant with several stems to 50cm; leaves fleshy, to 10cm long. Flowers blue with tube 8–15mm and petals 6–9mm. For dry well-drained soil in full sun. This grows well in the Royal Botanic Gardens, Edinburgh, in a sunny border. Hardy to −20°C.

Mertensia ciliata (James) G. Don **Mountain Bell** (*Boraginaceae*)   Native of C Oregon, east to C Idaho and W Montana, W Colorado and N New Mexico, growing by streams and in wet meadows and scrub, flowering in May–August. Rhizome short-creeping, forming clumps of leafy stems. Flowers with tube 5-lobed, 1.3–2cm long, narrower than *M. virginiana*. For moist, peaty soil in full sun or slight shade. Hardy to −20°C or less. Var. *stomatechoides* (Vell.) Jeps. is found in moist places in coniferous forest in the Sierra Nevada in California, from Tulare Co. northwards to Oregon and in Nevada, at 1500–3000m. Corolla tube 6–8mm; the expanded limb 4–10mm long.

Mertensia simplicissima G. Don syn. *M. asiatica* (Takeda) Macbr.   Native of Japan in N Honshu and Hokkaido, northwards to the Kurile Islands, Korea, Sakhalin and the Aleutian Islands, growing on sandy shores, flowering in May–September. Plant with

Pentaglottis sempervirens

Caccinea macranthera

Brunnera macrophylla 'Hadspen Cream'

Brunnera macrophylla

Brunnera macrophylla 'Variegata'

Trachystemon orientalis at Wisley

prostrate flowering stems to 1m, from a rosette of glaucous leaves 3–8cm long. Flowers 8–12mm long. The closely related *M. maritima* (L.) S. F. Gray is found in northern Europe and NE North America, south to Massachusetts, usually on shingle beaches. In Britain it is becoming rare but still found in several places around the coast of Scotland and northern Ireland. Hardy to −20°C or less.

Mertensia virginica (L.) DC. **Virginia Cowslip**, **Blue Bells**   Native of S Ontario to New Jersey and South Carolina, Minnesota, Nebraska and Kansas, growing in wet meadows and along streams, flowering in March–May. Plant with a thick fleshy root. Stem 30–60cm. Leaves up to 15cm long, soft, fleshy. Flowers about 2.5cm long with narrow tube and expanded limb. The plant dies down soon after flowering and is completely dormant by mid-summer. For moist peaty soil in part shade or sun. Grows well in the Savill Gardens at Windsor but otherwise uncommon in gardens in Europe. It is, however, a popular and most beautiful plant for wild flower gardens in North America.

Pentaglottis sempervirens (L.) Tausch syn. *Anchusa sempervirens* L. (*Boraginaceae*)   Native of SW Europe from C Portugal to SW France and naturalized in England, Ireland, Belgium and Italy, growing in damp, shady places or by roads and in hedges near the sea, flowering in April–June. A bristle-haired plant with a very deep tap root, with branched stems to 1m. Basal leaves 10–40cm, ovate-oblong, in a rosette. Flowers 8–10mm across, blue. Can become a weed if allowed to seed too freely, and the deep taproot is brittle and readily resprouts, making established plants difficult to remove. They are, however, easily killed by glycosate. Hardy to −10°C or less.

Trachystemon orientalis (L.) G. Don syn. *Borago orientalis* L. (*Boraginaceae*)   Native of E Bulgaria, N Turkey and W Caucasus in wet beech forest on shady river banks and on damp rocks at up to 1000m, flowering in March–May. Rhizome creeping; flower stems emerging before the leaves, elongating during flowering to 28–40cm. Leaves ovate-cordate, with petiole 10–25cm and blade *c*.20 × 18cm, ovate-cordate, acuminate. Flowers with petals 4–6mm, curled back. Easy in moist shade and naturalized in several places in England. Valued for its early flowering and tolerance of neglect. Hardy to −15°C, perhaps less.

Lamium galeobdolon
'Variegatum'

Lamium galeobdolon
'Herman's Pride'

Lamium galeobdolon
'Silberteppich'

Lamium maculatum 'Silbergroschen'

Ajuga reptans
'Atropurpurea'

Lamium maculatum
'Chequers'

Lamium maculatum
'Roseum'

Lamium maculatum
'Aureum'

Ajuga reptans 'Multicolor'

Specimens from Eccleston Square, London, 12 April. ⅓ life size

Lamium galeobdolon 'Herman's Pride'

Ajuga reptans L.   Native of most of Europe
except N Scandinavia and Russia and of North
Africa eastwards to the Caucasus, Turkey and
Iran, growing in woods, grassy places and on
sunny banks, flowering in April–June.
Flowering stems 10–30cm. Bracts ovate, tinged
with blue, the upper shorter than the flowers.
Flowers deep blue, rarely pink or white, 14–
17mm long. Plant producing stolons at least
15cm long in summer. Forms with different leaf
variegation and shape have been selected, and
are usually grown for groundcover in rather dry
shade, producing a mass of rosettes of rather
spoon-shaped leaves.
'Atropurpurea' syn. 'Purpurea' has dark-purple
leaves, with a shining surface.
'Multicolor' syns. 'Tricolor', 'Rainbow' has
leaves variegated with pink and white.
'Jungle Beauty' and 'Jumbo' not shown here,
are extra large with green leaves, possibly
hybrids with *A. genevensis*.

Lamium album L. (*Labiatae*) **White Dead
Nettle**   Native of Europe and Asia from
Turkey eastwards, though rare in the
Mediterranean region, growing in hedgerows,
waste places, forests, rocky slopes and by
streams, and often as a weed of gardens,
flowering in April–August. Plant with creeping
stolons and upright flowering stems to 60cm.
Flowers white 20–27mm long in whorls of 8–10.
A rather weedy plant for highly cultivated parts
of the garden, but very pretty on a grassy bank
with forget-me-nots and primroses and other
wild flowers. Hardy to −25°C or less. There is a
variegated form, 'Friday', and 'Pale Peril', with
new shoots gold.

Lamium galeobdolon (L.) L. syns. *Galeobdolon
luteum* Hudson, *Lamiastrum galeobdolon* (L.)
Ehrend & Polatschek **Yellow Archangel**
Native of Europe from Ireland eastwards to
European Russia, and south to Spain, N Turkey
and the Caucasus, in woods and hedgerows on
grassy banks, marshes and moist, rocky slopes,
flowering in April–June. Two subspecies are
common in Europe and a third is rarer.
Subsp. *luteum* is commonest in N & E Europe,
and is known in England only in Lincolnshire.
It has leaves and bracts usually with blunt teeth,
1–2 times as long as wide, and up to 8 medium-
sized (17–21mm) flowers in a whorl. It is
diploid. Subspecies *montanum* (Pers.) Hayek has
leaves with sharp acute teeth, upper bracts
1.8–3.5 times as long as wide, and 9–15 often
large (to 2.5cm long) flowers in a whorl. It is
commonest in southern Europe, and is the plant
generally found wild in England and Ireland. It
is tetraploid. A third subspecies, *flavidum* (F.
Hermann), is also diploid, and is commonest in
the central-eastern Alps, the Apennines and N
Yugoslavia. It has sharply serrate or biserrate
leaves, and more than 10 small flowers in a
whorl. It is usually found on subalpine screes
and rocky slopes. To subsp. *argentatum* (Smejkal)
belongs the commonly cultivated and very
rampant clone 'Variegatum'. It is a native of E
Europe and now widely naturalized elsewhere.
'Silberteppich' syn. 'Silver Carpet'   A variety
of *Lamium galeobdolon* in which the leaves are
almost entirely silvery. Flowers yellow. Much
less invasive than 'Variegatum' and often
damaged by slugs. It is a form of subsp.
flavidum, found by E. Pagels in Yugoslavia.
'Herman's Pride'   A much more robust form
with even more beautiful silver leaves. It does
not suffer from the purple-leaf disease as does
'Silberteppich'.

Ajuga genevensis L. (*Labiatae*)   Native of
Europe from S Sweden to France (and long
naturalized in England), east to European
Russia, Turkey and the Caucasus, growing in
scrub, in moist meadows and on steppe
grassland, chalk downs and limestone
grassland, flowering in May–July. Plant with
creeping underground stolons. Stems 6–30cm,
with white hairs. Leaves obovate with a long
petiole. Flowers bright blue; upper bracts
shorter than the flowers. The closely related *A.
orientalis* L. from SE Europe and SW Asia
differs in its more woolly stems, shorter bracts
and stamens which are not exserted from the
corolla which is said to be twisted through 180°.
Hardy to −20°C.

Lamium orvala and 'Album' at the Royal Botanic Gardens, Kew

Lamium garganicum L. subsp. *laevigatum*
Arcangeli syn. *L. longiflorum* Tenori A very
variable species, native of Europe from S France
and NW Africa east to Romania, Turkey and
NW Iran, growing on rocks, screes, shady cliffs
and banks, often on high mountains, flowering in
March–September. Plant mat-forming, with
sprawling stems 6–45cm high. Flowers with
upper lip of corolla bifid, 26–40cm long usually
purplish pink: shown here is subsp. *laevigatum*,
one of the larger subspecies with stems more than
10cm high, and leaves with few hairs. It is native
of the northern part of the species range. Most
distinct is subsp. *pulchrum* R. Mill from
mountains in C Turkey, in which the leaves are
densely silky and the large flowers are white with
bluish-purple veins and blotches. Easily grown
in well-drained soil.

Lamium maculatum L.   Native of most of
Europe, excluding the British Isles and
Scandinavia, and of N Iran, the Caucasus,
Turkey (mainly in the north and Amanus
Mountains), growing in woods, on banks and
subalpine meadows, flowering in February–
June. Plant with mat-forming, creeping and
rooting non-flowering stems, and flowering
stems 15–40cm tall. Leaves 1–8cm, often with a
white blotch. Flowers usually pinkish purple,
sometimes brownish purple, pale pink or white,
20–35mm long. Easily grown in partial shade or
cool places in full sun. Hardy to −20°C.
Lamium maculatum cultivars:
'Album'   Flowers white; leaves with silver
flash.
'Aureum'   Flowers pinkish; leaves bright
yellow-green, with silver flash.
'Chequers'   Flowers purplish pink, leaves with
silver flash – close to the commonest form of the
species.
'Roseum'   Flowers pale pink, leaves with white
flash. The distinction between the colour of this
and the normal variety is clearer than appears in
the photograph.
'Silbergroschen' syn. 'Beacon Silver'   White
leaves and pinkish-purple flowers. Leaves often
with purple blotches caused by a disease.
'White Nancy'   Leaves silver, usually without
purple blotches. Flowers white.

Lamium orvala L.   Native of N Italy and W
Austria east to W Yugoslavia and S Hungary,
growing in scrub and on the edges of woods,
flowering in April–May. Flowering stems 30–
100cm, usually *c.*40cm. Leaves 4.0–15cm long.
Flowers dark purple to pink or white, 'Album'
2.5–4.5cm long. An attractive plant for well-
drained soil in partial shade, slowly forming wide
mats. Hardy to −15°C.

Meehania urticifolia (Miq.) Makino (*Labiatae*)
Native of NE China, Korea and Japan (except
Hokkaido), growing in damp woods in the
mountains, flowering in April–May. Plant with
long stolons rooting at the nodes, spreading
quickly to form a large patch. Flowering stems
upright, 15–30cm long. Leaves 2–5cm long;
flowers 4–5cm long. An attractive, early-flowering
ground cover plant for partial shade, deciduous
in cold winters. *M. cordata* (Nutt.) Britton,
native of moist woods in SW Pennsylvania to
Illinois, Tennessee and North Carolina, is
smaller, less far creeping, with pinkish-purple
flowers 2.5–3cm long, in dense clusters. A third
species, *M. montis-koyae* Ohwi, does not have
creeping stolons and is nearly hairless. It is
confined to S&W Honshu, and is close to *M.
fargesii* from W China, shown in vol. 2, p. 209.

Lamium maculatum 'White Nancy'

Lamium album

Lamium garganicum subsp. *laevigatum*

Meehania urticifolia at Harry Hay's, Surrey

Ajuga genevensis

Lamium galeobdolon subsp. *montanum*

Lathraea clandestina with *Equisetum*

Latheraea squamaria and *Anemone nemorosa*

Jaborosa integrifolia

Hyoscyamus aureus L. (*Solanaceae*) Native of the E Mediterranean region from Crete, Rhodes and SW Turkey east to NW Iraq and south to Egypt, growing on cliffs, old walls and ruins, at up to 1200m, flowering in February–July. An attractive, tufted plant around 60cm across with softly hairy and glandular leaves, the blade orbicular to ovate, 3–5cm long. Flowers 3–4cm across, with exserted stamens. For a hot, dry position in a wall or rock crevice. Hardy to −10°C, perhaps. *Hyoscyamus albus* L., which is also often seen on classical ruins, has greenish or yellowish flowers, and stamens not exserted. It may be annual or perennial.

Jaborosa integrifolia (*Solanaceae*) Native of S Brazil, Uruguay and NE Argentina, around Buenos Aires, growing on the pampas, in damp fields, flowering in November–December, but in May–June in gardens in the north. Plant spreading by underground rhizomes which produce rosettes of leaves *c.*15cm long on short shoots. Flowers *c.*5cm across. For well-drained soil in a warm position. Hardy to −15°C with protection in winter. Most of the 6 or 7 species of *Jaborosa* have deeply cut or toothed leaves.

Lathraea clandestina L. (*Scrophulariaceae*) Native of W Europe, from Belgium south to Spain and east to S Italy, and naturalized in England, growing in wet woods, or meadows by streams, parasitic on the roots of willow, poplar, alder or maple. A leafless plant with crowded fleshy stems to 5cm, usually less. Flowers often emerging directly from the ground, 40–50mm. Seeds large, *c.*5mm. across, expelled explosively. Can be established by sowing fresh seed near the roots of suitable trees, or by transplanting roots and soil from where the plant is growing; I suspect seed lying in the soil is thereby kept moist, and so germinates well. Hardy to −15°C.

Lathraea squamaria L. **Toothwort** Native of most of Europe, from Ireland eastwards to the Himalayas and south to Spain and Turkey, growing in moist woods, and parasitic on many different trees, but usually on hazel, alder or beech, flowering in March–June. A leafless plant with few fleshy stems to 30cm. Flowers 14–17mm long. Not often cultivated, but possibly seed sown on the surface roots of suitable trees would establish itself. Hardy to −20°C or less.

Mandragora autumnalis Bertol. (*Solanaceae*) **Mandrake** Native of the Mediterranean coastal regions, from Portugal to Turkey and North Africa and Israel, in rocky places in pine woods and olive groves (at up to 600m in Turkey), flowering from January–April (var. *microcarpa* Bertol. flowers in autumn). The deep, thick, usually forked root was the famous Mandrake, which was said to shriek when it was pulled out of the ground; the leaves are sparsely hairy and sometimes even prickly, to 40cm long when fully developed. Flowers purplish, 4–8cm across. Fruit like a small, slightly elongated tomato, yellow or orange, with a long calyx. Hardy to −15°C, perhaps. *M. officinalis* L. has hairier leaves, smaller greenish-white flowers and round yellow fruit. It is found only in N Italy and W Yugoslavia. *M. caulescens* C. B. Clarke is a remarkable species from the Himalayas at 3000–4500m, with nodding, bell-shaped flowers *c.*2–5cm across, on leafy stems

which reach 30cm high. It is illustrated in Polunin & Stainton's *Flowers of the Himalaya.*

Phelypaea tournefortii Desf. (*Orobanchaceae*) Native of E Turkey and the S Caucasus in Georgia and Armenia, growing on mountain steppes at 1600–2660m, parasitic on *Achillea* and *Tanacetum*, flowering in June–July. Flowering stems 10–20cm, few to several, from a stout base on the root of the host. Stems and calyx glandular-pilose, with whitish hairs. Flowers to 5cm across, the petals velvety in texture. As far as I know, this exciting plant has never been cultivated successfully, but should be tried from seed sown around the roots of a suitable host, in a position in full sun, hot and dry in summer, moist in autumn and spring, and cold and dry in winter. Hardy to −20°C or less.

Physochlaina alaica Korolk. ex Kovalevsk (*Solanaceae*) Native of Central Asia, in the Pamir-Alai, growing on rocky slopes at *c.*1800m, flowering in April–May. Stem *c.*30cm. Leaves and stem softly hairy. Flowers yellowish, *c.*2cm long, in a rounded head. For well-drained soil in sun or partial shade, kept rather dry in summer. Hardy to −20°C or less.

Physochlaina orientalis (M. Bieb.) G. Don syn. *Hyoscyamus orientalis* Bieb. Native of the Caucasus, NW Iran and NE Turkey near Gümüşane, apparently often found in the mouths of caves and in rock crevices, at *c.*1500m, flowering in May. Plant with densely and softly hairy stems to 60cm from a stout rootstock. Leaves triangular ovate 4–13cm long, long-stalked. Flowers *c.*1.5cm long, purplish. For well-drained soil in sun or part shade. Unusual and valuable for its early flowering, usually in April in S England. Although rare in gardens, it has been grown at least since 1823. *Physochlaina* is a small genus of about 4 species, mainly in C Asia. *P. praealta* (Decne.) Miers, from the Himalayas, is taller, to 120cm, with greenish-yellow, purple-veined flowers in a cluster to 10cm across.

Rehmannia glutinosa Libosch. ex Fisch. & Mey. syn. *R. chinensis* Fisch. & Mey. (*Scrophulariaceae*) Native of N China, especially the area round Beijing, where it is common on old walls in the Forbidden City and the Ming tombs, and of Korea, growing in well-drained, stony ground on roadsides and in woods, flowering in April–July. Stems 15–30cm. Leaves softly pubescent. Flowers 5–7.5cm long, reddish brown to yellow, veined with purple. Probably hardy to −25°C at least if dry, but the softly hairy leaves are susceptible to warm damp in winter, so it is often grown in a greenhouse.

Scopolia carniolica Jacq. syns. *S. tubiflora* Kreyer, *S. ?caucasica* Kolesn. ex Kreyer (*Solanaceae*) Native of Austria, Italy and Yugoslavia, eastwards to Baltic Russia and the Caucasus, growing in moist rocky beech woods at *c.*1000m, flowering in April–May. Rhizome fleshy, horizontal; stems 20–60cm, with ovate or obovate leaves, all glabrous. Flowers 1.5–2.5cm long, usually brownish-purple or brownish-orange outside, paler inside, but sometimes all greenish-yellow as here. Fruit a capsule, not a berry as in so many *Solanaceae* (Nightshade family).

Mandragora autumnalis at Wisley

Physochlaina orientalis at Kew

Scopolia carniolica at Wisley

Physochlaina alaica near Ferghana

Rehmannia glutinosa in woods near Beijing

Rehmannia glutinosa on a ruined Ming tomb

Hyoscyamus aureus on ancient walls near Kaş, SW Turkey

Phelypaea tournefortii near Erzurum

Doronicum carpetanum

Doronicum plantagineum with *Allium ursinum*

Doronicum 'Miss Mason'

Doronicum pardalianches

Doronicum carpetanum Boiss. & Reut. ex
Willk. (*Compositae*) Native of the Pyrenees,
N & C Spain, N & C Portugal, growing in
mountain meadows and among rocks, flowering
in May–June. Plant forming large clumps of
stems, 40–80cm tall. Basal leaves cordate, with
long petioles. Stem leaves 6–8. Flowers 2–3 per
stem, rarely more, 4–5cm across. A fine plant
for a moist and partially shady position. Hardy
to −15°C, probably less.

Doronicum orientale Hoffm. syn. *D.
caucasicum* M. Bieb. Native of SE Europe,
from Italy, Sicily and Yugoslavia east to
Hungary and the Caucasus, and south to
Turkey and Lebanon, growing in woods and
scrub, in places dry in summer, at 50–1900m in
Turkey, flowering in March–July, normally in
April in S England. Plant spreading slowly by
fleshy underground rhizomes to make wide
patches. Basal leaves ovate or cordate, with a
long stalk. Flower head solitary, 2.5–5cm across
on a glandular and hairy stalk, 10–60cm tall,
usually *c*.30cm. Stem leaves 1 or 2. For a
partially shaded position, and tolerant of
drought in summer, when the leaves die down.
Hardy to −15°C or less.

Doronicum pardalianches L. **Great Leopard's
Bane** Native of W Europe from Belgium
south to Spain, and east to Germany and Italy
(and naturalized in Austria, Britain and
Czechoslovakia), growing in woods, flowering
in May–July. Plant forming spreading patches

by tubers produced at the end of underground
stolons. Stems to 90cm. Basal leaves cordate,
upper amplexicaul. Flower heads usually 2–6,
3–5cm across. A tall, softly hairy plant for moist
soil in partial shade. Hardy to −20°C or less.

Doronicum plantagineum L. Native of
Portugal and Spain, W Italy and France, and
naturalized in Britain, especially in E Scotland,
in woods, meadows and heathland, flowering in
April–June. Rhizome spreading and somewhat
tuberous, with tufts of hairs, the plant forming
extensive colonies. Stems to 80cm. Basal leaves
ovate-elliptical, often weakly cordate, with a
long stalk, sometimes toothed; upper leaves not
amplexicaul. Flower heads 1 or 2, rarely more,
3–5cm across. Easily grown in sun or semi-
shade, and very pretty naturalized in grass.

Doronicum cultivars: There are several
cultivars, usually dwarf and early flowering, and
often double. Shown here are:
'Miss Mason' Stems to 45cm. Flowering in
April and early May.
'Frühlingspracht' syn. 'Spring Beauty' Stems
to 45cm, usually less, with hideous double
flowers.

Petasites fragrans (Vill.) C. Presl. (*Compositae*)
Winter Heliotrope Native of the
Mediterranean region in Italy, Sardinia, Sicily
and North Africa, in damp shady woods and
gorges, flowering in December–March;
commonly naturalized on roadsides in other

Doronicum 'Frühlingspracht'

Doronicum orientale near Fethiye, SW Turkey

Petasites fragrans beautiful, but unwanted at Sellindge, Kent

parts of western Europe. Flowering stem up to 50cm. Leaves to 20cm across, reniform-cordate, green but hairy beneath. Flowers strongly scented of Heliotrope; pale lilac to purple. Only the male plant is naturalized or cultivated, and the female, according to *Flora Europea*, is unknown. This plant is a terrible spreader by fleshy underground rhizomes, and is a weed in many old gardens. The flowers, however, which are freely produced in mild winters, are most welcome. Cold below −10°C will kill the top growth, but the roots survive.

Petasites palmatus (Ait.) Gray **Sweet Coltsfoot**   Native of North America from Newfoundland to Massachusetts, west to Alaska and south to to S California along the coast, growing along streams in woods, flowering in February–April. Plant creeping by underground rhizomes. Flowering stems to 50cm, produced before the leaves. Flowers scented. Leaves 10–40cm wide, palmately lobed with 7–11 toothed lobes. For a moist, shady position. Hardy to −20°C and less. *P. japonicus* (Sieb. & Zucc.) Maxim., from Japan, Korea and China, has similar flowers, but huge orbicular leaves which may be 1.5m across, on stems 2m tall in var. *giganteus*; used by Japanese children as umbrellas.

Petasites paradoxus (Retz) Baumg. syn. *P. niveus* (Vill.) Baumb.   Native of Europe, from France and Spain in the Pyrenees, east to the Carpathians and C Yugoslavia, growing by streams in woods in the mountains, usually on limestone, near melting snow, flowering from May–July. Flowering stem up to 25cm. Leaves when mature, triangular-cordate to hastate, densely white-hairy beneath. Attractive with its pinkish-red bracts, which distinguish it from the commoner ghostly white and green *P. albus* (L.) Gaerten, also frequent in alpine woods. Both are too rampant underground for all but the wildest part of the garden.

Petasites paradoxus in the Valais

Petasites palmatus in California

Clintonia umbellulata at Washfield Nurseries

Clintonia uniflora in Yosemite, California

Clintonia andrewsiana in NW California

Clintonia borealis at Wisley

Clintonia andrewsiana Torr.
(*Convallariaceae*)   Native of California from
Del Norte Co. northwards to SW Oregon, in
Redwood forests in moist, shady places,
flowering in May–July. Plant without runners,
forming clumps. Leaves 5 or 6, 15–25cm long,
5–12cm across. Stem 25–50cm; flowers in both
terminal and lateral umbels, deep reddish; the
petals with nectaries at the base, 10–15mm long.
Berries bluish black, 8–12mm long. For semi-
shade and moist peaty or leafy soil. This species
grows well in E Scotland at the Royal Botanic
Garden, Edinburgh and at Glendoick. Hardy to
−10°C, probably lower with a good mulch.

Clintonia borealis (Ait.) Raf.   Native of E
North America, from Newfoundland to
Manitoba south to North Carolina and
Wisconsin, growing in moist woods and scrub,
often in the mountains, flowering in May–June.
Stems creeping underground to form extensive
colonies. Leaves 2–5; stems 15–35cm, with 3–6
drooping, greenish-yellow flowers. Petals 16–
20mm long. Berries blue. For loose leafy or
peaty soil in shade or partial shade. Hardy to
−25°C, or less, but damaged by late frosts.

Clintonia umbellulata (Michx.) Morong syn.
C. umbellata Torrey   Native of E North
America, from New York and New Jersey south
to Georgia and Tennessee, growing in woods in
the hills, flowering from May–June. Stems 15–
40cm, shortly creeping underground to form
dense patches. Leaves 2–5, oblong, oblanceolate
or obovate. Flowers sometimes purple-spotted,
scented, 8–12mm long. Berries black. For a
slightly moist position in partial or deciduous
shade. The fine clump shown here was growing
on acid clay in Kent. Hardy to −25°C.

Clintonia uniflora (Schultes) Kunth **Bride's
Bonnet**   Native of N & E California, north to
British Columbia and east to Montana, in pine
forest and under *Sequoiadendron*, at 1000–
1800m in California, flowering from May–July.
Plant with slender underground runners.
Leaves 2–3, 7–15cm long; 2.5–6cm wide.
Flower stems 7–10cm; flowers solitary, with
petals pubescent, 1.8–2.2cm long. For well-
drained, moist leafy soil in part shade. Hardy to
−15°C. The fifth species of the genus, *C. udensis*
Trautv. & C. A. Meyer syn *C. alpina* Baker,
from the Himalayas in N India and Nepal east
to SW China and Japan, has pale-mauve or
white flowers 6–10mm long, in a nodding umbel
of 2–6; it grows in alpine forests and scrub,
flowering in April–July.

Helonias bullata L. (*Melanthiaceae*)   Native of
E North America, from N New Jersey and S
New York south to North Carolina, growing in
swamps and bogs, flowering April–May.
Rhizome tuberous. Leaves 15–45cm long, up to
5cm wide, evergreen, crisp and shiny.
Flowering stems 4–20cm; flower heads 2–3cm
long, of 25–30 minute flowers. This is the only
species in the genus and differs from *Helionopsis*
in its smaller flowers in a tight head. For moist
acid and peaty soil. Hardy to −20°C.

Heloniopsis orientalis (Thunb.) Tanaka
(*Melanthiaceae*)   Native throughout Japan, but
commonest in the north, in Korea and Sakhalin,
growing in woods, scrub and meadows in the
mountains, flowering in April–June. Leaves

Heloniopsis orientalis at Wisley

Heloniopsis orientalis var. *flavida*

Helonias bullata at Wisley

evergreen, 7–15cm long, rather leathery.
Flowering stems 10–60cm, elongating after
flowering, with 3–10 flowers. Petals 1–1.5cm
long, pink, becoming purplish or greenish in
fruit. Easily grown in a cool shady position in
leafy soil, kept moist in summer. Hardy to
−15°C. Var. *breviscapa* (Maxim.) Ohwi, in spite
of its name, differs mainly in its smaller, white
or pale pink flowers. It is found in Kyushu and
Yakushima, in the mountains. Var. *flavida*
(Nakai) Ohwi, from C Honshu, is a taller plant
with thinner leaves, and white or greenish
flowers, green in fruit.

Scoliopus bigelovii Torr. **Slink Pod**
(*Liliaceae*)   Native of SW Oregon and N
California, from Humboldt Co. to Santa Cruz
Co., growing in moist, shady places in Redwood
forest below 500m, flowering in February–
March. Plant with 2 broad leaves to 10cm wide,
20cm long, from a slender rootstock. Flowering
stems 3-angled, leafless, 3–12 in an umbel at
ground level, 10–20cm tall, recurving in fruit.
Flowers with greenish sepals and narrow, erect
petals, 14–17mm long, smelling of bad meat.
For careful cultivation in moist, peaty soil in
shade. Hardy to −10°C or so, and requires
protection in cold winters. A second species, *S.
hallii* Watson, from Oregon, is similar but
smaller.

Streptopus roseus Michx. **Liverberry**
(*Convallariaceae*)   Native of E North America,
from Newfoundland to Manitoba and south to
Georgia and Michigan, growing in moist woods,
flowering in May–July. Plant with several very
graceful and slender stems, 25–60cm tall,
branched above. Leaves ciliate. Flowers
6–12mm long; anthers forked. Berries red. For
cool leafy soil in shade or partial shade. Hardy
to −20°C or less. *S. amplexifolius* (L.) DC. from
wet subalpine woods in the Alps, eastwards to
Japan and North America, has taller stems,
amplexicaul leaves and greenish-white flowers
c.1cm long.

Scoliopus bigelovii at the Royal Botanic Gardens, Kew

Streptopus roseus at Cruickshank Botanic Garden, Aberdeen

Uvularia sessilifolia

Disporum trachycarpum at the Savill Gardens, Windsor

Uvularia perfoliata

Uvularia grandiflora

Disporum bodinieri (Lvl.) Wang & Tang (*Convallariaceae*)   Native of W China, in Guizhou, Yunnan and Sichuan at 1000–1800m, growing in lush, wet scrub on steep mountains, flowering in April–May. Plant with few, much-branched stems to 2m. Leaves *c*.7cm long; flowers pale yellowish green, to 3cm long, with exserted stamens. For rich, moist soil in shade or partial shade. Hardy to −15°C perhaps.

Disporum cantoniense (Lour.) Merrill syn. *D. pullum* hort.   Native of W China, in Yunnan to Hubei, of Japan and SE Asia, growing in open woods and scrub, flowering in May–June. Plant with few stems to 2m, elongating after flowering. Flowers on short pedicels, *c*.2.5cm long, white or reddish. For well-drained soil in shade or partial shade. Hardy to −15°C perhaps.

Disporum megalanthum Wang & Tang Native of W China, in Sichuan, growing in bamboo and *Rhododendron* scrub at 1600–2500m, flowering in May–June. Plant with few, upright stems to 30cm at flowering, elongating later. Flowers white, *c*.3cm long, stamens not exserted. Hardy to −15°C.

Disporum sessile subsp. *flavens* Kitagawa Native of Korea and Heilonjiang (Manchuria) growing in deciduous woods, flowering in May–June. Flowers 2cm long.

Disporum smithii (Hook.) Piper   Native of the coast ranges of California, from Santa Cruz Co. north to British Columbia, growing in cool, moist places in Redwood and evergreen forest, flowering in March–May. Stems 30–90cm, in clumps. Leaves ovate to ovate-lanceolate, rounded or subcordate at the base, 5–12cm long. Flowers 2–6 in a group, whitish, the petals 1.5–2.5cm long. Berries obovoid, orange to red. Easily grown in a moist shaded position. Hardy to −15°C, perhaps less.

Disporum trachycarpum (Wats.) Benth. & Hook.   Native of W North America, from British Columbia to NE Oregon and south along the Rockies from North Dakota to S Arizona and W New Mexico, at up to 3000m in Arizona, growing in woods, often along streams, flowering in May–July. Plant with several

branched stems to 60cm. Leaves 4–12cm long, ovate, ciliate glabrous above. Flowers creamy white, 9–15mm long, with exserted stamens. Style smooth. Berry yellow, becoming red. For moist, leafy soil in shade. Hardy to −20°C.

Disporum uniflorum Baker   Native of W China, in Yunnan, especially near Lijiang, growing among bracken in *Rhododendron* and mixed deciduous scrub at 2000m, flowering in May. Plant with few stems to 1m, elongating after flowering. Flowers on long, *c*.6cm, pedicles, to 4cm long, stamens not exserted. For well-drained, leafy soil in sun or partial shade. Hardy to −15°C.

Uvularia grandiflora Smith (*Convallariaceae*) Native of Quebec to Ontario, south to Minnesota, Georgia, Tennessee and Kansas, growing in woods on rich soils, flowering in April–June. Stems to 75cm, glabrous. Leaves perfoliate, 5–13cm long, downy beneath, at least when young. Flowers 2.5–5cm, bright yellow, inner surface of petals smooth. Easily grown in well-drained but moist, leafy soil; in deciduous shade; needs protection from slugs when young. Hardy to −20°C.

Uvularia perfoliata L. **Straw Bell**   Native of Quebec to Ontario, south to Florida and Mississippi growing in moist woods and scrub, flowering in April–June. Stems 20–60cm, glabrous. Leaves perfoliate, 5–9cm, long, glabrous and paler beneath. Flowers 2–3.5cm, pale yellow; inner surface of petals with minute glands. Easily grown in moist, leafy soil in partial shade. In the wild it usually does not form dense clumps as here. Hardy to −20°C or less.

Uvularia sessilifolia L. **Straw Lilies**   Native of New Brunswick and Ontario, west to Minnesota, south to Georgia and Arkansas, growing in moist woods and scrub, flowering in May–June. Rootstock creeping; stem to 40cm, glabrous. Leaves 3.5–7.5cm, not perfoliate, glabrous, paler beneath. Flowers pale greenish yellow, 1.5–3cm long; inner surface of petals smooth. Capsule ovate, 3-angled, tapering into its stalk. Easily grown in moist, leafy soil in deciduous shade. Distinguished from *U. caroliniana* by its thin leaves and smooth stem.

Disporum bodinieri in the Min River Valley, Sichuan

Disporum bodinieri

Disporum uniflorum at Lijiang, Yunnan

Disporum flavens at Kew

Disporum megalanthum at Wolong, Sichuan

Disporum cantoniense

Disporum smithii

Lysichiton americanus at Chyverton, Cornwall

Symplocarpus foetidus near New York

Orontium aquaticum

Acorus calamus at Leeds Castle, Kent

Acorus calamus 'Variegatus'

Lysichiton camschatcensis

Acorus calamus L. (*Araceae*)   Native of
Siberia, China, Japan and W North America,
and naturalized from Iran and Turkey
westwards since the 16th century, growing in
shallow water by lakes and slow rivers; in
Europe especially associated with moats and
lakes around old castles. Leaves and leaf-like
stems upright to 1.5m, striped in 'Variegatus',
tinged pink at the base, often with wavy
margins, 6–15mm wide. Flowers minute,
greenish, on an apparently lateral spadix which
is about 7cm long, produced in May–July.
'Variegatus' has a cleaner, longer-lasting
variegation than any of the striped water irises.
The plant was grown for its aromatic foliage and
the Oil of Calamus extracted from the leaves and
rhizomes. Hardy to −25°C. *Acorus gramineus*
Solander, from India, China and Japan, is
smaller, to 50cm, has evergreen leaves without a
midrib and an almost erect spadix 5–10cm long.
It is the dwarf form, var. *pusillus* Engl., that is
generally cultivated, and the striped 'Argenteo-
striatus' is also common.

Lysichiton americanus Hult. & St. John
(*Araceae*) **Yellow Skunk Cabbage**   Native of
NW California, from near San Francisco in the
Santa Cruz mountains, north to Alaska and east
to Montana in bogs and wet woods near the
coast, flowering in April–June. Leaves when
mature 30–150cm tall, oblong to elliptical,
short-stalked. Flowers emerging before or with
the leaves, on stalks 30–50cm tall. Spathe
10–20m long, yellow. Easily grown in wet soil
and valuable for its early flowering and large
handsome leaves. The flowers smell unpleasant,
but not foul enough to upset anyone who grows
the plant well.

Lysichiton camschatcensis (L.) Schott
Native of Japan, in N Honshu and Hokkaido
northwards to E Siberia, Sakhalin, Kamchatka
and the Kurile Islands, growing in bogs and wet
places and by ponds and lakes, flowering in
April–July. Like *L. americanus*, but smaller and
white flowered. Mature leaves 40–80cm long.
Flowers emerging before or with the leaves, on
stems 10–30cm long. Spathe 8–12cm long.
Flowers sweetly scented. Easily grown in moist,
acid soil but rarer than *L. americanus* in gardens.
Young plants of both species require protection
from slugs. The probable hybrid between the
two species has a pale-yellow or creamy spathe.

Orontium aquaticum L. (*Araceae*) **Golden
Club**   Native of E North America, from
Massachusetts and Kentucky south to Florida
and Louisiana, growing in peaty swamps and
ponds, flowering in April–June. Leaves either
emerging or floating on the water surface, the
blade 15–30cm long; flowering stems 15–60cm
long. Spadix 2.5–5cm long. Spathe bract-like
and usually dropping off before flowering. For
pools and shallow water. Hardy to −20°C.

Symplocarpus foetidus (L.) Nutt. syn.
Spathyema foetida (L.) Raf. (*Araceae*) **Skunk
Cabbage**   Native of Nova Scotia, west to
Manitoba, south to Georgia, growing in swampy
woods and by streams, flowering in February–
April, as soon as the frost departs the soil.
Leaves 30–90cm long, *c*.30cm wide, ovate,
truncate at base, developing during and after
flowering into handsome rosettes. Spathe
emerging before the leaves, 7.5–15cm tall, solid,
fleshy, stinking. Spadix becoming large, up to
15cm in diameter when ripe in August–
September. Hardy to −25°C and less.

Aquilegia canadensis near Charlottesville, Virginia

Aquilegia caerulea James (*Ranunculaceae*)
Native of SW Montana to N Arizona and N New
Mexico, growing in the mountains at 2200–
3000m, commonly in aspen groves, flowering in
June–August. Stems to 90cm. Flowers 5–7.5cm
across; sepals spreading, blue; petals blue or
white, with spur 3–5cm, and the well-developed
petal limb commonly white. This is the state
flower of Colorado, where it grows on the north
rim of the Grand Canyon. For a sheltered
position in sun or partial shade.

Aquilegia canadensis L. **Wild Columbine**
Native of North America from Nova Scotia to the
Northwest Territories, south to Nebraska,
Texas and Florida, growing in rocky woods and
on shady banks and damp roadsides, flowering in
April–July. Stem 25–60cm, glabrous or slightly
pubescent. Leaflets deeply lobed; flowers
2.5–5cm long, including the straight spurs which
are c.12mm long, usually scarlet, very rarely
white or yellow. Sepals pointing downwards,
c.15mm long. Style and stamens exserted.
Pollinated by hummingbirds. For well-drained,
sandy, soil in deciduous shade, or in cool areas
with some sun. Hardy to −25°C.

Aquilegia chrysantha Gray   Native of S
Colorado to New Mexico, Arizona and N
Mexico, growing in moist places in pine forests,
scrub and along streams at 1000–3200m,
flowering in April–September. Stems to 60cm.
Flowers facing upwards 4–7.5cm across, with
spurs 4–7cm long; sepals spreading. *Aquilegia
longissima* Gray, from mountains in W Texas, S
Arizona and NE Mexico, is an even more striking
species with pale yellow flowers and spurs
9–15cm long. Both require moist, well-drained
soil in a warm and sheltered position.

Aquilegia 'Crimson Star'   An attractive hybrid
with red and white flowers. Plants short-lived.
Hardy to −15°C perhaps.

Aquilegia elegantula Greene   Native of the
Rocky Mountains from SW Colorado and SE
Utah to N Mexico in rocky places at c.3000m,
flowering in June–July. Plant slender to 60cm.
Flowers with spurs less than 3cm long; sepals
greenish at the apex. For a warm, sheltered
position. Hardy to −15°C perhaps.

Aquilegia formosa Fisch.   Native of California,
north to Alaska and east to W Montana and
Utah, in moist woods and damp places in scrub
and on banks from near sea level to 3000m,
flowering in April–August, according to altitude
and latitude. Stem 50–100cm, glandular above;
basal leaves, bluish, biternate; leaflets divided to
about the middle. Flowers to 5cm across, spurs
10–20mm usually scarlet, with yellow limbs to
the petals, 3–5mm long. Sepals 15–25mm long,
spreading or reflexed. Var. *formosa* is a mountain
form, found at 1000–3000m in the Sierra
Nevada; var. *truncata* (Fisch. & Mey.) Baker,
with glabrous or sparingly pubescent stems, and
the yellow lamina only 1–2mm long, is also
shown here; it grows at lower altitudes also, and
is common in the coast ranges of California. For a
warm position in full sun or partial shade, with
moisture at the root. Hardy to −15°C.

Aquilegia olympica Boiss.   Native of the
Caucasus, N & W Iran and N & E Turkey,
growing in alpine meadows, scrub and spruce
forest at 1700–2800m in Turkey, flowering in
June–July. Plant forming small clumps with
several upright stems to 60cm. Flowers with
bluish sepals 25–35mm long and somewhat
hooked spurs. For moist but well-drained peaty
soil. Hardy to −20°C or less. The name comes

Aquilegia canadensis

Aquilegia elegantula

Aquilegia formosa var. *formosa*

Aquilegia 'Crimson Star'

AQUILEGIA

Aquilegia formosa var. *truncata*

Aquilegia formosa var. *truncata* in the Salmon Mountains, NW California

Aquilegia chrysantha

Aquilegia chrysantha in Arizona

Aquilegia ottonis subsp. *amaliae*

from Armenian Olympus, today called Keşiş Dağ in NE Turkey.

Aquilegia ottonis Orph. ex Boiss. subsp. **amaliae** (Orph. ex Boiss.) Strid   Native of NE Greece where it is common on Olimbos Or (Thessalian Mount Olympus) at 900–2300m, and possibly of neighbouring Yugoslavia and Albania, growing in damp rocky places in gorges, flowering in June–August. Plant with several flowering stems to 45cm from a tough, woody rootstock. Leaflets 1.5–3cm long. Flowers 18–28mm long, with limb of spurred petals, white, a little shorter than the blue sepals. Seed capsules 12–15mm long. The other subspecies of *A. ottonis* are found in the Peloponnese and in Italy. For a cool position in partial shade. Hardy to −15°C.

Aquilegia olympica

Aquilegia caerulea

87

'Hensol Harebell'

Aquilegia
'Long-spurred Hybrids'

Aquilegia vulgaris
'Flore Pleno'

'Olympia'
Blue and White

Aquilegia vulgaris
(reddish seedling)

'Olympia'
Red and Gold

Aquilegia
'Mrs Scott Elliott
Hybrids'

'Hensol Harebell'

Aquilegia vulgaris
'Nora Barlow'

'Dwarf Fairyland
mixed'

Specimens from Wisley, 12 May. ⅔ life size

Aquilegia 'Dwarf Fairyland Mixed'

Aquilegia 'Biedermeier Mixed'

Aquilegia 'Dragonfly hybrids'

Aquilegia 'Music' (white seedling)

Aquilegia 'Biedermeier mixed' A short-stemmed strain with upward-facing flowers close to *A. vulgaris*, but stems around 50cm high.

Aquilegia 'Mrs Scott Elliott hybrids' *A. caerulea* James is described on p. 86. In this strain the flowers vary somewhat in colour from the typical blue and white form. Height around 80cm.

Aquilegia 'Dwarf Fairyland mixed' A low-growing compact, many stemmed strain with stems *c*.45cm, in which the upward-facing flowers may be single or double with numerous tubular petals and short spurs. Unusual, but if not positively ugly, then lacking the grace which is one of the main charms of the Columbines.

Aquilegia 'Hensol Harebell' A hybrid strain between *A. vulgaris* and *A. alpina*. Large rich-blue flowers on branched stems to 75cm, raised at Mossdale, Castle Douglas, Scotland, by a Mrs Kennedy in the early 1900s.

Aquilegia 'Long-spurred hybrids' and **'Dragonfly hybrids'** These long-spurred hybrids, in various shades of blue, yellow, red and bicolours, are derived from the American species *A. caerulea*, *A. chrysantha* and *A. formosa*. They are good plants for a sunny position and well-drained, but not dry soil, and are generally rather short-lived perennials,

easily raised from seed. 'Long-spurred hybrids' are tall, *c*.75cm, with flowers in rather pale shades. 'McKana' hybrids are similar. 'Dragonfly' hybrids are smaller, *c*.50cm with flowers of deeper shades.

Aquilegia 'Music' A strain of medium height, *c*.60cm tall, with long-spurred flowers in various colours.

Aquilegia 'Nora Barlow' This is a variant of *A. vulgaris*, with flowers with numerous narrow petals in pale green and red. It is curious rather than beautiful, and has been in cultivation since probably the 17th century, when it was known as the 'Rose Columbine'.

Aquilegia 'Olympia' 'Blue and White', 'Red and Gold' and **'Violet and Yellow'** In these seed strains, the striking bicolours have been stabilized. Stems to 60cm.

Aquilegia vulgaris 'Flore Pleno' In this double-flowered deep purple plant the sepals are normal, but there are at least twice the usual number of petals. Other strange mutants that are known are the spurless ones, called 'Stormy Columbines', and an upside-down one, with numerous spurs facing downwards on a nodding flower, which is shown in *Gerard's Herball* (1633). It appears to be lost at present but may recur.

Aquilegia 'Olympia' violet and yellow

Aquilegia 'Hensol Harebell'

Aquilegia fragrans near Vishensar, Kashmir

Aquilegia fragrans

Aquilegia alpina L. (*Ranunculaceae*)   Native of the Alps in France, Switzerland, Austria and Italy, and in the N Apennines, growing in open woods and on shady rocks on cliffs at 1300–2000m, flowering in July–August. Stems 15–60cm usually with 1–3 flowers, pubescent above. Leaflets deeply divided. Flowers nodding; sepals blue, 30–45mm. Spurs 18–25mm, blue, straight or curved, limb paler 14–17mm. For moist soil in a cool shaded position. Hardy to −20°C.

Aquilegia atrata Koch   Native of the Alps, from France to Austria and the Apennines, growing in subalpine hay meadows, flowering in May–July. Stems 40–80cm, densely pubescent above. Flowers nodding, deep reddish purple, 3–5cm across; sepals 15–24mm; petals with limb 8–12mm, spur 10–15mm, hooked. Easily cultivated in moist or rather dry soil in partial shade, and striking with its tall stems and almost black flowers. Hardy to −20°C.

Aquilegia bertolonii Schott syn. *A. reuteri* Boiss.   Native of SE France and NW Italy, in the Alpes Maritimes and neighbouring ranges, growing in scrub on rocky hillsides at 750–1600m, flowering in June–July, in warmer places and at lower altitudes than *A. alpina*. Stems 10–30cm, glandular above; stem leaves linear, usually entire. Flowers 1–5, nodding; sepals, spurs and lamina the same colour, usually purplish blue; sepals 18–33mm; spurs 10–14mm, straight or slightly curved; limb 10–14mm. This should be tolerant of a warmer and drier position than *A. alpina*. Hardy to −15°C.

Aquilegia flabellata Sieb. & Zucc. var. **pumila** Kudo **'Mini star'**   Native of Honshu and Hokkaido, north to Sakhalin, the Kurile Islands and North Korea, growing in scrub in the mountains, flowering in June–August. Flowers with limb 1.5cm, white spurs incurved, 1–5cm. An attractive plant for a sunny position. 'Mini star' is a dwarf strain with stem *c*.15cm tall. *A. flabellata* itself is not known in the wild, but has long been cultivated in Japan. It is larger, with very glaucous leaves and stems 20–50cm, with flowers 3–5cm across. A white form is also known. Hardy to −20°C perhaps.

Aquilegia fragrans Benth.   Native of N Pakistan to N India (Uttar Pradesh) and frequent in Kashmir, growing in scrub and subalpine meadows at 2400–2600m, flowering in June–August. Stems 40–80cm, not much branched; whole plant glandular. Flowers pale yellowish, white or pale blue-green, scented sweetly but with a hint of cat, 3–5cm long. Sepals 2.5–3cm, spreading; spur 15–18mm, straight or hooked. A beautiful species for good, well-drained soil in sun or partial shade. Hardy to −20°C.

Aquilegia vulgaris L.   Native of most of Europe from England and Ireland, Spain and Portugal to Yugoslavia, Poland and N Russia, growing in woods and meadows at up to 1700m in the Alps, flowering in May–July. Stems 30–60cm, much branched. Flowers nodding, usually purplish blue, pink or rarely reddish purple or white, *c*.5cm across, with spurs 15–22mm, and limb 10–13mm. This hybridizes freely with other species in the garden. The bicoloured variant, shown here, is one such hybrid. Easily grown in sun or partial shade. Hardy to −25°C or less.

Aquilegia yabeana Kitag.   Native of Korea and NE China, in Heilonjiang (Manchuria), growing in the mountains, flowering in May. Plant forming a small clump of delicate stems to 60cm. Leaflets *c*.1.5cm across. Flowers pinkish purple or reddish, *c*.2.5cm across. For a cool position in leafy soil. Hardy to −20°C.

Semiaquilegia ecalcarata (Maxim.) Sprague & Hutch. (*Ranunculaceae*)   Native of W China, in Gansu, W Sichuan and Shensi, growing in damp, mossy woodland and scrub, flowering in May–June. Plant forming small clumps of branching stems to 40cm; Flowers *c*.2.5cm across. For moist, leafy soil in sun or partial shade. Hardy to −20°C.

Aquilegia flabellata 'Mini star'

Aquilegia vulgaris seedling

Aquilegia atrata in the Valais

Semiaquilegia ecalcarata

Aquilegia alpina in the Valais, with *Geranium sylvaticum* and *Trollius*

Aquilegia yabeana

Aquilegia bertolonii

Thalictrum aquilegifolium in Switzerland

Thalictrum minus with plumes of *Ferulago* in C Asia

Thalictrum flavum subsp. *glaucum* at the Savill Gardens, Windsor

Thalictrum delavayi 'Hewitt's Double'

Thalictrum lucidum at Wisley

Thalictrum delavayi

Thalictrum aquilegifolium by the waterlily pool in Monet's garden, Giverny, Normandy

Thalictrum aquilegifolium L.
(*Ranunculaceae*)   Native of Europe from
France and Spain eastwards to W Russia,
Romania and Turkey (where it is rare), growing
in meadows, often in the mountains, and on
shady rocks, flowering in May–July. Stems to
150cm; leaves green; flowers with sepals which
soon fall, but conspicuous stamens; the
filaments swollen towards the apex, purplish
pink or white. An attractive plant easily grown
in good moist soil. Hardy to −25°C.

Thalictrum delavayi Franch. syn *T.
dipterocarpum* hort. non Franch.   Native of SW
China, in Yunnan and growing in alpine
meadows and scrub, flowering in June–
September. Stems to 200cm. Leaflets 3, lobed,
to 2.5cm across. Flowers with hanging stamens,
sepals to 12mm long, purple. 'Hewitt's Double'
has flowers with petaloid stamens forming a
dense rosette. There is also a white form in
cultivation. *T. chelidonii* DC. from the
Himalayas of Bhutan and Sikkim differs in its
leaflets 1–4cm across, coarsely and bluntly
toothed. Sepals 8–15mm long, purple. Both
species are best in a cool position with moist
peaty soil. Hardy to −15°C.

Thalictrum diffusiflorum Marquand & Airy
Shaw   Native of China in SE Xizang, growing
in scrub and woods, in grassy places, at 3600m,
flowering in July. Similar to *T. chelidonii* DC.
but with smaller leaflets and flowers on a very
lax inflorescence. Stems to 3m; sepals *c*.12mm
long. For rich peaty soil. Hardy to −20°C.

Thalictrum flavum L. subsp. **glaucum** (Desf.)
Batt. syn. *T. speciosissimum* L.   Native of
Spain, Portugal and North Africa, growing in

Thalictrum diffusiflorum at Kew

damp meadows and by streams, flowering from
June to August. Stems to 150cm. Whole plant
bluish green; leaflets with prominent veins on
the underside. A most beautiful plant for the
herbaceous border or wild garden, requiring
rich, moist soil to reach full size. Subsp. *flavum*
is native of most of Europe including England,
Ireland and Scotland, east to Turkey and
Siberia, in wet meadows, fens and by rivers. It
is similar but usually rather smaller, with bright
green stems and leaves, the leaflets without
prominent veins on their underside.

Thalictrum lucidum L.   Native of C & E
Europe to Turkey and W Russia, growing in
ditches, marshes and wet meadows, flowering in
June–August. Stems to 120cm. Plant shining
green; leaflets narrowly oblong, or linear in the

upper leaves. Inflorescence with long branches.
Stamens upright, *c*.7mm long. A robust plant
forming large clumps of pointed leaflets and tall
stems with rather greenish-yellow flowers. For
moist rich soil. Hardy to −25°C.

Thalictrum minus L.   Native of Europe from
Scotland and Ireland to North Africa eastwards
to C Asia, China, Japan, with related species in
North America, growing on limestone rocks, in
chalk grassland, on sand dunes and shingle, in
damp meadows and in shady places by streams,
on mountain steppes and tundra, flowering in
May–August. Plants with small yellowish or
brownish hanging flowers and long anthers
dangling on slender filaments, well adapted for
wind pollination.

Paeonia rhodia on Rhodes

Paeonia rhodia

Paeonia cambessedesii

south and eastwards to Greece, the Caucasus, Turkey, N Iran and Iraq, growing in oak, pine and beech forest, often among bracken, or on rocky limestone slopes, usually north-facing, and at up to 2200m in E Turkey, flowering in April–June. Plant forming a large clump of thick, fleshy roots, with many stems to 60cm. Leaves with basically 9 elliptic leaflets, but often some are divided so there may be as many as 15, all glabrous or sparsely hairy on the veins beneath. Flowers 8–14cm across, red or pinkish. Capsules 3–5, white tomentose. Easily grown in dry, well-drained soil in full sun; in moist soils the roots are liable to slug damage. Hardy to −15°C.

Paeonia mascula subsp. ***arietina*** (Anders.) Cullen & Heywood   Native of E Europe, from Italy (but not recorded from Greece), to Turkey, growing in oak scrub and on rocky slopes, at up to 2000m in Turkey, flowering in June–July. Differs from subsp. *mascula* in its narrower leaflets which are hairy beneath, and usually have 12–16 segments, typically 15. Possibly less drought-tolerant than subsp. *mascula*. Hardy to −15°C.

Paeonia mascula subsp. ***hellenica*** Tzanoudakis   Native of Sicily, especially on mountains in the north, and of Greece, in Attica, Evvia, Andros and the C Peloponnesos (with var. *icarica* on Ikaria), growing among bracken in *Abies* forest, in scrub or on open rocky slopes, usually on schist, at 450–850m, flowering in April–May. Differs from all other subspecies in its white flowers 10–13cm across; the leaves usually have 9 segments, but may have as many as 21. Although known for many years (I took this photograph in 1968), this subspecies was only described in 1977. I have never seen it in cultivation in N Europe, but Stearn's *Paeonies in Greece* records that it has been cultivated in the garden of the Goulandris Natural History Museum in Athens; it is said to come into growth very early, as does *P. rhodia*, and will require protection from late frosts. Hardiness unknown.

Paeonia mascula subsp. ***russii*** (Biv.) Cullen & Heywood   Native of Corsica, Sardinia, Sicily, the Ionian islands and C Greece, in forests in the mountains, in vineyards and in *Quercus coccifera* scrub on rocky limestone slopes, flowering in March–May. Differs from subsp. *mascula* in having even broader, ovate to obovate leaflets, hairy beneath. The stem is usually shorter, 25–45cm, and not fully extended at flowering time, and both stems and leaves are purplish when young. Flowers 9–12cm across, usually pinkish mauve. Easily grown in a warm position and well-drained but deep, rich soil; hardy to −15°C.

Paeonia rhodia W. T. Stearn   Native of Rhodes, in open *Pinus* and *Cupressus* forest at 500–700m, flowering in February–April. Plant forming clumps of smooth, reddish stems to 50cm, and leaves with up to 29 glabrous leaflets. Flowers 7–8cm across. This species is still easily found on Rhodes. Plants grown from seed have survived in SE England for twenty years, surviving −15°C, both at the foot of a wall, and in a frame in the open. They are susceptible to botrytis, but otherwise grow and flower well. The closely related *P. clusii* Stern & Stearn from Crete and Karpathos has many more (40–80) narrower leaflets, which are usually stiffer than the soft leaves of *P. rhodia*. The white flowers are 7–10cm across. It requires similar conditions to *P. rhodia*, and hybrids between the two are in cultivation.

Paeonia cambessedesii (Willk.) Willk. (*Paeoniaceae*)   Native of the Balearic islands, in E Majorca and Minorca, growing on limestone rocks and cliffs, flowering in April. This species is now becoming rare in the wild. Stems to 45cm, but usually around 25cm. Leaves biternate, with glabrous, lanceolate leaflets, greyish shining green above, purplish beneath. Flowers 6–10cm across, with 5–8 carpels. Easily grown in a sheltered position or frame, but needs protection from late spring frosts, and too much wet in summer. The smallest and one of the most distinct species. Hardy to −10°C.

Paeonia mascula (L.) Mill. subsp. ***mascula*** Native of Europe from France and Austria

Paeonia mascula subsp. *hellenica* in Evvia, with *Abies cephalonica*

Paeonia mascula subsp. *russii*

Paeonia mascula subsp. *mascula* near Muş, E Turkey

Paeonia mascula subsp. *arietina*

Paeonia anomala in the Maili Tau Mountains, near Yumin, NW China

Paeonia anomala

Paeonia 'Smouthii' at Kew

Paeonia anomala L. syns. *P. hybrida* Pall., *P. intermedia* C. A. Meyer   Native of Russia from the far north-west in the Kola peninsula, south to C Asia in the Tien Shan and Pamir-Alai, and east to the Altai, south to Mongolia and N China, in the W Gobi, growing in coniferous woods, on rocky hillsides among shrubs, and in dry steppe grassland, flowering in May–July. Stems to 50cm, forming clumps. Leaves biternate, with the leaflets divided into numerous narrow segments, usually 5–25mm wide; dark green above with minute bristles on the top of the veins. Flowers 7–9cm across, red. Carpels glabrous. *P. hybrida* Pall. is said to differ in its narrower leaflets, 10–15mm wide. *Paeonia intermedia* var. *intermedia* (C.A.M.) B. Fedtsch. has pubescent follicles. This should be the hardiest species, and is very beautiful with its large rather flat flowers of rich pinkish red. It will require deep, sandy, well-drained soil in full sun. Hardy to −25°C or less.

Paeonia coriacea Boiss.   Native of S Spain and Morocco in the middle Atlas, and doubtfully recorded from Corsica and Sardinia, growing in scrub and cedar forests, and among rocks and old walls, flowering in April–May. Stems to 60cm. Leaves biternate, with 9 leaflets and up to 16 segments, all glabrous beneath. Flowers 7–15cm across, usually pinkish. Carpels usually 2, 4.5cm long, glabrous, attenuate at apex. In gardens some forms of this species can appear too early and be damaged by late frosts. It requires a warm position, in rather dry soil. *P. broteroi* Boiss. & Reut., which also grows in S Spain and Portugal, differs in its softer, more divided leaves, usually red flowers and 2–4 densely tomentose carpels.

Paeonia mollis Anderson   A garden variety, probably a hybrid, known since 1818, but still in cultivation. Said to have been raised by Messrs Loddiges from seed sent by Pallas from Russia. Stem to 45cm. Leaves with narrow segments, with a bluish sheen. Flowers 7cm across, hairy beneath and said to sit down among the foliage, although that is not apparent in our illustrated specimen which was growing at Kew. Hardy to −20°C.

Paeonia officinalis L. subsp. **officinalis** Native of S France, east to Hungary and south to Albania, growing in woods, scrub and rocky slopes, usually on limestone, at up to 1800m in the S Alps, flowering in May–June. Leaves with the terminal 3 leaflets each deeply 3-lobed, and the lateral leaflets each 5-lobed; the lobes lanceolate, acuminate, pubescent beneath. Flowers 7–13cm across, red, opening flat. Easily grown in good garden soil. Hardy to −25°C. There are several cultivars of this old garden peony; the commonest is 'Rubra Plena', a huge, double very deep red, which is easily grown and long lasting in gardens and the edges of Victorian shrubberies. There is also a double white, a double pink, 'China Rose', a salmon-pink single, and 'Anemoniflora Rosea', with red, yellow-edged petaloid stamens and deep-pink petals. All except the doubles are rare in cultivation.

Paeonia mollis at Kew

Paeonia coriacea near Ronda, SE Spain

Paeonia officinalis L. subsp. *villosa* (Huth) Cullen & Heywood syn. *P. humilis* Retz var. *villosa* (Huth) F. C. Stern   Native of S France, especially around Montpelier, to C Italy, around Florence, growing in rocky places and scrub, flowering in May–June. Stems to 40cm. Lower leaves with leaflets cut into segments up to ⅓ of total leaflet length. Flowers 7–13cm across, red, opening rather flat. Carpels pubescent, 2–3. Subsp. *officinalis* differs in its more deeply divided leaflets. Subsp. *humilis* differs in its glabrous carpels. Easily grown in ordinary garden soil.

Paeonia peregrina Mill. syn. *P. decora* G. Anderson   Native of Italy (Calabria) to Romania, Greece, Bulgaria and W Turkey, growing in rough fields and scrub, among limestone rocks and in oak forests at up to 1200m, flowering in April–May. Stems to 50cm, from a clump of narrow roots with swollen ends. Lower leaves with 9 main obovate-cuneate leaflets, each divided into 3 or more pointed lobes, with minute bristles along the veins on the upper surface. Flowers usually dark red, sometimes pink, cup shaped, 9–12cm across. Carpels 1–4, with long white hairs. Easily grown in a sunny position and well-drained soil. Hardy to −20°C. Mathew & Brickell 7563.

Paeonia 'Smouthii' syn. *P. laciniata* hort.   A hybrid between *P. tenuifolia* and *P. lactiflora*, known since 1843. Plant forming large clumps, with stems *c.*60cm tall and very free-flowering in well-drained soil and full sun. The flowers are scented, and *c.*10cm across. Hardy to −20°C.

Paeonia tenuifolia L.   Native of SE Europe from Yugoslavia and Bulgaria to Romania and SW Russia in the Crimea and the neighbouring steppes near Stavropol, growing in dry grassland, flowering in May. (It is also recorded from Soviet Armenia.) Stems to 60cm. Leaves divided into filiform segments, less than 5mm wide. Flowers bright red, 6–8cm across: carpels 2–3 hairy. Easy to grow and very hardy, to −25°C or so, in full sun and well-drained soil. There is also a pale-pink cultivar, 'Rosea', and a double.

Paeonia officinalis subsp. *villosa*

Paeonia officinalis subsp. *officinalis*

Paeonia tenuifolia

Paeonia peregrina

Paeonia mlokosewitschii in Aberdeenshire, with *Berberis thunbergii* 'Atropurpurea' behind

Paeonia wittmanniana at Kew

Paeonia obovata var. *alba* at Aylburton, Gloucestershire

Paeonia mairei near Baoxing, Sichuan

Paeonia emodi Wall. (*Paeoniaceae*) Native of
Pakistan and N India from Chitral to Kashmir
and W Nepal, growing in forests and scrub, at
1800–2500m, flowering in April–June. Stems to
75cm. Leaves deeply dissected into lanceolate
segments, which are usually glabrous. Flowers
white, 2–4 per stem, 8–12cm across, with 5–10
petals. Carpels 1–2, hairy or glabrous. This is
said to grow in large colonies in the wild and
must be a fine sight when in flower. In
cultivation it grows happily in sandy soil in a
normal, moist herbaceous border. Hardy to
−20°C.

Paeonia mairei Léveillé Native of China, in N
Yunnan and W Sichuan, growing in steep open
woods, scrub, and on mountainsides at 800–
2900m, flowering in May–June. Stems 50–
100cm, usually 1-flowered; leaflets long-
acuminate or caudate at the apex, glabrous, thin
in texture. Flowers 8–15cm across. Carpels
glabrous or covered with short golden-brown
hairs, 2–2.5cm long, attenuate towards the
stigma. Close to *P. obovata*, but with narrower
leaves, and found further south. This species
should grow best in areas with a cool, moist
summer in well-drained leafy soil. Hardy to
−15°C.

Paeonia mlokosewitschii Lomakin Native of
SE Caucasus in the valley of Lagodeki (which is
now a nature reserve), growing on sunny slopes
in hornbeam–oak forest, flowering in April.
Stems to 60cm. Leaves biternate, with leaflets
oval to obovate, often obtuse or rounded at
apex, glaucous especially beneath. Flowers
8–12cm across, yellow. Carpels tomentose.
Easily grown in well-drained soil in sun or
partial shade. Hardy to −20°C, but the buds can
be killed by late frosts, and grows well in cold
parts of E Scotland. Christopher Lloyd has a
memorable comment on this plant: 'It flowers
for about five days in early May, and is at its
ravishing best for about four hours in the
middle of this period.'

Paeonia obovata Maxim. var. **alba** Saunders
Native of E Siberia, N China, in Heilongjiang
(Manchuria), Shaansi, Sichuan, Sakhalin and
Japan, in Hokkaido, Honshu and Shikoku;
growing in woods and scrub in mountains,
flowering in April–June. Stem to 60cm. Young
leaves purplish, biternate with rounder leaflets.
Flowers white, cream or pale pinkish purple
(the white form is the one usually cultivated),
c.7cm across. Carpels glabrous. Easily grown in
semi-shade in sandy, well drained but rich soil.
Hardy to −20°C. Var. *willmottiae* (Stapf) Stern,
from W Hubei and E Sichuan, has hairy
undersides to the leaf, larger flowers, to 10.5cm
across and is earlier flowering, in May in
gardens in S England. *P. japonica* Mak., from
Japan, Korea and Heilongjiang, also has white
flowers, but short recurved stigmas.

Paeonia veitchii Lynch Native of NW China,
in Gausu, Sichuan and Shensi, growing in
subalpine meadows and scrub and on mountain
steppes at 2500–3500m, flowering in May–June.
Rhizomes creeping to form large dense clumps a
metre or more across. Stems to 50cm. Leaflets
cut deeply into narrow, pointed segments, with
minute bristles, flowers, 2 or more per stem,
pink, 5–9cm across. Carpels 2–4, hairy. Easily
grown in well-drained soil in sun or part shade.
There is also a white form. Hardy to −20°C.
Var. *woodwardii* (Stapf & Cox) F. C. Stern, a
native of Gansu and NW Sichuan, growing in
yak pastures at *c*.3000m, differs from the
normal variety in its shorter stems to 30cm, and
leaves with longer, bristly hairs on the veins.

Paeonia wittmanniana Hartwiss ex Lindl.
Native of W & S Caucasus, the Talysh in S
Azerbaijan and NW Iran, and in the Elburz,
growing in alpine pastures, on rocky slopes,
probably among bracken, and in beech woods,
at up to 1700m, flowering in April–August
according to altitude. Stems to 1m. Leaves
biternate with leaflets 4.5–10cm wide, acute to
acuminate, glabrous and shining above, lighter
green beneath, with some hairs on the veins.
Flowers 10–12cm across, pale yellow. Carpels
2–3, tomentose or glabrous (var. *nudicarpa*
Schipczinsky). A robust leafy plant (especially
the var. *macrophylla* (Albor) Busch (which also
has almost-white flowers), easily grown in rich
soil in sun or partial shade among shrubs.
Hardy to −15°C, perhaps less.

Paeonia emodi at Wisley, Surrey

Paeonia veitchii at Kew

Paeonia veitchii var. *woodwardii*

Double White *Paeonia lactiflora* in late May in the Old Imperial Summer Palace near Peking

'Kelways' Unique'

'Bowl of Beauty'

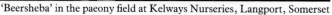

'Beersheba' in the paeony field at Kelways Nurseries, Langport, Somerset

***Paeonia lactiflora* cultivars**   These are the common garden paeonies which reached the peak of their popularity in Edwardian gardens, as the names Lord Kitchener and Sarah Bernhardt indicate. They were well developed as a garden flower in China by the 18th century, and first introduced to Europe in 1784. They are all very hardy, originating as they did in N China, and can tolerate −50°C or lower without damage to the roots. They prefer a rich, heavy soil, with good drainage, but moist in summer. The crowns should be planted just below the surface, with the resting buds not more than 3cm below the soil. If they are planted too deeply, they will not flower freely.

'Beersheba'   Stems to 100cm. Early flowering. Raised by Kelways.

'Bowl of Beauty'   Stems to 90cm. Flowers scented, mid- to late season. Raised by Hoogendoorn in 1949. Probably the commonest of the 'Imperial' paeonies in which the stamens are replaced by narrow petaloid filaments.

'Kelways' Unique'   Raised by Kelways.

'Lorna Doone'   Raiser not recorded.

'Madelon'   Stems to 90cm. Raised by Dessert in 1922.

'Pink Delight'   Stems to 70cm. Flowers especially beautiful and well-scented in mid- to late season. Raised by Kelways.

'White Wings'   Stems to 80cm. Raised by Hoogendoorn in 1949.

'Madelon'

'White Wings'

'Lorna Doone'

'Pink Delight'

'Ballerina'

'James Kelway'

'Barrymore'

'Shirley Temple'

'Laura Dessert'

'Festiva Maxima'

'Jan van Leeuwen'

'Gleam of Light'

'Kelway's Supreme'

'Countess of Altamont'

Specimens from Kelways Nurseries, Langport, Somerset, 26 June. ⅓ life size

Paeonia lactiflora 'Whitleyi Major'

'Duchesse de Nemours'

'White Innocence'

'Alice Harding'

'Heirloom'

'Mme Claude Tain'

Paeonia lactiflora Pallas syns. *P.* 'Whitleyi Major', *P. albiflora* Pallas (*Paeoniaceae*) *P. lactiflora* is the herbaceous paeony from which most of the large garden peonies have been bred. It is native of Siberia from south of Lake Baikal eastwards to Vladivostock and in NW China and Mongolia to near Beijing, growing on steppes and in scrub, flowering in May–June. Stems to 60cm, usually with 2 or more flowers. Leaves divided into lanceolate lobes, basically 9, but with the terminal lobes of the lateral leaflets usually further divided, glabrous or sparsely pubescent with a papillose and rough margin. Flowers 7–10cm across in the wild, white to pink; carpels 3–5, glabrous. 'Whitleyi Major' is a garden clone, similar to the wild type. For good, sandy well-drained soil, moist in summer. Hardy to −25°C or less.

'Alice Harding'   Stems to 100cm; well-scented flowers in mid-season. Raised by Lémoine in 1922.

'Ballerina'   Stems to 90cm; flowers bluish pink, fading to white in early to mid-season. Raised by Kelways.

'Barrymore'   Stems to 90cm; flowers palest pink when first open. Raised by Kelways.

'Countess of Altamont'   Stems to 100cm; flowers scented, in mid-season. Raised by Kelways.

'Duchesse de Nemours'   Stems to 80cm; very free-flowering and well scented. Raised by Canlot in 1856 .

'Festiva Maxima' Stems robust, to 90cm. Flowers scented, white with crimson blemishes. Raised by Miellez in 1851.

'Gleam of Light'   Stems to 90cm. Flowers mid- to late season. Raised by Kelways.

'Heirloom'   Rather short, with stems to 70cm. Raised by Kelways.

'Jan van Leeuwen'   Raised by van Leeuwen in 1928.

'Kelways' Supreme'   Stems to 90cm, freely branched and so with a long flowering season. Flowers palest pink fading to white. Raised by Kelways.

'Laura Dessert'   Stems to 75cm. Flowers white with yellow petaloid stamens, in early to mid-season. Raised by Dessert in 1913.

'Mme Claude Tain'   Stems to 75cm. Raised by Doriat in 1927.

'Shirley Temple'   Stems to 75cm. Very well-scented flowers, palest pink to white.

'White Innocence'   A hybrid between *P. lactiflora* and *P. emodi* raised by Dr A. P. Saunders in New York in 1947. Stems 120–150cm, arching, with several flowers, greenish in the centre.

'Knighthood'

'Magic Orb'

'Beacon Flame'

'Crimson Glory'

'Mr G. F. Hemerick'

'Kelways' Majestic'

'Inspecteur Lavergne'

'Kelways' Brilliant'

'Shimmering Velvet'

'Auguste Dessert'

'Sir Edward Elgar'

Specimens from Kelways Nurseries, Langport, Somerset, 24 June. ⅓ life size

'Sarah Bernhardt'

'Silver Flare'

'Polindra'

'Albert Crousse'

Paeonia lactiflora cultivars (continued):

'Albert Crousse' Stems to 90cm; late-flowering. Raised by Crousse in 1893.

'Auguste Dessert' Stems to 75cm. Flowers mid- or late season, with good autumn colours on the leaves. Raised by Dessert in 1920.

'Beacon Flame' Stems to 75cm. Raised by Kelways.

'Crimson Glory' Stems to 80cm. Late flowering. Raised by Sass in 1937.

'Inspecteur Lavergne' Stems to 80cm. Flowers mid- or late season. Raised by Doriat in 1924.

'Kelways' Brilliant' Stems to 90cm. Raised by Kelways.

'Kelways' Majestic' Stems to 90cm. Flowers extra large. Raised by Kelways.

'Knighthood' Raiser not recorded.

'Magic Orb' Stems to 95cm. Flowers well scented. Raised by Kelways.

'Mr G. F. Hemerick' Probably raised by van Leeuwen.

'Polindra' Raiser not recorded.

'Sarah Bernhardt' Stems to 90cm. Flowers very large, in mid- to late season. Raised by Lémoine in 1906.

'Shimmering Velvet' Stems to 85cm. Flowering season extending into summer. Raised by Kelways.

'Silver Flare' Stems to 90cm. Flowers early season. Raiser not recorded.

'Sir Edward Elgar' Flowers in mid- to late season. Stems to 75cm. Raised by Kelways.

Single paeonies in Claude Monet's garden at Giverny, in June

Corydalis flexuosa near Wolong, NW Sichuan

Corydalis wilsonii

Corydalis lutea

Corydalis thrysiflora by streams below the glacier on Lake Vishensar

Corydalis scouleri at Kew

Corydalis anthriscifolia at Baoxing, Sichuan

Corydalis nobilis

Corydalis nobilis near Yumin, NW China

Corydalis ochroleuca

Corydalis anthriscifolia Franch.
(*Fumariaceae*) Native of W Sichuan, especially around Baoxing, growing in shady places in woods and below cliffs, at *c*.2000m, flowering in April–May. Stems spreading from a thick rootstock to 40cm. Leaves glaucous. Flowers *c*.2.5cm, opening purplish, fading to buff, with upward-pointing spurs and buff seed capsules. A pretty plant with an unusual colour combination; suitable for a shady cool place in leafy soil. Hardy to −15°C or less?

Corydalis flexuosa Franch. Native of China, in W Sichuan, especially the Baoxing and Wolong valleys, growing on steep shady slopes with *Matteuccia*, at *c*.2000m, flowering in April–July. Plant upright from a thin rootstock with fleshy leaf bases, and thin stolons, dormant in summer. Leaves glaucous, sometimes marked with purple. Stems to 40cm. Flowers *c*.2.5cm long, blue, sometimes purplish. Capsule slender. For moist, loose leafy soil in shade or partial shade. Hardy to −10°C, perhaps less. Source: CD&R 528.

Corydalis lutea (L.) DC. Native of the foothills of the S Alps in Switzerland, Italy and Yugoslavia, growing on shady rocks and screes, usually on limestone, and frequently naturalized elsewhere, especially on old walls, flowering in May–October. Plant forming a mound of delicate green leaves, from a thin fleshy rootstock. Stems to 40cm. Flowers up to 16 in a dense, elongated raceme, yellow, 12–20mm long. Fruits pendant; seeds shining. Easily

grown and self-seeding in shady crevices in walls and among rocks. Hardy to −20°C.

Corydalis nobilis (L.) Pers. Native of Soviet C Asia, in the Saur and Tarbagatay mountains and in China, in W Sinjiang, in the Maili mountains near Yumin, growing in scrub and grassy places by streams in the mountains, flowering in April–May. A robust upright plant, with numerous stems up to 60cm, from a central rootstock, dormant if dry in summer. Flowers 20–30 in a dense head, *c*.20mm long, yellow (or white?), with a dark point on the inner petals. For good sandy soil in full sun or partial shade. Hardy to −20°C or less.

Corydalis ochroleuca Koch Native of Italy and Yugoslavia, Albania and N Greece; growing in rocky woods, and naturalized especially on old walls elsewhere in Europe, flowering in May–September. Plant with several erect stems to 40cm from a central rootstock. Leaves glaucous. Flowers up to 14, rarely more, in a dense raceme, creamy white, *c*.15mm long. Fruit erect; seeds dull, not shining. A delicate plant for growing in walls or crevices in pavement, in sun or shade. Hardy to −15°C. Shown here is subsp. *leiosperma* (Conr.) Hayek which has bracts at least ⅓ as long as the pedicels, and shiny seeds.

Corydalis scouleri Hook. Native of W North America from British Columbia south to N Oregon, growing in damp shady woods, flowering in June–July. Plant with stems to

60cm or more from a stout rootstock, forming large clumps of delicate leaves. Flowering stems little taller than the leaves, with short racemes of 15–35 pinkish-mauve flowers, about 2.5cm long. The closely related *C. caseana* Gray, from NE Oregan and California to Idaho and Colorado, has paler pink or white flowers with purple tips, 50–200 in the raceme. For moist leafy soil in partial shade, and a sheltered position. Hardy to −15°C.

Corydalis thrysiflora Prain Native of the W Himalayas, from Pakistan to Kashmir, where it is very common, growing in mountain streams, among rocks and below glaciers, at 3000–4300m, flowering in July–August. Plant with a rosette of leaves from a deep rootstock. Stems 15–30cm, branched, with dense terminal flower clusters. Flowers 12–15mm long. Spur about ½ as long as the flower. Capsule 5–7mm, broadly ovate, with a long curved style. Not difficult to grow in moist gritty, peaty soil in sun or partial shade. If too shaded the plant becomes leggy. Hardy to −20°C.

Corydalis wilsonii N. E. Br. Native of China, in W Hubei, growing on shady limestone cliffs at *c*.1500m, flowering in April–May. Plant with a rosette of many deeply divided fern-like leaves to 25cm long, from a central rootstock. Flowering stems to 20cm, upright, with *c*.20 flowers, each *c*.15mm long. Easily grown in a cool position, in a wall or rocky place in the shade. Hardy to −15°C or so.

Geranium libani 'Wakehurst'

Geranium aristatum

Geranium × *monacense* var. *monacense*

Geranium monacense var. *anglicum*

Geranium reflexum

Geranium phaeum var. *phaeum*

Geranium phaeum var. *phaeum*

Geranium phaeum var. *lividum* 'Majus'

Specimens from the University Botanic Garden, Cambridge, 20 June. ⅓ life size

Geranium aristatum Freyn & Sint.
(*Geraniaceae*) Native of S Albania, S
Yugoslavia and NW Greece growing in damp
shady places in the mountains, usually on
limestone, at 1650–2100m, flowering in June–
September. Plant tufted, with stems to 60cm,
more or less erect, glandular above. Leaves with
7 or 9 rather broad lobes. Flowers nodding;
petals 13–16mm, strongly reflexed, pale with
lilac-pink veins. Easily grown in ordinary
garden soil in partial shade.

Geranium libani Davis Native of S Turkey
(Hatay), W Syria and Lebanon, growing in
maquis and *Abies* forest, flowering in April–
May. Leaves glossy above, appearing in
autumn, dying down in summer. Hardy to
−15°C. For a warm position, dry in summer.

Geranium × monacense Harz (syn. *G.
punctatum* hort.) var. **anglicum** Yeo A hybrid
between *G. reflexum* and *G. phaeum* var.
lividum. Petals 11–14mm, pinkish lilac, with a
very small white base. Leaves usually
unblotched. *G. × monacense* var. *monacense* is
the hybrid between *G. reflexum* and *G. phaeum*
var. *phaeum*. Flowers purplish red with a large
pale base. Leaves often blotched.

Geranium phaeum L. Native of Europe from
the Pyrenees and the Alps east to W Russia, N
Yugoslavia and Czechoslovakia, growing in
subalpine meadows and woods and on banks,
flowering in May–August. Naturalized
elsewhere on roadsides and by rivers, especially
commonly in E Scotland. Plant tufted with
thick rhizomes forming large clumps. Leaves
with 7–9 lobes, often spotted reddish purple,
10–20cm across. Stems 60–80cm, glandular
above. Petals 11–14mm long, pinkish, lilac to
purple or almost black; or white in the
cultivated form 'Album'. Hardy to −20°C. Var.
lividum (L'Her.) Persoon 'Majus' is a tall, large-
flowered clone of var. *lividum* with petals to
16mm long. Var. *lividum* differs from var.
phaeum in having pale flowers with a bluish
border to the white base.

Geranium pogonanthum Franch. Native of
SW China, in Yunnan and Sichuan, and WC
and N Burma, growing in scrub, or on the edges
of forest, flowering in July–September. Plant
with stout rootstock and long creeping stems.
Leaves marbled, deeply divided into 5 or 7
lobes, with acute tips. Peduncles 4–8cm.
Flowers nodding, 2.5–3.5cm across, pink or
purple to almost white. Filaments red. For cool
moist soil in sun or shade. Hardy to −15°C.

Geranium reflexum L. Native of Italy in the
Apennines, N Yugoslavia and N Greece,
growing in mountain meadows, shady rocks and
clearings in woods, flowering in May–June.
Plant clump-forming; stems 40–80cm. Leaves
5–7 lobed, with pointed shallowly toothed
lobes. Flowers with petals reflexed, 11–13mm
long, pink with a white base. Like *G. phaeum*
but with narrower, more strongly reflexed
petals, and with young fruits pointing
downwards. For semi-shade, and tolerant of
rather dry soil. Hardy to −15°C.

Geranium sinense Knuth Native of W China,
in Yunnan and Sichuan, growing in alpine
meadows, flowering in August–October. Plant
with few ascending or creeping stems from a
stout rootstock. Basal leaves long-stalked,
divided to the base into 7 rather narrow lobes;
upper leaves short-stalked. Flowers up to 2cm
across, commonly visited by wasps. Hardy to
−15°C or less.

Geranium phaeum

Geranium phaeum

Geranium phaeum 'Album'

Geranium pogonanthum

Geranium sinense

Geranium sanguineum var. *striatum*

Geranium sanguineum on the Burren, Co. Clare

Geranium swatense in the Royal Botanic Garden, Edinburgh

Geranium maculatum L. (*Geraniaceae*) Native of E North America west to Manitoba and Kansas, growing in wet places in woods, on wet rocks and in swamps, flowering in April–July. Stems 50–70cm, few from a stout rootstock. Leaves with 5 or 7 rather narrow lobes, each toothed and lobed near the apex, *c*.10cm across. Flowers pink, often very pale and white at the base. A graceful species, useful for its early flowering and its ability to tolerate waterlogged soil. Hardy to −25°C or less.

Geranium oreganum Howell Native of Washington south to N California in meadows, scrub or open woods at 800–1500m, in California flowering in June–July. Stems to 60cm, spreading. Leaves 10–20cm across, divided nearly to the base into 7 lobes, each deeply dissected. Inflorescence loose; flowers 4.3–4.7cm across, upward-facing. An attractive species for sun or partial shade, but with rather a harsh colour. Hardy to −15°C.

Geranium orientalitibeticum Knuth Native of Sichuan near Kanding (Tatsienlu), growing in screes at 2250–3750m, flowering in June–July. Plant growing from strings of small underground tubers, which are pink with a white centre. Leaves emerging in spring, dying down in late summer, around 10cm across, pale greenish, marbled with cream. Stems 20–35cm. Flowers pinkish, 2.3–2.7cm across. Easily grown in ordinary well-drained garden soil in full sun, kept moist in early summer, and spreading to make small patches. Hardy to −20°C.

Geranium palustre L. Native of C & E Europe from France and Sweden eastwards to Russia, the Caucasus and NE Turkey, growing in damp places, and in scrub and the edges of woods, flowering in June–August. Stems spreading from a central rootstock, up to about 40cm. Leaves 5–10cm across, with 7 lobes, each with rather few deep teeth. Flowers 3–3.5cm across, magenta with dark-purple veins. Easily grown in any good soil, in sun or light shade. Hardy to −20°C.

Geranium pylzowianum Maxim. Native of W China, in Gansu, Shaanxi, Sichuan and Yunnan, growing in alpine meadows and rocky places at 2400–4250m, flowering in May–June in gardens. Plant with underground stolons and chains of small tubers, forming slowly spreading patches. Stems 12–25cm, rarely taller. Leaves *c*.5cm across, not marbled, darker green and more deeply divided into narrower segments than *G. orientalitibeticum*. Flowers not opening flat, with petals 1.6–2.3cm long, deep rose pink. Easily grown in well-drained soil in a sunny position. Hardy to −20°C.

Geranium sanguineum L. **Bloody Cranesbill** Native of Europe, from NW Ireland and Scotland eastwards to the Caucasus and N Turkey, growing in sunny grassy places, in scrub, among rocks, usually on limestone, and on coastal dunes, flowering in April–August. Stems several from a slowly increasing rootstock, spreading or creeping to *c*.30cm long. Leaves very deeply divided into 5 or 7 lobes, each lobe further divided into 3–5 nearly to the base. Flowers 2.5–4.2cm across, usually purplish red, sometimes pink, especially in var. *striatum* Weston syn. var. *lancastriense* (Mill.) Druce from Walney Island off the coast of Cumbria, NW England. Easily cultivated in sun or, in very warm climates, in partial shade. Low-growing, and suitable for the edge of a border or in a path; it has an exceptionally long flowering season. Hardy to −20°C.

Geranium swatense Schonbeck-Temesy Native of N Pakistan, in Dir and Swat, and of Kashmir, growing on grassy hillsides at 2000–2500m, flowering in August. Plant with creeping but not rooting stems to 50cm from a central rootstock. Leaves divided to ⅔ into 3 or 5 rather widely separated lobes, on stalks *c*.10cm long. Flowers *c*.2cm across, deep pink to white, with a white centre, on pedicels with long soft glandular hairs. Easily grown in a sunny position in well-drained soil. Hardy to −20°C or less.

Geranium wlassovianum Fisch. ex Link Native of Mongolia, NE China and E Siberia, growing in damp grassland and scrub, flowering in July–August in gardens. Stems to 30cm, covered with eglandular hairs, spreading from a stout central rootstock. Leaves short-stalked, often brownish. Flowers usually deep purplish, rarely pale pink, with petals 1.7–2.2cm long, veined with deep violet. For sun or partial shade in any ordinary soil. Hardy to −25°C.

Geranium oreganum

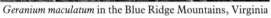

Geranium maculatum in the Blue Ridge Mountains, Virginia

Geranium pylzowianum

Geranium orientalitibeticum

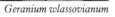

Geranium wlassovianum

Geranium palustre

Geranium
viscosissimum

Geranium ibericum
subsp. *jubatum*

Geranium erianthum

Geranium renardii

Geranium
richardsonii

Geranium himalayense
'Plenum'

Geranium himalayense

Geranium macrorrhizum
'Bevan's Variety' (p. 114)

Geranium pratense
subsp. *stewartianum* (p. 117)

Specimens from the University Botanic Garden, Cambridge, 4 June. ⅓ life size

Geranium erianthum DC. (*Geraniaceae*)
Native of British Columbia and Alaska
westwards through the Kurile Islands to Japan
(Hokkaido) and E Siberia, growing in subalpine
meadows and scrub and on grassy slopes near
the sea, flowering in June–August. Stems to
30cm, from a compact rootstock. Leaves
divided to about ¾ into 7 or 9 lobes, each
deeply and irregularly toothed and overlapping;
non-glandular hairs appressed. Flower 2.5–
3.7cm across, often very pale blue with darker
veins, in a compact inflorescence. Hardy to
−20°C. Shown here is a plant from NE
Hokkaido.

Geranium himalayense Klotsch   Native of the
Pamirs and the Himalayas from NE
Afghanistan to C Nepal, growing in open
forests, scrub and on grassy slopes, at 2100–
4300m, flowering in May–July. Plant forming
spreading mats with underground rhizomes.
Stems to 30–45cm. Leaves to 20cm across,
divided to ¾ or ⅘, into 7 overlapping lobes,
each with blunt lobes and teeth. Flowers deep
blue, with overlapping petals, 4–6cm across, the
largest in the genus. This is a good garden plant,
tolerant of drought and a certain amount of
shade. Of the several clones in cultivation,
'Gravetye' has the largest flowers, of a good rich
blue. It is a parent, with *G. pratense*, of the
excellent hybrid 'Johnson's Blue' (see p.117).
'Plenum' syn. 'Birch Double' is a smaller plant,
with rather more purplish double flowers about
3.5cm across. Known since 1928. Hardy to
−20°C.

Geranium ibericum Cav. subsp. **jubatum**
(Handel-Mazetti) Davis   Native of N Turkey,
from Bolu to Trabzon, where it grows in scrub,
meadows, and on rocky igneous hillsides, at
1900–3000m, flowering in July and August.
Stems, with both long glandular and eglandular
hairs, to 40cm. Clump-forming, with
overlapping and deeply incised leaves with 9 or
11 lobes, to 20cm across. Flowers 4–4.8cm
across, bluish with purplish veins, facing
sideways. Subsp. *jubatum* differs from subsp.
ibericum from NE Turkey and the Caucasus in
having glandular hairs on the pedicels, like *G.
magnificum* and *G. platypetalum*. Easily grown in
well-drained soil and sun. Hardy to −20°C.

Geranium renardii Trautv.   Native of the
Caucasus, on cliffs and in rocky meadows at
c.2000m, flowering in July (June in gardens in
England). Plant with short thick rootstock
forming low mounds. Leaves to 10cm across,
greyish, strongly rugose with impressed veins,
divided halfway into 5 or 7 toothed lobes. Stems
to about 20cm. Flowers flat, 30–36mm across,
white or bluish with conspicuous blue veins.
Petals notched, well separated from each other.
Easily grown in full sun and well-drained soil.
The common clone in gardens is named 'Walter
Ingwersen', after its introducer. Hardy to
−20°C.

Geranium richardsonii Fisch. & Trautv.
Native of British Columbia, east to
Saskatchewan, south to California, South
Dakota and New Mexico, growing in damp,
grassy places and meadows, at 1000–3000m (in
California), flowering in July–August. Stems
few, much-branched, to 60cm from a thick
rootstock. Leaves slightly glossy, 5–10cm
across, deeply divided into 5 or 7 lobes each
shallowly lobed or toothed with broad teeth.
Flowers 2.4–2.8cm across, usually white,
sometimes pale pink and veined, their surface
hairy towards the centre of the flower. A
variable species, good forms of which are very

Geranium himalayense in Kashmir   *Geranium himalayense* 'Gravetye'

Geranium renardii

beautiful, as is the one shown here, collected by
Peter Yeo in Colorado in 1973. Good in moist
soil in full sun. Hardy to −20°C.

Geranium viscosissimum Fisch. & Meyer
Native of British Columbia, east to Alberta and
south to N California (at an altitude of about
1800m), South Dakota and Wyoming, growing
in open woods and meadows, flowering in May–
July. Stems 30–80cm, much-branched, very
glandular from a deep woody rootstock.
Flowers about 4.5cm across, pale pink to
pinkish purple with dark veins. Leaves 7-lobed
to about ⅘, the lobes with rather few teeth,
about 7.5cm across. For any good soil in sun or
partial shade. Hardy to −25°C.

Geranium erianthum from Japan

Geranium macrorrhizum

Geranium platypetalum from the Caucasus

Geranium 'Ann Folkard' (*Geraniaceae*)   This beautiful hybrid between *G. procurrens* and *G. psilostemon* was raised by the Revd O. G. Folkard at Sleaford, Lincs., in around 1963 from seed of *G. procurrens*. It has a compact rootstock and shortly creeping stems. Leaves always bright yellowish green; flowers 3.5–4cm across, produced with great freedom. Easily grown in sun or partial shade.

Geranium canariense Reut.   Native of the Canary Islands, in Tenerife, Palma, Gomera and Hierro, growing along streams and in moist partially shaded places in the laurel forest, flowering in March–May (and later). Plant with a beautiful large rosette of many wide leaves, borne on a stem up to 15cm tall in old plants. Leaf blades to 25cm across, sparsely hairy, divided to the base into three lobes, the two lateral lobes being further divided almost to the base, with the central lobe not stalked; all the lobes are deeply dissected and toothed, with curved teeth. Flowers 2.3–3.6cm across, on much-branched, glandular inflorescences from the leaf axils. This is one of the hardier of the giant Herb Roberts from the Canary Islands and Madeira, and survives outside in sheltered places in warm gardens, surviving perhaps at −5°C. The most magnificent species *G. maderense* Yeo, from Madeira, is more tender and requires greenhouse treatment. It can make a plant up to 1.5m high and across.

Geranium × cantabrigiense Yeo   A hybrid between *G. macrorrhizum* and *G. dalmaticum*, which was raised in the University Botanic Garden, Cambridge, by Dr Helen Kiefer in 1974. It has bright-pink flowers. Other pink-flowered clones have arisen by chance in gardens. One was found in the wild in the Biokova mountains in S Yugoslavia, and is called 'Biokovo'. It has white flowers and longer runners than the Cambridge form. Plant mat-forming with stems to 30cm. Leaves up to 10cm wide; flowers 2.5–2.8cm across, like those of *G. macrorrhizum*, borne during June and July in gardens. Does well in sun, or dry areas in partial shade in hot climates. Hardy to −15°C, perhaps.

Geranium eriostemon DC.   Native of E Siberia, W China in E Xizang, Sichuan and W Hubei, Korea and N Japan, growing in grassy places in the mountains and in open woods, flowering in May–June, although often in April in gardens, and intermittently later. Plant with a thick rootstock: stems few, upright to 50cm or to 1m in gardens. Flowers 2.5–3.2cm across. Leaves with 3 or 5 lobes cut to about ⅔, with shallow teeth, and with spreading hairs on the veins on the underside of the lower leaves. Photographed in Sichuan in May. This species is sometimes wrongly called *G. sinense* (q.v.) which has a smaller very purple-red flower and spreading and creeping stems, and is very late flowering. It is confusingly similar to *G. erianthum* which, however, has appressed hairs on the lower leaves, and leaf lobes deeply toothed. Hardy to −20°C.

Geranium macrorrhizum L.   Native of the S Alps in France and Italy and the SE Carpathians in Romania, south to Greece, growing among limestone rocks, screes, in woods and scrub, at up to 2100m in Greece, flowering in April–August. Plant with fleshy underground rootstock and thick rhizomes which creep across the ground forming dense mats. Stems to 50cm. Leaves 10–20cm across, very aromatic, and used in the past as a source of Oil of Geranium. Flowers 2–2.5cm across, magenta to pale pink or white. Easily grown in dry or moist situations in sun or shade, forming very effective, weed-smothering ground cover. Several named cultivars are grown in gardens:
'Album'   Petals white; sepals and stamens pink. Introduced from the Rodope mountains in Bulgaria by Walter Ingwersen.
'Bevan's Variety'   Petals deep magenta; sepals deep red. Collected by Dr Roger Bevan and distributed by Washfield Nurseries.
'Ingwersen's Variety'   A pale-pink-flowered variety from Mount Koprivnik in Montenegro, introduced by Walter Ingwersen in 1929.
'Spessart'   Should have dark-pink petals, although I have bought a very pale-flowered form under this name. All are hardy to −15°C.

Geranium × magnificum Hylander   A hybrid between *G. platypetalum* and *G. ibericum* subsp. *ibericum* of unknown origin, but known to have been cultivated since 1871. This is a very good garden plant, forming large clumps and spreading also by short underground stolons. Its one drawback is its short flowering season, in June, from early to late according to district in the British Isles. Peter Yeo describes three cultivated clones of this cross in his monograph: the commonest has stems up to 70cm; leaves divided to more than ½ with about 9 major lobes. Stem with glandular and eglandular hairs. Flowers 4.5–5cm across; petals often slightly notched, purplish-blue with dark veins, slightly overlapping. This is a common cottage garden plant in E Scotland, growing exceptionally well in well-drained soil in full sun and exposure. It survives, but is much weaker and less free-flowering, in shade. Hardy to −20°C, perhaps less.

Geranium platypetalum Fisch. & Meyer   Native of the Caucasus, south to NE Turkey and NW Iran, growing in meadows and on rocky slopes in the N Caucasus and in spruce and hazel woods in Turkey, flowering in June–August. Plant forming small clumps with thick short rhizomes. Stems glandular to about 40cm. Leaves green, rugose above with 7 or 9 lobes, the main lobes divided into 3, to about ⅓. Flowers blue with darker raised veins, 30–45mm across; petals broadest at apex, and notched or slightly 3-lobed. Hardy to −20°C.

Geranium psilostemon Ledeb. syn. *G. armenum* Boiss.   Native of NE Turkey and the SW Caucasus, growing in scrub, open spruce forest and the subalpine hay meadows which consist mainly of large herbaceous plants and lilies, at 400–1200m, flowering in June–September. Stems to 1.2m from a short rootstock. Leaves divided to ¾ or ⅘ into 7 lobes, each lobe deeply incised and toothed. Flowers about 3.5cm across on a much-branched inflorescence. A strong-growing species for the back of an herbaceous border or for the wild garden. It grows particularly well in the cool summer climate and well-drained soils of E Scotland. Its leaves turn red in autumn. 'Bressingham Flair' is an attractive selection, generally shorter with slightly paler flowers. It is very free-flowering. Introduced in 1973. Hardy to −20°C.

Geranium × *magnificum* growing in shade

Geranium eriostemon above Baoxing, Sichuan

Geranium psilostemon from near Trabzon

Geranium × *cantabrigiense*

Geranium 'Ann Folkard' at Wakehurst Place, Sussex

Geranium canariense by a stream in the forest in Tenerife

Geranium canariense

Geranium 'Johnson's Blue'

Geranium 'Sellindge Blue'

Geranium sylvaticum 'Album'

Geranium pratense 'Plenum Violaceum' at Charleville, Co. Offaly

Geranium pratense 'Mrs Kendal Clarke'

Geranium rivulare in the Valais

Geranium clarkei in the Gadsar Valley, Kashmir

Geranium sylvaticum by the River Don, Aberdeenshire

Geranium clarkei Yeo (*Geraniaceae*) Native of Kashmir, growing in alpine meadows and valleys in well-drained soil at 2100–4200m, flowering in July. Plant creeping with underground rhizomes. Stems to 50cm, usually *c*.30cm, spreading. Leaves cut nearly to the base into 7 lobes, each deeply dissected, to 15cm across. Flowers 4.5–5.5cm across, purplish blue, white or pale pink, with pink veins. An attractive plant, easily grown in sun or partial shade, with a long flowering season from June to September. The pale-flowered form is very distinct; the blue-flowered form can be clearly distinguished from *G. himalayense*, which has less-divided leaves with broader lobes, and sideways-facing flowers, and from *G. pratense* which has stouter upright stems. Hardy to −20°C. Photographed in the Gadsar Valley, Kashmir, where it grows in great quantity on the grassy valley floor. This is the pale form of the species, known as 'Kashmir White'.

Geranium 'Johnson's Blue' This is almost certainly a hybrid between *G. himalayense* and *G. pratense*. It originated in a nursery in Holland in about 1950 from seed sent there by A. T. Johnson. It is shorter than *G. pratense*, more spreading, with stems to 70cm and flowers of purer blue. Petals *c*.25mm long. Because this is a sterile hybrid it has a longer flowering season than *G. pratense*, generally in June–July.

Geranium pratense L. Native of Europe from Ireland eastwards, south to Spain and the Caucasus, east to Siberia, the Himalayas and the Altai, growing in meadows and grassy places, flowering in June–September. Plant with tufted rootstock and deep fleshy roots. Stems robust, upright, much-branched to 130cm, usually about 75cm. Leaves deeply divided into 7 or 9 lobes, each lobe further divided into narrow

pointed divisions. Flowers 3.5–4.5cm across, blue or white, usually with pinkish veins. This species is common on grassy roadsides especially on limestone in N England, flowering first in June, and again later if the verges are cut: it is thus an ideal plant for the wild garden as it can grow happily in quite rank grass. It is also good in a border, and will seed itself around an untidy garden. Many cultivars are grown, including:
'Galactic' With large white flowers – there is also a double white, 'Plenum Album'.
'Mrs Kendal Clarke' Which should be 'pearl-grey flushed with softest rose', but is the name often given to a pale-flowered form with white veining.
'Silver Queen' White with a pale-blue tinge.
'Striatum' Has white flowers, spotted and streaked with blue: it comes partly true from seed.
Two good doubles are 'Plenum Caeruleum' and 'Plenum Violaceum': the former has light-blue, loosely double, rather untidy flowers; the latter deep-purplish-blue flowers, neater, with purple petaloids surrounded by normal petals.
Subsp. *stewartianum* Nasir, shown on p. 112, from Kashmir, is close to *G. clarkei*, and has narrow leaf-lobes and pinkish-purple flowers.

Geranium rivulare Villars Native of the Alps in France, Switzerland, N Italy and Austria, growing in alpine meadows, among dwarf shrubs and rocks, and in open conifer woods, usually on acid soil, flowering in June. Plant tufted. Stems to 45cm. Leaves deeply divided into 7 to 9 lobes, each further dissected into narrow, acute elongated teeth. Flowers white with fine purplish veins, 1.5–2.5cm across. A graceful plant similar to a small, pale *G. sylvaticum*. Hardy to −20°C.

Geranium 'Sellindge Blue' This is probably a hybrid between *G. pratense* and *G. regelii*, which arose in the author's garden at Sellindge, Kent, in around 1986, as a seedling in a path. It forms a rounded plant with numerous glandular branching and rather floppy stems. The basal leaves are smaller than those of *G. pratense*, to 12cm across, and the flowers 3cm across, intermediate between those of *G. pratense* and *G. regelii* growing in the same garden.
'Brookside', another *G. pratense* hybrid, is very similar, with more prostrate stems and a long flowering period. Flowers a good blue, 4cm across.

Geranium sylvaticum L. Native of most of Europe from Scotland and Ireland, east to Siberia, and south to the Caucasus and Turkey, growing in grassy places, by roads and rivers, and in open woods flowering in May–July according to locality. It is especially common in parts of N England and E Scotland, with pinkish-purple upward-facing flowers, in contrast to the purple-blue flowers of *G. pratense*. Plant with tufted rootstock and deep roots. Stems to 70cm. Leaves deeply divided into 7 or 9 lobes, each further lobed and toothed. Flowers rather crowded, 2.2–3cm across. Peter Yeo records that in NE Europe, white- and pink-flowered become commoner further north, and we saw populations in central Finland, almost entirely pink and white. Pink forms are rare among the normal purple in Scotland. The pure white form 'Album' is very attractive and comes true from seed.
'Mayflower' is said by Yeo to have flowers of a good rich violet blue with a smaller white zone. Grows up to 60cm high, flowering in May–June. Easily grown in sun or partial shade in any good, moist, well-drained soil. Hardy to −25°C or less.

Pelargonium endlicherianum at Nurse's Cottage, North Mundham, Sussex

Geranium magniflorum on Mont-aux-Sources, Orange Free State

Geranium brycei at Carlyle's Hoek, NE Cape

Geranium incanum var. *multifidum*

Pelargonium quercetorum at Harry Hay's, Surrey

Biebersteinia multifida DC. (*Geraniaceae*)
Native of Lebanon and SE Turkey, eastwards to
Afghanistan and Soviet C Asia, growing in
rocky places, flowering in May–June. Plant with
few upright stems to 70cm, from a thick root,
dormant in summer. Leaves aromatic. Flowers
nodding, with petals *c*.10mm long. For a dry,
well-drained position. Hardy to −15°C, or
lower? *Biebersteinia orphanidis* Boiss., with small
pink flowers in a congested spike-like
inflorescence, is found in the Peloponnese and C
Turkey.

Erodium acaule (L.) Becherer & Thell.
(*Geraniaceae*) Native of S Europe, from
Portugal and Spain to Turkey, and around the
Mediterranean, growing in dry grassy places
and scrub, flowering in February–May, and
until September in gardens. Plant with stems
and leaves from a stout rootstock, to 25cm.
Leaves to 15cm long. Petals 7–12mm,
unmarked. For a well-drained sunny position.
Hardy to −10°C, possibly less.

Erodium carvifolium Boiss. & Reut.   Native
of WC & NC Spain, especially round Soria, in
pine woods and mountain meadows, at
c.1500m, flowering in May–June. Leaves up to
10cm long, finely divided, with non-glandular
hairs. Flowers to 4cm across. Easily grown in
well-drained soil. Hardy to −15°C.

Erodium manescavi Cosson   Native of W & C
Pyrenees, mainly in France, possibly also in
Spain, growing in mountain meadows,
flowering in July–August. Leaves to 50cm, with
deeply cut leaflets. Umbels with 5–20 flowers,
the bracts green, joined to form a cup. Petals
15–20mm. Easily grown in well-drained but
moist soil. Hardy to −15°C.

The African species Geranium   Twenty-six
species of perennials, found mostly in the
summer-rainfall areas of Africa. The four shown
here are now in cultivation; the rest are
described in a recent paper by Hilliard & Burtt.
G. pulchrum has the largest flowers, as well as
being the tallest.

Geranium brycei N. E. Br. (*Geraniaceae*)
Native of the Drakensberg, in Lesotho, Orange
Free State, Natal and the NE Cape, growing in
damp and rocky, usually sunny, places,
roadsides or on open mountainsides, at 2200–
3000m, flowering in December–March. Plant
robust or subshrubby, up to 1m, with numerous

stems, forming large mounds of silvery leaves. Leaflets 5–7, hairy on both sides, deeply lobed. Flowers in a much-branched inflorescence, pink, pale purple or bluish, 1.8–4.0cm across, the petals shallowly notched. Easily grown in a sunny position, flowering in midsummer. Hardy to −10°C.

Geranium incanum Burm. fil. var. **multifidum** (Sweet) Hilliard & Burtt   Native of Cape Province, from Port Alfred west to the Cape peninsula, growing in scrub, on dunes and in clearings in forest, flowering in September–March. Plant with stout rootstock and perennial, sometimes woody sprawling stems to 1m, often climbing through scrub. Leaves 5–7-lobed to the base, each lobe further divided and divided again into linear segments *c.*1mm wide, green above, silvery beneath, the margins revolute. Flowers violet to magenta, with petals 12–16 × 6–12mm; in var. *incanum*, the petals are white with dark veins, only 10–12 × 6–7mm. Although this comes from the winter rainfall area of the Cape, it is easily grown in a sunny position. Hardy to −10°C, but if killed by lower temperatures, usually appearing again, from seed?

Geranium magniflorum Knuth   Native of the Drakensberg in Lesotho, Natal and Orange Free State, growing in damp places among rocks, and on grassy slopes, at 1800–3200m, flowering in December–February. Plant with a stout rootstock and decumbent stems to around 30cm. Leaves many from the rootstock, deeply divided into 5 lobes, with each lobe further divided, green above, silvery below, the margins revolute. Flowers pink to bluish or rarely white with dark veins, 2.5–3.2cm across. This should be one of the hardiest African species, as it dies down in winter. Summer-flowering in gardens in England.

Geranium pulchrum N. E. Br.   Native of the C Drakensberg and nearby mountains in W Natal, growing in damp places and streambeds among scrub, at 1500–2285m, flowering in December–March. A robust subshrubby perennial, up to 1.2m. Leaves up to 12cm across, 5–7-lobed nearly to the base, silvery silky, especially beneath, the lobes coarsely toothed. Flowering stems much branched, hairy and glandular, with flowers 3.2–4.4cm across, pink or pale purple. This species has grown well in cultivation in the Chelsea Physic Garden in London, and is easily grown from cuttings and seed. Hardy to −10°C perhaps.

Pelargonium endlicherianum Fenzl (*Geraniaceae*)   Native of S, NE & C Turkey, Syria and Iraq (?), growing on dry limestone rocks, often in shade or partial shade at 650–1500m, flowering in June–July. Plant forming small clumps of leaves to *c.*6cm across. Flowering umbels on stems with few branches to 35cm; each with up to 10 flowers. Hardy to −10°C, but liable to attack by botrytis in winter. For a very well-drained, sunny position, and poor soil, so that the leaves do not grow too large.

Pelargonium quercetorum Agnew   Native of N Iraq and SE Turkey (Hakkari), growing on limestone rocks in oak and *Celtis* scrub at 1200–2000m, flowering in June, and intermittently until September in cultivation. Plant forming large mounds of leaves to 18cm tall, the blades *c.*12cm across: flowering umbels on stems up to 1m, with few branches and up to 30 flowers. For a dry position in full sun or partial shade, but not drought-tolerant as a seedling. Hardiness uncertain, possibly to −10°C for short periods, if kept rather dry in winter.

Geranium pulchrum on Ngeli Mountain

Biebersteinia multifida near Samarkhand

Erodium carvifolium at Corsley Mill, Warminster

Erodium acaule

Erodium manascavi

Geranium × *oxonianum* 'Claridge Druce'

Geranium × *riversleaianum* 'Russell Prichard'

Geranium endressii

Geranium endressii 'Wargrave Pink'

Geranium asphodeloides N. L. Burman subsp. **asphodeloides** (*Geraniaceae*)   Native of Sicily east to Greece, N Turkey, the Caucasus and N Iran, growing in open woods and meadows, flowering in June–October. Stems to 60cm or more, from a stout rootstock, the plant forming a mound of interlacing stems. Basal leaves divided to ¾ into 5 or 7 lobes. Flowers pale to deep pink or white, rather small, but numerous with narrow petals 10–15mm long. A distinct and quietly attractive species with a long flowering season. Subsp. *crenophilum* (Boiss.) Bornm., from Lebanon and Syria, has deep-pink flowers with broad petals; subsp. *sintenisii* (Freyn) Davis, from N Turkey, has pale-pink to purple flowers, and the whole plant is covered with red-tipped glandular hairs. Hardy to −20°C, perhaps.

Geranium collinum Willd.   Native of SE Europe, N & E Turkey, Iran and C Asia eastwards to Siberia and the NW Himalayas, growing in damp meadows and open woods, flowering in June–September. Stems spreading and sprawling to 60cm. Leaves deeply divided into 5 or 7 narrow, deeply cut lobes. Immature fruits held erect on reflexed pedicels. Flowers 25–30cm across, pinkish. A reliable plant, suitable for the wildish garden in partial shade or possibly in a moist meadow.

Geranium endressii Gay **'Wargrave Pink'**   *G. endressii* is native of SW France and NW Spain, in the western end of the Pyrenees, growing in damp places, flowering in June–July. 'Wargrave Pink' is a selection found in the nursery of Waterer Sons and Crisp in 1930. It has several upright or spreading stems, to 50cm or more, from a branching rootstock. Leaves usually 5-lobed nearly to the base, with each lobe rather broad, shortly 3-lobed and toothed. Flowers *c*.35mm across. Easily grown in sun or partial shade. *G. endressii* itself differs in having deeper pink flowers, and rhizomes which spread underground so that the plant forms considerable patches. Hardy to −15°C.

Geranium nodosum L.   Native of the Pyrenees eastwards to Italy and C Yugoslavia, growing in woods in the mountains and hills, flowering in June–October. Plant forming spreading patches, with elongated rhizomes. Leaves with 3 to 5 shallowly toothed lobes. Flowers 2.5–3cm across, bluish or purplish. A hardy and modest plant for the wild garden, tolerant of dry shade and valuable for its late flowering in hot weather. Hardy to −15°C.

Geranium × **oxonianum** Yeo **'Claridge Druce'**   A hybrid between *G. endressii* and *G. versicolor*, which is fertile and now found wild in places in England. Plant strong-growing, forming mounds of deep-green leaves and flowering from May to October. Petals *c*.2.5 × 1.4mm, pink with darker veins, white at the base. All varieties of *Geranium* × *oxonianum* are good garden plants with a long flowering season, forming weed-proof clumps which are easily propagated by division. Hardy to −15°C, perhaps less.
'Thurstonianum' is a form of *G.* × *oxonianum*, known since before 1914. Petals often very narrow, 3–6mm wide, *c*.1.8cm long, often with deformed and petaloid stamens. Plant with a very long flowering season, in June–September, and tolerant of sun or shade and drought.

G. × **riversleaianum** Yeo **'Mavis Simpson'**   This is one of several hybrids between *G. endressii* (q.v.) and *G. traversii* from Chatham Island, New Zealand. 'Mavis Simpson' was

Geranium versicolor

Geranium nodosum

Geranium collinum

Geranium×oxonianum 'Thurstonianum'

Geranium asphodeloides

found as a seedling at Kew. It has a stout rootstock and ascending creeping stems. Basal leaves 5–10cm across, soft and greyish, silky hairy. Flowers 20–30cm across, pale pink, with a silvery sheen. A small and low-growing plant for full sun. 'Russell Prichard' is probably the best known of the group, with magenta flowers *c*.3cm across. Hardy to −15°C.

Geranium versicolor L.   Native of S Europe, in C & S Italy, Sicily and Yugoslavia, south to Greece, growing in woods and on shady banks, and naturalized on roadsides and hedges in parts of England, flowering in May–October. Plant with spreading stems to 60cm from a compact rootstock. Basal leaves 5–20cm across, evergreen, deeply 5-lobed, usually with brown patches between the lobes. Flowers erect with petals broadest at the apex, deeply notched, white with a fine network of magenta veins. Easily grown in a rather dry, shady position. Hardy to −15°C.

Geranium × riversleaianum 'Mavis Simpson' at Washfield Nursery

Geranium lambertii on the rock garden at Wisley

Geranium lambertii

Geranium procurrens

Geranium kishtvariense

Geranium wallichianum 'Buxton's Variety'

Geranium 'Salome'

Geranium wallichianum at Axeltree Nursery, Rye, Kent

Geranium kishtvariense Knuth (*Geraniaceae*)
Native of Kashmir, growing in grassy, open
forests and in scrub, flowering in June–
September. Plant with creeping underground
stolons, but not strong enough to be invasive;
stems creeping and forming a mound to 30cm
across. Basal leaves 5-lobed to ⅔, lobes and
teeth acute. Flowers to 4cm across, reddish
purple or intense rich pink, with a small pale
centre. Easy in a cool position in sun or partial
shade, in moist, leafy soil.

Geranium lambertii Sweet   Native of C Nepal
to Bhutan and SE Xizang, growing in clearings
in coniferous forest, and in juniper scrub at
2350–4200m, flowering in July–September.
Stems creeping from a stout rootstock to about
1m, but not rooting. Leaves divided into 5 wide
and deeply toothed lobes. Flowers 4–6cm
across, saucer-shaped, the petals elegantly
curved at their margins, pale lilac, deep pink or
white, crimson-stained at the base. A beautiful
plant for a cool position, preferably raised up so
that the nodding flowers can be seen at their
best. Very difficult to increase by division, but
comes true from seed. 'Swansdown' is the name
given to the white form; the normal form has
pale-pink flowers. The white form is sometimes
erroneously called *G. candicans* or even *G.
candidum*. Hardy to −20°C.

Geranium procurrens Yeo   A native of E
Nepal, Sikkim, and Bhutan, growing in
hemlock and fir forest at 2440–3600m, flowering
in July–September. Few long creeping and
rooting, or climbing stems are produced from a
stout rootstock. Basal leaves (produced in
spring) divided to ⅔ into 5–7 deeply toothed
lobes. Flowers, 2.3–4cm across, magenta with
black veins, to November in gardens. The
creeping stems may reach 2m in a season and
root at the nodes to form young plants, making
rampant ground cover for a cool moist area in
partial shade. This is especially useful for
growing in areas where spring-flowering bulbs
are planted, and for providing the shady root
area so enjoyed by lilies.

Geranium 'Salome'   A hybrid between *G.
lambertii* and *G. procurrens* which occurred at
Elizabeth Strangman's Washfield Nurseries at
Hawkhurst, Kent, in around 1981. It has a long
flowering season, beginning in mid-summer.
The flowers are about 4cm across, with dark-
purple veins on a cool-purple ground. The plant
dies back to a central rootstock in winter, and
so, like *G. lambertii*, is difficult to propagate.

Geranium wallichianum D. Don ex Sweet
Native of the W Himalayas from NE
Afghanistan to Kashmir, growing in subalpine
meadows and open wooded hillsides at 2400–
3600m, flowering in June–September, and into
October in gardens. Stems several from a
central rootstock, creeping to 120cm, but not
rooting; leaves and flower stalks to 30cm tall.
Leaves 5-lobed, each lobe divided to about ½.
Flowers in pairs, usually pinkish or purplish
blue, with a white centre, *c*.3.5cm across.
'Buxton's Variety' or 'Buxton's Blue' has nearly
pure blue flowers with an extra large white
centre; it is a selected form, raised by E. C.
Buxton in North Wales in *c*.1920, and comes
more or less true from seed. Some forms with
rich pinkish flowers have recently been
introduced from Kashmir. Hardy to −20°C or
lower, and grows best in a position which is cool
and moist in summer, but not heavily shaded.

Geranium species near Gadsar, Kashmir

Geranium wallichianum in open woodland in Kashmir

Helianthemum 'Henfield Brilliant'

Helianthemum nummularium in Kent

Pegamum harmala

Helianthemum hybrids, *Geranium sanguineum* and *Alchemilla mollis* at Barnsley House

Ruta graveolens at the Savill Gardens, Windsor

Haplophyllum latifolium

Dictamnus albus (pink and white forms)

Dictamnus angustifolius

Dictamnus albus L. (*Rutaceae*) **Burning Bush**
Native of Spain northwards to Italy and
Germany and east to Turkey, the Caucasus and
W Himalaya, with very closely related species in
C Asia, growing on steppes, open woods and
dry rocky places at up to 2700m, flowering in
May–July. Plant forming dense clumps, with
stems 40–80cm, glandular and aromatic.
Leaflets 6–12. Petals 2–2.5cm long, usually
pinkish, often white. The leaves are so highly
aromatic that they can be set alight on hot, still
evenings, the hot gases burning for a second or
two.

Dictamnus angustifolius G. Don ex Sweet
Native of much of Soviet C Asia and NW China,
growing in grassy steppes and rocky woods,
flowering in May–August. Stems several,
upright, to 1m from a stout rootstock. Similar to
D. albus, but shorter, neater in habit, and with
narrower, more clearly veined petals. Hardy to
−20°C or less.

Haplophyllum latifolium Kar. & Kir.
(*Rutaceae*)   Native of Soviet C Asia and NW
China, in the Tarbagatai, the Dzungarian Alatau, the Tienshan and the Pamir Alai, growing
in rich steppes among fennels and other large
herbs, flowering in May–June. Plant with a
tough rootstock and spreading, branching stems
to 60cm. Flowers *c.*1cm across. For dry soil in
full sun, hot in summer. Hardy to −20°C or
less. The genus *Haplophyllum*, related to *Ruta*,
contains many species from E Europe to
Siberia; most have yellow flowers and entire or
few-lobed leaves.

Helianthemum nummularium (L.) Mill. syn.
H. chamaecistus Mill. (*Cistaceae*) **Rock Rose**
Native of most of Europe except N Scandinavia
and Russia, of North Africa, Turkey, the
Caucasus and N Iran, growing in grassland,
usually on chalk or limestone, and dry rocky
places and dunes, flowering from May–
September. A very variable species in the wild,
divided in 8 subspecies in Europe. Stems to
50cm, woody below. Leaves to 5cm long, 1.5cm
across, green or white tomentose. Flowers red,
orange, yellow to pink or white, up to 3.5cm
across. The form found wild in Britain is subsp.
nummularium with yellow flowers and leaves
greyish beneath. Numerous garden varieties
have been raised from this and from subsp.
pyrenaicum, which has pink flowers. Large
flowers with petals up to 18mm long are found
in subsp. *grandiflorum* from S Europe.

H. croceum (Desf.) Pers. with roundish, fleshy
stellate-tomentose leaves and variably coloured
flowers has also probably had influence in those
garden hybrids with whitish leaves.
'Henfield Brilliant' shown here, is one of the
best, with bright orange-red flowers. For well-
drained, limy soil in full sun. Hardy to −20°C.

Linum narbonense L. (*Linaceae*)   Native of S
Europe, from NE Portugal and Spain eastwards
near the Mediterranean to Yugoslavia, Sicily
and North Africa, growing on dry hills,
flowering in May–July. Stems to 50cm. Leaves
long, acuminate, glaucous. Flowers with sepals
10–14mm, longer than the capsule; petals
2.5–4cm long, bright blue. Bracts with a papery
white margin. Very beautiful, but requiring a
warm position in full sun. Hardy to −10°C
perhaps. 'Heavenly Blue' and 'Six Hills Variety'
are two named forms, but we have seen neither.

Linum perenne L. **Perennial Flax**   Native of
most of Europe from England (subsp. *anglicum*
(Mill.) Ockenden) and Spain eastwards to
Russia and C Asia, growing in grassland and dry
subalpine meadows, flowering in May–July.
Stems up to 60cm, erect, spreading or
decumbent. Flowers with petals 1–2.5cm;
sepals 3.5–6mm, usually shorter than the
capsule. Bracts without a white papery margin.
For dry, well-drained soil in full sun.

Pegamum harmala L. (*Zygophyllaceae*)
Native of S Europe and North Africa eastwards
to C Asia, NW China and Tibet, growing on dry
steppes, especially where grazing is heavy, at up
to 1500m in Turkey, flowering in May–July.
Plant with several branching stems to 70cm
from a tough rootstock. Leaves divided into
linear segments, greyish, very pungent. Flowers
25–40mm across. For dry soil in full sun. Hardy
to −20°C when dry. A very poisonous plant,
said to cause hallucinations, and to have been
used as a truth drug.

Ruta graveolens L. (*Rutaceae*)   Native of
Yugoslavia to Greece, Bulgaria and the Crimea,
growing in dry stony places, flowering in June–
July. Plant with a rather woody base and
branching stems to 45cm. Leaves greyish,
pungent, the terminal segments 2–9mm wide.
Flowers *c.*1cm across, the petals deeply toothed
and waved. For a dry position in full sun. Hardy
to −10°C, possibly less when dry. 'Jackman's
Var.' is a dense, extra-bluish form. Shown here
is a prostrate variety with creeping stems.

Linum perenne

Linum narbonense in S France

Boykinia aconitifolia

Aceriphyllum rossii

Saxifraga stolonifera

Saxifraga fortunei in Hokkaido

Saxifraga spathularis

Aceriphyllum rossii (Oliv.) Englemann (*Saxifragaceae*)   Native of N China and Korea, growing in moist, shady places among rocks, flowering in May, usually earlier in gardens. Plant forming clumps of deeply lobed leaves with blades *c*.15cm across, flowers *c*.8mm across. For cool, moist soil in a partially shaded position. Hardy to −20°C.

Boykinia aconitifolia Nutt. syn. *Saxifraga aconitifolia* Field (*Saxifragaceae*)   Native of North America, from S West Virginia to North Carolina, Tennessee and Georgia, growing in woods in the mountains, flowering in July. Plant forming wide-spreading sheets several metres across. Stems 30–60cm; leaves *c*.15cm across, flowers 4mm across. Easily grown in a leafy soil in partial shade. Hardy to −20°C.

Lithophragma parviflora (Hook.) Nutt. (*Saxifragaceae*)   Native of the Rocky Mountains and from S California to British Columbia, growing on dry, rocky hills at 600–1800m, flowering in March–June. Roots with bulblets. Stem 20–35cm. Flowers 1–2cm across, with petals cut into 3–5 narrow lobes. For good soil, dry in summer. Hardy to −25°C. *Lithophragma affinis* Gray, with stems to 60cm, is common in California and S Oregon below 1000m. It is probably less hardy.

Saxifraga aquatica Lapeyrouse (*Saxifragaceae*)   Native of the E & C Pyrenees, growing in wet places by mountain streams at 1500–2400m, in acid soil, flowering in June–

August. Plant forming mats to 2m across by spreading stolons. Stems 25–60cm. Leaves to 35mm across. Petals 7–9mm long. This species is like a large mossy saxifrage, and is a marsh rather than a rock plant. It requires wet, damp, acid soil by running water. *S. irrigua* M. Bieb. from the Caucasus and Crimea is similar but smaller.

Saxifraga fortunei Hook. fil.   Native of Japan, Sakhalin, Korea, E Siberia and N China, growing on wet, shaded rocks by streams in the mountains and to sea level in the north, flowering in July–October. Plants forming small clumps but often solitary. Leaves 4–20cm wide. Flower stems 5–45cm tall; petals unequal, the lowest 5–15mm long. The stems are usually reddish, but the whole plant is reddish in 'Wada's Variety' and 'Rubrifolia'. The Japanese plants shown here are called var. *incisilobata* (Engl. & Irmsch) Nakai, to distinguish them from the original Chinese *S. fortunei*. 'Windsor' is a tall clone with stems to 60cm. Hardy to −15°C, perhaps less.

Saxifraga granulata L.   Native of W Europe and North Africa, from Norway and Sweden, south to Spain, Sicily and Morocco and east to Yugoslavia, W Russia and Finland, growing in grassland usually on limestone or sandy soils but in damp places at high altitudes in the south, flowering in April–July. The double-flowered form, 'Flore Pleno', has long been known in gardens. Plant dormant in summer with small bulbils. Stems 10–30cm, or rarely, to 50cm.

Saxifraga granulata near Sherborne, Dorset

Saxifraga granulata

Lithophragma parviflora at Kew

Saxifraga granulata 'Flore Pleno'

Saxifraga aquatica at Inshriach

Leaves up to 3cm across. Flowers with petals 7–16mm long, produced in late spring. Very pretty for naturalizing in a well-drained meadow as can be seen at Kew. Hardy to −20°C or less.

Saxifraga hirsuta L.   Native of SW Ireland, in Kerry and Cork, and in the Pyrenees and N Spain, growing in rocky places in woods, on shady cliffs and by streams and waterfalls, flowering in May–July. Plant forming mats of loose rosettes. Leaves with lamina 15–40 × 10–50mm, and petiole 2–3 times as long, hairy all over. Petals 3.5–4mm, with a yellow patch and faint pink spots. Easily grown in a moist, shaded or partially shaded position, but not tolerant of drought. Hardy to −15°C.

Saxifraga spathularis Brot.   Native of NW Spain, N Portugal and W Ireland, especially around Killarney and Killarney harbour, growing on shady rocks, in woods and on shaded cliffs on acid soils, flowering in May–July. Plant forming loose clumps of rosettes. Leaves rather fleshy, the lamina 15–50 × 12–30mm, the petiole 25–55mm long with sparse, glandular hairs. Flowers with petals *c*.5mm long, each with 2 yellow and several crimson spots. *S.* × *urbium* 'D. A. Webb', the London Pride, is the hybrid *S. spathularis* × *S. umbrosa*. It has more rounded teeth on the lamina and more glandular hairs on the petiole. *S. umbrosa* L. itself, from the C Pyrenees, has leaves with a longer lamina with shallowy crenate lobes and dense hairs on the petiole. All are easily grown in moist soil in partial shade. *S.* × *polita*, the hybrid between *S. spathularis* and *S. hirsuta*, is also common in W Ireland. Hardy to −15°C.

Saxifraga stolonifera Meeburgh syn. *S. sarmentosa* L. **Mother of Thousands**   Native of W China (naturalized in Darjeeling), and in Japan, growing on shady cliffs and on mossy rocks at low altitudes, flowering in May–July. Plant forming rosettes of rather fleshy leaves, and spreading by long red stolons. Leaf blade 3–9cm across. Stems up to 40cm, usually *c*.25cm; flowers with the lowest petals longest, 10–20mm long. Easily grown in a moist, shady position and commonly seen as a house plant in cottage windows. Hardy to −10°C or lower in some forms.

Saxifraga hirsuta at Littlewood Park, Aberdeenshire

Tiarella polyphylla (pink form) near Baoxing, Sichuan, W China

Tiarella cordifolia at the Valley Gardens, Windsor

Tiarella wherryi at Washfield Nurseries, Kent

Heuchera cylindrica 'Greenfinch', with variegated *Symphytum*

Tiarella trifoliata at Washfield Nurseries, Kent

Heuchera cylindrica Dougl. ex Hook.
(*Saxifragaceae*)   Native of N Nevada,
Wyoming and Montana westwards to NE
California and British Columbia, growing on
cliffs and among rocks, flowering in April–
August. Plant forming mats of wavy-edged
leaves 2.5–7.5cm wide. Flower stem 15–90cm.
Flowers cream or greenish, 6–13mm long, with
very small or without petals. Hardy to −20°C,
perhaps. For sun or partial shade in well-
drained soil.
'**Greenfinch**'   A green-flowered selection,
made by Alan Bloom, with stiff upright stems
around 90cm.
'Hyperion' has pinkish flowers.

Heuchera micrantha Dougl. ex Lindl. var.
diversifolia (Rydberg) Rosendahl, Butters &
Lakela syn. *H. diversifolia* Rydb.   Native of
North America from Vancouver Island, British
Columbia and W Washington to N California,
growing in rocky places at up to 800m,
flowering in May–July. Plant forming mounds
or small mats of leaves to 20cm high, those
produced in winter nearly round, summer
leaves lobed. 'Palace Purple' is striking with its
blackish-purple leaves with a metallic sheen and
white flowers. Hardy to −15°C perhaps.

Heuchera pilosissima Fisch. & Mey.   Native
of California, along the coast from San Luis
Obispo Co. to Humboldt Co., growing in pine
and Redwood forests below 300m, flowering in
April–June. Plants with creeping rhizome.
Leaves 3–7cm across, hairy. Flowering stems
20–60cm, brown-hairy, with flowers in a narrow
and compact raceme. Calyx tube 3–4mm long;
petals pinkish white, 2mm long. For well-
drained soil in partial shade. Hardy to −15°C.

Heuchera villosa Michx.   Native of E North
America, from Virginia and Kentucky to
Georgia and Tennessee, growing in rocky places
in the mountains, flowering in June–September.
Plant clump-forming; leaves 7.5–12.5cm across,
with 7–9 acute lobes, the terminal lobe usually
longer than wide. Flowers 2–3mm long; petals
whitish; stamens exserted. For a partially
shaded position and well-drained leafy soil.
Hardy to −25°C or so.

Tiarella cordifolia L. (*Saxifragaceae*) **Foam
Flower**   Native of E North America from
Nova Scotia to Ontario and Minnesota, south to
Georgia, Indiana and Michigan, growing in
rich, moist woods in the mountains, flowering
in April–May. Plants forming large spreading
mats, by creeping underground stolons. Leaves
5–10cm long, with scattered hairs, flowers in
simple or, rarely, few branched racemes, each
around 6mm across. *T. cordifolia* subsp. *collina*
Wherry (see p. 131) differs in its non-creeping
rhizome.

Tiarella polyphylla D. Don   Native of Sikkim
and Bhutan, eastwards to W China, Taiwan and
Japan, growing in moist woods, on shady banks
and by streams in the mountains, flowering in
April–August. Plants spreading by seed not
forming dense mats. Leaves 5-lobed, cordate at
base, to 7cm across, hairy and glandular
beneath. Flowering stems 10–40cm, with small
(4mm long) white, pinkish or green flowers in a
simple or few branched, narrow raceme. An
attractive plant for a cool moist shady position.
Hardy to −15°C or less.

Heuchera micrantha 'Palace Purple'

Tiarella cordifolia subsp. *collina*

Heuchera villosa

Tiarella trifoliata L.   Native of Oregon
northwards to British Columbia and Alaska,
east to N Montana and W Idaho, growing in
moist woods by streams, flowering in May–July.
Plant forming clumps with petioles up to 17cm
high, and leaves with terminal leaflets 3–8cm
long; flowering stems 25–50cm high, usually
c.30cm.

Tiarella wherryi Lakela   Native of Tennessee,
North Carolina and Alabama, growing in shady
ravines, and rocky woods, flowering in July–
August. Plant without stolons, forming small
patches, up to 20cm tall; leaves with 5 major
acute, and other lesser blunt lobes, 7–14cm
long. Flowering stems 15–35cm tall. Flowers
often tinted with purple. An attractive plant for
a cool sheltered position. Hardy to −15°C.

Heuchera pilosissima

Heuchera × brizoides
'Edge Hall'

Heuchera sanguinea
'Alba'

Heuchera sanguinea

Heuchera micrantha

Mitella diphylla

Tiarella cordifolia subsp. *collina*

× *Heucherella alba*

Tolmiea 'Taff's Gold'

Tellima breviflora

Tellima grandiflora

Tiarella trifoliata

Heuchera cyclindrica 'Greenfinch'

Tolmiea menziesii

Heuchera cylindrica

Specimens from Kew, 3 June. Life size

Heuchera × brizoides hort. ex Lémoine **'Red Spangles'** (*Saxifragaceae*)   *H. × brizoides* is a group of hybrids between *H. sanguinea* and *H. americana* L. (with small greenish flowers) and possibly also *H. micrantha*, raised in France in the late 19th century. 'Red Spangles' was raised by Alan Bloom in 1958. It flowers in late May and again in late summer. Stems 40–60cm tall; each flower 9mm across. Another good hybrid raised about the same time is 'Scintillation', with crimson flowers; 'Edge Hall' is a good, pink hybrid, others are white. All are good in sun or light shade. Hardy to −15°C or less.

Heuchera cylindrica **'Greenfinch'**   Text on p.129.

Heuchera micrantha Dougl. ex. Lindl. Native of W North America from C Oregon to C Washington in the Cascades, and east to W Idaho, growing in moist woods by creeks and falls, flowering in June. Plant forming clumps of roughly-hairy leaves usually *c*.15cm tall; flowering stems up to 1m, much branched; leaves with shallow, inconspicuous lobes, nearly round, 2–8cm long (compare 'Palace Purple' p.129). Flowers greenish or reddish 1–3mm long, petals white or pinkish. Easily grown in sun or partial shade in moist, leafy soil. Hardy to −15°C perhaps.

Heuchera sanguinea Engelmann   Native of S Arizona and N Mexico, growing on moist shady rocks, flowering in March–October. Plant forming low mats of dark-green leaves 2.5–7.5cm wide. Flowering stems 25–50cm with numerous red flowers 6–13mm long. 'Alba' is a white-flowered cultivar. Although this plant inhabits shady places in its native habitat, it requires sun or partial shade in cooler, northern climates and flowers from May onwards. Hardy to −20°C.

× *Heucherella alba* (Lémoine) Stearn **'Bridget Bloom'** (*Saxifragaceae*)   A hybrid between *Tiarella cordifolia* and *Heuchera × brizoides*, sometimes listed under × *Heucherella tiarelloides*, raised by Alan Bloom around 1958. An attractive plant forming mats of rather small leaves 4–8cm long, deeply cordate, 5–7 lobed and toothed, the terminal lobe largest. Inflorescence branched, to 45cm. Flowers with a glandular deep pink tube and calyx 6mm long, and narrowly ovate white petals *c*.4 × 1mm. For light leafy soil in partial shade, flowering from May to October. × *H. tiarelloides* (Lémoine) Wehrhahn ex Stearn was originally raised by Lémoine at Nancy in 1917. The *Tiarella* parent of 'Bridget Bloom' is usually said to be *T. cordifolia*, but Alan Bloom records that *T. wherryi* was used.

Mitella breweri Gray (*Saxifragaceae*)   Native of C California, north to British Columbia and Montana, growing on damp shady slopes in conifer forest above 1800m, flowering in June–August. Plant tufted; leaves 2–6cm wide, the petioles with curled brownish-yellow hairs. Flowering stems 10–30cm tall; flowers 3mm across the tube, the petals with 5–7 hair-like lobes. *M. pentandra* Hook. is found as far north as Alaska and in the Rockies, and differs in having straight hairs on the petioles, and more rounded seeds. Both are easily grown in shady, leafy soil. Hardy to −20°C or so.

Mitella diphylla L.   Native of E North America, from Quebec west to Minnesota, south to North Carolina and Missouri, growing in cool places and by streams in woods, flowering in April–May. Plant forming small

clumps. Leaves shallowly 3–5-lobed, 2.5–5cm long. Flowering stems 25–45cm tall, with a pair of rather pointed short- stalked leaves, and a narrow raceme of small flowers with white, fimbriate petals. For a cool moist position, in light leafy soil. Hardy to −25°C or below.

Tellima breviflora Rydb. (*Saxifragaceae*) Native of British Columbia and Alaska to N California, growing by streams, flowering in April–June? Very similar to, and not generally considered distinct from *T. grandiflora*, but differs in having the shorter (5mm long) calyx tube a little, not much, longer than the oblong sepals.

Tellima grandiflora (Pursh.) Dougl. **Fringe Cups**   Native of California from San Luis Obispo Co. northwards, and in the Sierra foothills north to Alaska, growing in cool moist coniferous woods and rocky places below 1500m, flowering in April–June. Plant forming spreading clumps; basal leaves hairy, 3–7-lobed, 5–10cm wide. Flowering stems 40–80cm tall; flowers on short (1–3mm) pedicels, with petals at first whitish, later red, pinnatifid, reflexed: flower tube very broad, campanulate. For moist, shady places. Hardy to −15°C perhaps. Var. *purpurea*, syn. var. *rubra*, has purplish-red leaves.

Tiarella cordifolia subsp. **collina** (*Saxifragaceae*)   Text on p.129.

Tiarella trifoliata   Text on p.129.

Tolmiea menziesii (Pursh.) Torrey & Gray (*Saxifragaceae*)   Native of W North America from N California (Glenn Co.) to Alaska, growing in coniferous forest below 1800m, in cool shady places, flowering in May–June. Plant forming large clumps. Leaves lobed, hairy, 3–10cm wide, pale green or spotted in 'Taff's Gold', often with young plants growing in the sinus. Flowering stems 30–80cm tall; flowers with a tube 5–6mm long, the brown recurved filiform petals 5–7mm long, and only 3 stamens. For moist, cool places in shade or semi-shade. Hardy to −15°C perhaps.

Mitella diphylla in New York State

Heuchera × brizoides 'Red Spangles'

Tellima grandiflora

Mitella breweri

Tolmiea menziesii

Chloranthus fortunei near Ya-an, Sichuan

Houttuynia cordata

Houttuynia cordata 'Plena'

Anemopsis californica near Bishop, E California

Houttuynia cordata 'Variegata'

Rheum 'Ace of Hearts'

Rheum ribes in Hakkari, Turkey

Rheum spiciforme in Kashmir

Anemopsis californica (Nutt.) Hook. fil. &
Arnott syn. *Houttuynia californica* Benth. &
Hook. (*Saururaceae*) Yerba Mansa   Native of S
California and west of the Sierra Nevada,
eastwards to Nevada and Texas, and south to
Baja California and Mexico, in wet, often saline
or alkaline fields, sometimes growing in large
numbers, below 2000m, flowering in March–
September. Stems 10–50cm, woolly, with one
broadly ovate clasping leaf. Basal leaf blade
4–18cm, elliptic-oblong, equalling the long
stalks. Petal-like bracts 1–3cm long. For warm
wet soil or shallow water, probably requiring
summer heat to grow well. Hardy to −15°C and
below?

Chloranthus fortunei (A. Gray) Solms-Lamb.
(*Chloranthaceae*)   Native of China, growing in
damp woods at *c*.1800m, flowering in May.
Plant with 1 or 2 fleshy stems to *c*.30cm from a
stout rootstock. Leaves in 2 opposite pairs,
forming a whorl of 4, about 15cm long. Flowers
with no petals or sepals and 3 stamens. Fruits
berry-like. Hardy to −10°C, perhaps. There are
at least ten *Chloranthus* species, some *Aucuba*-
like shrubs, mainly found in forests in E Asia
and Japan, others herbaceous perennials, grown
for their scent.

Houttuynia cordata Thunb. (*Saururaceae*)
Native of Japan, China, SE Asia (to Java) and
the Himalayas, west to Himachal Pradesh in N
India, growing in damp shady places, woods
and scrub, at up to 2400m, and as a weed in wet
fields, flowering from June–July. Plant with
slender creeping rhizomes and erect stems 20–
50cm high. Leaves 3–8cm long. Flowers minute
in an elongated head 1–2cm long, subtended to
4–6 petal-like bracts. Easily grown in moist,
shady places, creeping harmlessly between
ferns. Three forms are shown here: the wild
form with one whorl of bracts; a double with
numerous bracts becoming smaller upwards,
'Plena'; and a form with multicoloured leaves,
'Variegata' syn. 'Chameleon'. The leaves can be
eaten like spinach, or raw, and are much
collected in the mountains of W China, and sold
in local markets. Hardy to −15°C, perhaps less.

Rheum 'Ace of Hearts' (*Polygonaceae*)   A
hybrid between *R. kialense* and *R. palmatum*,
with heart-shaped leaves, reddish-veined

beneath. Flowers white or very pale pink, on stems to 125cm. For rich moist soil. Raised in c.1970 by The Plantsmen in Dorset.

Rheum alexandrae Batalin. (*Polygonaceae*) Native of W China, in W Sichuan above Kanding (Tachienlu), growing in lush marshy meadows and by streams, especially where yak have been kept, at c.4000m, flowering in June. Plant with deep roots and upright stems to 1.2m tall. Basal leaves ovate, shining-green. Bracts creamy yellow, overlapping and protecting the flowers against the monsoon. For rich, damp soil in full sun. Hardy to −20°C. *R. nobile* Hook. & Thoms. from Nepal and Bhutan grows on rock ledges at c.4000m. It has rounded basal leaves to 30cm across, and even more impressive tightly overlapping bracts on a stem to 1.5m high, but has proved very difficult to grow in gardens.

Rheum palmatum L. Native of W China, in Yunnan, W Sichuan, E Xizang and Gansu, growing in scrub and rocky places and by streams at 2500–4000m, flowering in May–June. A huge plant, from a very stout rootstock. Leaves to 100cm across, deeply lobed and toothed. Flowering stems to 3m, in late spring. Flowers usually white. 'Atrosanguineum' syn. 'Atropurpureum' has young leaves rich crimson-purple and flowers rich pink. In var. *tanguticum* Maxim., from NW China, in Gansu and N Xizang, the side shoots of the inflorescence are said to be erect, and the leaves and shoots are also red when young. This was one of the most valuable Chinese herbal drugs, and Roy Lancaster writes that it is still cultivated for medicine. All *Rheums* require very rich, moist soil, well-manured each year, to grow and flower to their full potential. Hardy to −20°C, or less.

Rheum ribes L. Native of S & E Turkey south to Israel, and east to N Iraq, Soviet Armenia and NW Iran, growing in dry gorges among rocks, at 2300–2700m, flowering in May–June. Plant with a very stout, woody rhizome. Leaves to 40cm across, with stems c.15cm, prickly, the leaf blades drying crisply in summer and rustling as they blow around in the wind. The stalks are eaten raw by the locals. Flower stems 30cm. Fruits with very broad wings. For a dry position, where it is very long-lived. Hardy to −15°C, possibly less.

Rheum spiciforme Royle Native of C Asia in the Tien Shan and the Pamir Alai east to Afghanistan and Bhutan and SE Xizang, at 3600–4800m in scrub, on open slopes and among rocks, flowering from January–July. Plant with a stout rootstock and a rosette of leaves 15–30cm across, on short stalks to 18cm. Spikes 5–30cm, with flowers turning reddish as they mature. For ordinary garden soil in a well-drained position. Hardy to −20°C or less.

Rumex alpinus L. (*Polygonaceae*) Native of the mountains of C & S Europe, from France and Spain to Poland, W Russia, the Caucasus and Turkey, and naturalized in Scotland and N England, growing in damp grassy places by old farms, and near cowsheds, at up to 2500m, flowering in June–August. Plant slowly forming large patches, with a creeping rhizome. Leaves to 40cm long and wide. Flowering stems to 1m. For very rich, cool, moist soil. Hardy to −20°C or less. The leaves were formerly used for wrapping butter, and the young shoots are edible. The red-veined dock, *R. sanguineus*. L. var. *sanguineus*, is also worth growing, for its beautiful leaves.

Rheum palmatum in flower at Beth Chatto's Garden

Rheum palmatum 'Atrosanguineum'

Rheum palmatum (young leaves)

Rumex alpinus in Perthshire

Rheum alexandrae at the Savill Gardens

Silene dioica (wild form) in Aberdeenshire

Silene dioica (compact garden form)

Silene schafta

Silene fimbriata from Itkol, C Caucasus

Silene caroliniana

Lychnis flos-cuculi at Gibbon's Brook, Sellindge

Lychnis flos-cuculi L. (*Caryophyllaceae*)
Ragged Robin Native of Europe from Iceland
and Scotland, east to Siberia and the Caucasus,
south to Spain, Sicily and Greece and
naturalized in NE North America, growing in
marshes and bogs, flowering in May–July. Plant
creeping at ground level. Flowering stems
upright, 30–75cm. Flowers 3–4cm across.
Petals pink with 4 very thin narrow lobes or
white with less deeply 2-lobed petals in subsp.
subintegra Heyek in Greece and the Balkans. A
pretty plant for a damp meadow, moist border
or bog garden, especially in its double form.

Silene asterias Griseb. (*Caryophyllaceae*)
Native of Albania, Yugoslavia, Bulgaria and
Greece, growing in damp places by streams at
1200–2000m, flowering in June–July. Plant
forming clumps of rosettes of thin leaves to
15cm long. Stems to 100cm, with 1 or 2 pairs of
leaves. Heads of flowers 4–6cm across. A
striking and unusual plant for moist, peaty soil
in full sun. Hardy to −20°C or less.

Silene caroliniana Walt. **Wild Pink** Native of
Maine south to Georgia along the mountains,
west to C New York, Pennsylvania and
Kentucky, growing in dry rocky or sandy
places, often in shallow soil on rock outcrops,
flowering in April–June. Stems 10–25cm,
glandular-pubescent and sticky. Basal leaves
5–10cm long. Flowers *c*.2.5cm across. An
attractive plant for poor, shallow, dry soil.
Hardy to −25°C.

Silene dioica (L.) Clairv. syn. *Lychnis dioica* L.
Red Campion Native of most of Europe, east
to Bulgaria and of North Africa, growing in
woods, rocky slopes, hedges and sea cliffs,
flowering in March–June. Plant forming clumps
of rosettes with several stems 30–90cm tall,
softly hairy. Flowers 1.8–2.5cm across, bright
pinkish, very rarely white. A very floriferous
dwarf form is common in cottage gardens in E
Scotland. It is probably subsp. *zetlandica*
(Compton) Clapham, found in Orkney and
Shetland; similar plants are found on coasts and
mountains in other parts of Europe. It has stems
c.30cm and is hairier with a denser
inflorescence. Two double-flowered forms are
also cultivated: 'Flore Pleno', an old cultivar
known since the 16th century, and 'Richmond',
a semi-double found in Richmond Park near
London in *c*.1978. For any position that is not
hot and dry. Hardy to −25°C.

Silene fimbriata Sims syns. *Oberna multifida*
(Adam) Ikonn., *Silene multifida* (Adam)
Rohrb. Native of the Caucasus at *c*.2000m,
growing in wet subalpine birch woods,
flowering in May–June. Stems 1–1.5m, swollen
at the joints. Flowers *c*.2.5cm across, with a
very swollen calyx. An attractive plant for the
wild garden or back of a cool shaded border.
Hardy to −25°C.

Silene laciniata Cav. Native of the mountains
of Mexico, with subsp. *major* Hitch. & Maguire
in S California from Santa Cruz Co. southwards,
growing in scrub, chaparral, and sandy places
along the coast, flowering in May–July. Stems
several, sprawling to 70cm from a deep taproot.
Leaves linear to lanceolate, 5–10cm long.
Flowers 16–30mm across, with appendages
1–1.5mm long. Capsule exserted from the calyx.
Silene californica Durand, from S California
north to Oregon, is very similar, but has
broader leaves and capsules not exserted from
the calyx. For dry, well-drained soil in full sun.
Hardy to −10°C, possibly lower.

Silene virginica near Charlottesville, Virginia

Silene laciniata at the Royal Botanic Gardens, Edinburgh

Silene schafta S. C. Gmel. ex Hohen. Native
of the Talysh and N Iran, growing on subalpine
rocks at 1500–1800m, flowering in July–
August, usually in June in gardens. Stems semi-
prostrate to 30cm long. Flowers *c*.2cm across,
usually bright pink but paler in 'Shell Pink'.
For the top of a wall or front of a border in full
sun. Hardy to −20°C.

Silene virginica L. Native of S New Jersey,
W New York and SW Ontario, west to
Minnesota, south to Georgia and Missouri,
growing in dry woods and on roadside banks,
flowering in April–September. Stem 30–60cm.
Flowers 2.5–3.75cm across; petals narrow, 2-
lobed or toothed at apex. A very striking plant,
but seldom cultivated. For well-drained soil in
partial or deciduous shade. Hardy to −20°C.

Silene asterias at Harry Hay's, Surrey

Lychnis coronaria 'Alba' with Viola cornuta 'Alba', delphiniums and 'Iceberg' roses

Lychnis coronaria 'Oculata'

Lychnis 'Abbotswood Rose'

Lychnis × arkwrightii hort. ex Heydt **'Vesuvius'** (*Caryophyllaceae*)   A hybrid between *L.* × *haageana* (*L. fulgens* × *L. coronata*) and *L. chalcedonica*. Stems to 45cm. Leaves purplish. 'Vesuvius' is a good selection, raised in around 1912. Hardy to −15°C.

Lychnis chalcedonica L. **Jerusalem Cross**
Native of W Russia, from Odessa to Moscow, and recorded also in NW China growing in woods and scrub, flowering in June–July. Plant with a spreading rootstock and several upright stems to 45cm, sometimes to 1.2m in cultivation. Flowers 10–50 in a flat-topped head, each 1.5cm across. Petals deeply lobed. Easily grown in good moist soil in sun or partial shade, in a sheltered position; cultivated in gardens in Europe since before 1593. Hardy to −20°C or less. Several forms are grown in gardens: e.g. 'Alba' and 'Alba Plena', white single and double; 'Rosea', a pale pink; 'Carnea', a flesh pink; a double pink; and 'Rubra Plena', a double red.

Lychnis coronaria (L.) Desv.   Native of Europe from Czechoslovakia and Yugoslavia south to NW Africa, Greece and NW Turkey, and eastwards to the Crimea, Iran and Turkestan, growing in scrub, woods and on rocky sunny slopes, flowering in May–September. Usually a rather short-lived perennial. Stems to 100cm, much branched. Leaves softly and densely white-hairy. Flowers usually purplish pink, *c.*3cm across. Long cultivated; and several colour forms are now common in gardens: 'Atrosanguinea', deep crimson; 'Oculata', white with pink eye; 'Alba', white, and a double 'Flore Pleno'. The pale-flowered single form comes more or less true from seed. 'Abbotswood Rose' is probably a hybrid between *L. coronaria* and *L. flos-jovis*, called *L.* × *walkeri*. It is shorter, to *c.*60cm, and more spreading than *L. coronaria* and has flowers of a piercing pink, with deeply emarginate petals. All these will survive on very poor, dry sandy soils in full sun; they will flower well, but be short-lived in rich soil and partial shade. Hardy to −20°C.

Lychnis flos-jovis (L.) Desv.   Native of France, Switzerland and N Italy in the W Alps, growing on dry sunny subalpine slopes on acid rocks at 1000–2000m flowering in June–August. Usually a short-lived perennial with stems 20–90cm. Leaves white hairy; flowers purplish or scarlet, in heads of 4–10. Petals deeply lobed; 'Hort's Variety' has paler rose-pink flowers, and there are also a white and a dwarf form. Best in well-drained, rather poor soil. Hardy to −15°C.

Lychnis viscaria L. syn. *Viscaria vulgaris* Bernh.   Native of Scotland and Wales, south to Spain and east to NW Turkey, Siberia and C Asia, growing in open sandy places, on dry hillsides, rocks and cliffs, flowering in May–August. Leaves narrow, not hairy, forming mats. Stems to 90cm, usually around 40cm; flowers purplish red, 18–20mm across. In cultivation there are several forms, including a double 'Flore Pleno' or 'Splendens Plena'; and a white 'Alba'; subsp. *atropurpurea* (Griseb.) Chater, from Romania to Yugoslavia and Greece, differs in minor details of the calyx and capsule stalk. For well-drained soil in full sun. Hardy to −25°C or less.

Lychnis × *arkwrightii* 'Vesuvius'

Lychnis chalcedonica at Cedar Tree Cottage, Sussex

Lychnis viscaria 'Alba'

Lychnis viscaria

Lychnis chalcedonica 'Rosea' at Wisley

Lychnis viscaria 'Flore Pleno'

Lychnis flos-jovis at the Savill Gardens, Windsor

Lupinus nootkatensis by the River Dee, near Braemar

Lupinus nootkatensis

Lupinus polyphyllus (naturalized)

Lupinus perennis in Maine

Lupinus 'La Chatelaine'

Lupinus 'My Castle'

Lupinus 'Magnificence'

Thermopsis mollis

Thermopsis ovata in Washington State

Baptisia australis (L.) R. Br. (*Leguminosae*)
Native of N Virginia to W Pennsylvania, east to
Missouri and Kansas and south to Georgia and
Texas, growing in rich soil, flowering in June–
August. Plant forming large clumps of glabrous
upright stems to 2m tall. Leaves very short-
stalked with 3 oblanceolate leaflets. Flowers
2–2.5cm long. Seed pod inflated. For rich,
moist soil in sun or light shade. Hardy to
−20°C. *B. cinerea* (Raf.) Feon. & Schub. is
minutely hairy, with yellow flowers about 2.5cm
long; *B. leucophaea* Nutt. and *B. leucantha* T. &
G. have white flowers; all are natives of prairies
and rich meadows in SE North America.

Lupinus nootkatensis Donn ex Sims
(*Leguminosae*)   Native of NE Asia and NW
America, from British Columbia to S Alaska,
and naturalized in Norway and on the Tay,
Dee, Spey and Beauly in Scotland, growing on
shingle banks in rivers, flowering in June–July.
Stems several, erect up to 80cm. Leaflets 6–8.
Flowers bluish, 6–18mm long. This species was
introduced into cultivation in Europe as long
ago as 1795 by Archibald Menzies on Captain
Vancouver's expedition. It has since died out in
gardens, probably because it is very susceptible
to slug damage. It is, however, a fine sight in
late June on some of the best salmon rivers in E
Scotland.

Lupinus perennis L.   Native of E North
America from Maine and Ontario westwards to
Minnesota and south to Florida, Missouri and
Louisiana, growing in grassy places in dry,
sandy soil, flowering in May–June. Stems few
from a compact rootstock to 60cm. Leaves with
around 8 narrowly oblanceolate leaflets. Flowers
blue, more rarely pink or white, 12–16mm long,
without a spot on the standard. A useful species
for meadow garden on poor sandy soil; hardier
than the western *L. polyphyllus*, to −25°C, or
less.

Lupinus polyphyllus Lindl.   This is the
forerunner of the large cultivated lupins. It is a
native of coastal California from Santa Cruz Co.
of San Francisco, northwards to British
Columbia (with subsp. *superba* (Heller) Munz
inland to Nevada), growing in wet grassy
meadows, flowering in May–July. In wild forms
the stems are up to 1.5m high, with 9–17
leaflets; the flowers are blue, purple or reddish,
11–14mm long, in whorls on racemes 15–60cm
long. Good for naturalizing in sandy soil in long
grass. Hardy to −25°C.

Garden lupins   Perennial lupins were
cultivated in English gardens from about 1826

when *L. polyphyllus* was first introduced from
North America. The great strides in their
improvement took place from 1911 onwards
when George Russell, gardener to a Mrs
Michlethwaite in York, began to grow lupins on
his allotment and select, every year, the best
seedlings that appeared. It is probable that the
annual *L. hartwegii* with magenta flowers
contributed to the improved range of flower
colours in Russell's hybrids. It was not until 1937
that Russell's lupins received wide recognition;
many distinct colours are still in cultivation, such
as 'Limelight' (yellow) and the blue-and-white
bicolour 'Vogue'. 'Mrs Michlethwaite' is named
after his former employer. Named lupin
cultivars require well-drained soil, preferably
slightly acid and sandy, without nitrogenous
manure; they should not be allowed to set seed,
or the plant will be weakened. The young shoots
are also commonly damaged by slugs. Recently
Russell's work has been continued by the
Woodfield brothers, who now produce fine
lupins in a wide range of colours and bicolours.
Shown here are:
'La Chatelaine' syn. 'Schlossfrau',
'Magnificence', and **'My Castle'** syn. 'Mein
Schloss'

Thermopsis caroliniana M. A. Curtis
(*Leguminosae*)   Native of North Carolina,
Georgia and Tennese, growing in open woods
and on river banks, flowering in April–May.
Stems 80–100cm, stout, with few branches and
leafy stipules. Leaflets obovate, 5–8cm long.
Flowers in a compact raceme. For good soil in
full sun or partial shade. Hardy to −15°C,
perhaps less.

Thermopsis mollis (Michx.) M. A. Curtis
Native of S West Virginia, E Tennessee, North
Carolina and Georgia, growing in the mountains,
flowering in July–August. Plant with few to
several erect stems, 60–90cm tall. Stipules not
leafy. Leaves stalked with 3 oval leaflets, 2–4cm
long. Flowers in an elongated raceme, c.20mm
long. Seed pod flat. For good soil in sun or partial
shade. Hardy to −20°C.

Thermopsis ovata (Rob.) Rydb.   Native of
Wyoming and Idaho west to Washington and
Oregon, growing in damp, grassy places, sandy
river banks, and in open woods, flowering in
May–July. Stems 60–80cm, stout, succulent.
Stipules leafy, obovate to ovate-cordate, 2–4cm
long. Leaflets obovate to broadly elliptic, 6–8cm
long. Flowers in a loose raceme. Seed pods
usually upright, 5–7cm long, silky-hairy. For
any good moist soil in sun or partial shade. Hardy
to −20°C.

Thermopsis caroliniana

Baptisia australis

Alchemilla conjuncta

Alchemilla mollis with box hedges in Gloucestershire

Alchemilla pedata at Harry Hay's, Surrey

Alchemilla conjuncta Babington (*Rosaceae*)
Native of the SW Alps and Jura in France and
Switzerland, and found wild also in Scotland,
growing in subalpine meadows and rocky places
by streams, flowering in June–July. Plant
forming spreading patches to 30cm across.
Leaves blue-green above, silky-silvery beneath,
the lobes joined in the lower ⅓ or so; flowering
stems to 40cm. Easily grown in well-drained,
moist soil in a sunny position. Hardy to −20°C
or less? *A. alpina* L., which is common on
granite mountains in Scotland, N England and
most of Europe, is smaller, with all the leaflets
separate to the base.

Alchemilla erythropoda Juz.   Native of the W
Carpathians, Yugoslavia and Bulgaria eastwards
to N Turkey, the Caucasus and N Iran, growing
in rocky mountain meadows, flowering in May–
August. Plant forming clumps up to 20cm
across. Flowering stems 20–30cm, often reddish
purple. Leaves bluish green, densely and softly
hairy on both sides, *c*.4cm across, with
characteristic deflexed hairs on the mature
petioles. A small, easily grown species for a
sunny position; suitable for gaps in paving or
other places near pathways. Hardy to −20°C or
less.

Alchemilla glabra Neygenf.   Native of N & C
Europe, including N England and Scotland,
and NE North America, growing in grassy
places, open woods and by streams in the
mountains, usually on acid soils, flowering in

May–September. Plant forming clumps with
flowering stems to 60cm. Leaves *c*.8cm across,
glabrous except for a few hairs on the apical part
of the veins beneath. In its deep green, glabrous
leaves, a contrast to *A. mollis. A. xanthochlora*
Rothm. is similar, but has hairy stems and
inflorescence, and leaves glabrous above, hairy
on the veins beneath. *A. glabra* is better than *A.
mollis* on damp, acid soils. Hardy to −25°C.

Alchemilla mollis (Buser) Rothm.   Native of
N Greece and the E Carpathians in Romania
and W Russia, south to the Caucasus, N
Turkey, Soviet Armenia and N Iran, growing
by streams in meadows and in fir and beech
forest, flowering in June–September. Plant
forming large clumps, and seeding freely.
Leaves to 15cm across, hairy on both sides,
lobed to ⅕. Flowering stems to 80cm long.
Easily grown in sun or partial shade. Hardy to
−25°C and tolerant of drought.

Alchemilla pedata A. Rich.   Native of
Ethiopia, particularly in the north-west,
growing in grassy places and on the edges of
forest. Plant spreading by runners to form
patches several metres across. Leaves *c*.4cm
wide. Inflorescence simple and very delicate.
Hardy to −5°C, but often needs reseeding after
cold winters.

Cornus canadensis L. syn.
Chamaepericlymenum canadense (L.) Asch. &
Graebn. (*Cornaceae*) **Bunchberry**   Native of

North America, from Newfoundland to Alaska,
south to West Virginia, Colorado and
California, of Japan, Korea and E Siberia,
growing in coniferous woods, flowering in May–
July. Plant creeping underground to form
extensive patches several metres across.
Flowering stems 7.5–20cm, with the leaves in a
whorl of *c*.6 at the top. Bracts white, 8–18mm
long. Flowers minute, green. Fruits bright red
and fleshy. Easily grown in peaty soil in shade or
partial shade. A good companion for heathers.
C. suecica L. is found all round the Arctic; it is a
smaller, more delicate plant with 3 pairs of
leaves up the stem, and blackish-purple flowers.

Gillenia trifoliata (L.) Moench. syn.
Porteranthus trifoliatus (L.) Britton (*Rosaceae*)
Native of E North America, from Ontario and
New York east to Michigan and south to
Georgia and Missouri, growing in rocky open
woods, flowering in May–July. Plant tufted
with many stems to 120cm from a woody
rootstock. Leaves trifoliate, the upper sessile,
with leaflets to 7.5cm long. Stipules, at the base
of the leaflets, small and narrow, to 8mm long.
Flowers white or pinkish, with petals 1.0–1.2cm
long. A most graceful and attractive plant, but I
have not found it easy to establish: the young
shoots are eaten by slugs and it should be
planted in a position that is neither too sunny
and dry, nor too shady. *G. stipulata* (Muhl.)
Bergmans differs in being usually smaller, with
leafy stipules about a third as long as the short-
stalked leaves.

Alchemilla mollis after rain

Gillenia trifoliata

Alchemilla glabra in Aberdeenshire

Alchemilla erythropoda

Cornus canadensis

Duchesnea indica

Geum chilense 'Mrs Bradshaw'

Geum coccineum

Fragaria 'Pink Panda'

Potentilla palustris

Potentilla nepalensis 'Rosana'

Potentilla 'Gibson's Scarlet'

Potentilla nepalensis 'Master Floris'

Duchesnea indica (Andrews) Focke (*Rosaceae*)   Native of S & E Asia, including China and Japan, but widely naturalized in North America, from New York southwards, and S Europe, growing in damp, shady woods and by streams, flowering in April–June and intermittently through the summer. Plant creeping by rooting runners, flowers yellow with petals 8mm long; fruits red, strawberry-like but insipid. *D. chrysantha* (Zoll. & Moritz) Miq. is a smaller plant with paler, pinkish-white fruit. *D. indica* is probably the hardier species, surviving to −15°C in the absence of snow cover.

Fragaria 'Pink Panda' (*Rosaceae*)   A hybrid between *F. × ananassa*, a garden strawberry, and *Potentilla palustris*, the wild marsh cinquefoil, raised by Dr Jack Ellis. The original cross was made in 1966, and, after repeated backcrossing, 'Pink Panda' was selected, and introduced by Blooms in 1989. Height 10–15cm. Flowers 2–2.5cm across, often with 6 or more petals, produced in May–November, seldom fruiting. For full sun or partial shade. Hardy to −20°C.

Geum chilense Balbis **'Mrs Bradshaw'** (*Rosaceae*)   Native of Chile, on Chiloe Island, and around Conception, growing in damp places by mountain streams, flowering in November–January. Plant forming clumps, with flowering stems to 45cm. Flowers orange-red to purplish red. Differs from *G. coccineum* in its taller, more branched stems, and leaves in which the leaflets increase gradually in size to the apex. Hardy to −20°C, perhaps.

Geum coccineum Sibth. & Sm. syn. *G. borisii* hort.   Native of the Balkan peninsula, and N Turkey, growing in wet meadows, and along streams in damp forests, at 1300–2000m flowering in May–August. Plant forming low clumps of pale green leaves with 2–4 pairs of lateral leaflets and a large terminal leaflet, 4–14cm across, orbicular-reniform. Flowering stems 10–45cm with 2–4 flowers. Petals 10–18mm long. Easily grown in moist peaty soil. Hardy to −25°C.

Potentilla nepalensis Hook. (*Rosaceae*) Native of the Himalayas from Pakistan eastwards to C Nepal, in alpine meadows and fields at 2100–2700m, flowering in June–September. Plant forming a loose mass of wiry branching stems 20–90cm long. Lower leaves with 5 leaflets. Flowers 1.3–2.5cm across, dark crimson to bright pink or orange. Easily grown in any good, moist soil. 'Rosana': flowers bright pink with a red centre. 'Master Floris': flowers creamy yellow with a pink edge and dark-red centre. 'Helen Jane': flowers pale pink with dark centres. *P. nepalensis* differs from *P. atrosanguinea* by having lower leaves with 5, not 3, leaflets, and is a taller, more spreading plant with smaller flowers in a more branched inflorescence. 'Miss Willmott' (not shown) is cherry pink with a dark centre.

Potentilla palustris (L.) Scop. syn. *Comarum palustre* L. **Marsh Cinquefoil**   Native of Europe, south to Bulgaria, eastwards to Siberia and Japan, and in North America from Greenland to New Jersey and N California, growing in wet places, by lakes, ponds and wet bogs, flowering in May–August. Plant with creeping rhizomes, forming extensive patches

Potentilla nepalensis 'Helen Jane'

Potentilla thurberi

many metres across. Stems 15–45cm. Leaves bluish green with 5–7 leaflets. Petals deep purple, *c*.1cm, shorter than the purplish sepals. A plant for the wet wild garden, attractive with its greyish leaves. Hardy to −25°C.

Potentilla × russelliana   A hybrid between *P. atrosanguinea* and *P. nepalensis*; lower leaves with 3–5 leaflets, narrower than *P. atrosanguinea*. Some of those generally considered cultivars of *P. atrosanguinea*, e.g. 'Gibson's Scarlet', probably belong to this hybrid. The following *Potentilla* cultivars are probably either selections of *P. atrosanguinea* or hybrids between this and other species. The flowers are in various shades of red, orange or yellow, on branching stems about 45cm tall, forming spreading plants about 60cm across: 'Yellow Queen'; 'Fireflame'; 'Hamlet'; 'Gibson's Scarlet', lower leaves 3–5; 'Monsieur Rouillard'.

Potentilla thurberi A. Gray ex Lehm.   Native of C Arizona to C New Mexico and N Mexico, growing in moist clearings in conifer forest, in damp meadows and along streams, flowering in July–October. Plant tufted with many stiff stems 30–75cm tall. Leaves pinnate with 5 or 7 close, toothed leaflets, 2.5–5cm long. Flowers *c*.2.5cm across, deep velvety red with a darker centre. For a good soil in a warm position. Hardy to −25°C perhaps, growing well in New England where it flowers in June.

Waldsteinia ternata (Stephan) Fritsch (*Rosaceae*)   Native of Europe in the Carpathians in Czechoslovakia and Romania, and, rarely, in SE Austria and NW Yugoslavia, and of E Asia and E Siberia, Sakhalin and N Japan, growing in woods in the mountains, flowering in May–June. Plant forming low mats by creeping rhizomes. Leaves 3-foliolate, the leaflets 2–3cm long. Stems to 20cm, 1–7 flowered. Flowers 1.5–2cm across. Easily grown in leafy soil in partial shade where it makes very attractive ground cover. From descriptions in the floras the Japanese plants appear to be more delicate with fewer larger flowers on the stems. *W. fragarioides* (Michx.) Tratt from NE North America has similar leaves but smaller flowers 6–10mm across.

Potentilla × russelliana

Potentilla 'Fireflame'

Potentilla 'Yellow Queen' with *Viola cornuta*

Potentilla 'Hamlet'

Waldsteinia ternata

Geum 'Lemon Drops'

Potentilla
rupestris

Geum rivale f. album

Geum rossii

Potentilla
atrosanguinea

Geum
'Georgenberg'

Geum
montanum

Potentilla nepalensis (p. 142)

Potentilla atrosanguinea
(pale form)

Specimens from Beth Chatto, Unusual Plants, 9 June. ½ life size

Geum rivale in Perthshire

Geum 'Leonard's Variety'

Geum triflorum

Geum elatum in Kashmir

Geum rivale f. *album*

Potentilla rupestris

Geum elatum Wall. ex D. Don (*Rosaceae*)
Native of the Himalayas from Pakistan to SE
Xizang, growing in scrub and alpine meadows
at 2700–4300m, flowering in June–August.
Very variable; as shown here a stemless plant
with congested pinnate basal leaves and single,
upright yellow flowers. At lower altitudes, a
taller plant with branched stems and nodding
yellow or more rarely reddish flowers. For well-
drained soil, in a sunny position, moist in
summer. Hardy to −20°C.

Geum 'Georgenberg' This is sometimes
quoted as *G.* × *heldreichii*, a hybrid between *G.
coccineum* and *G. montanum*, but the nodding
buds suggest that *G. rivale* or *G.* × *intermedium*
was one parent. *G. montanum* may well be the
other. The hybrid *G. rivale* × *G. montanum* is
called *G.* × *tirolense* Kerner; this is probably
also the parentage of 'Lemon Drops' from Beth
Chatto. Best in moist, peaty soil.

Geum montanum L. Native of the Pyrenees,
Alps, Corsica and Carpathians, eastwards to W
Russia and SW Greece growing in sub-alpine
meadows, at 1500–3000m, flowering in June–
July. Plant with a shortly creeping rhizome and
a rosette of leaves. Terminal leaflet *c*.6cm long.
Flowering stem 3–10cm long, 1–3 flowered.
Flowers 2.5–4cm across. Easily grown in well-
drained, rather peaty soil in full sun. *G. reptans*
L. is closely related, but usually found at a
higher altitude, above 2000m; it has long stolons
and the leaves are always pinnate, with the
terminal lobe not much larger than other lobes.
Both are hardy to −25°C.

Geum rivale L. **Water Avens** Native of most
of Europe except the far south, of the Caucasus
and N Turkey, N Asia east to the Altai in NW
China and N America from Newfoundland to
British Columbia and south to New Jersey and
Colorado, growing in wet meadows, by streams
and in marshes, flowering in May–June. Plant
forming low mats of irregularly pinnate leaves,
with flowering stems simple or with few
branches, usually *c*.30cm, rarely up to 1m.
Stems and flowers brownish red or pinkish, pale
yellow green in f. *album*. Styles 8–9mm, hairy.
Hybrids with Herb Bennett (*G. urbanum* L.) are
common, especially in shady places by rivers.
They have taller stems with paler flowers, and
are called *G.* × *intermedium* Ehrh.
'Leonard's Variety' is probably a hybrid
between *G. rivale* and another species, possibly
G. coccineum. It has masses of stems up to 45cm
tall, with nodding flowers of pinkish orange,
with a hint of brown. All are easily grown in a
moist or partially shady border.

Geum rossii (R. Br.) Sev. Native of W North
America, from Alaska south to NE Oregon,
Nevada, New Mexico and in E Asia, growing in
arctic tundra, and on screes and stony meadows
in the mountains, flowering in June–July. Plant
forming dense clumps to 30cm across. Basal
leaves 4–10cm long. Flowering stems 8–20cm
tall. Petals 10–12mm long, yellow. Easily grown
in well-drained soil. Hardy to −20°C or lower.

Geum triflorum Pursh. Native of North
America, from Newfoundland and New York
westwards to British Columbia, south to Oregon

and California and along the Rockies south to
Nevada, growing in damp places and mountain
screes, flowering in April–August, according to
altitude. Plant forming clumps to 30cm or more
across. Basal leaves 5–15cm, with up to 30
segments. Flowering stems to 30cm tall, with
1–9 flowers. Petals pale yellow to reddish or
purplish. Easily grown in rather damp soil.
Hardy to −20°C or lower.

Potentilla atrosanguinea Lodd. syn. *P.
argyrophylla* Wall. ex Lehm. (*Rosaceae*) Native
of the Himalayas, from Afghanistan eastwards to
Sikkim, growing in scrub, and on grassy open
slopes, at 2500–4500m, flowering in June–
August. Plant with few erect or spreading stems
to 60cm. Leaves trifoliate, variably silvery,
especially beneath, with leaflets 2 × 5cm long.
Flowers red in the west, orange or yellow (var.
argyrophylla (Lehm.) Grierson & Long) in the
east, 2–4cm across. A useful spreading plant for
the front of a border, in cool moist soil. Plants
grown as *P. argyrophylla* commonly have paler
red flowers. Hardy to −25°C.

Potentilla rupestris L. syn. *P. foliosa* Somm. &
Lev. Native of most of Europe including
Britain, the Caucasus, Turkey and eastwards to
C Siberia, growing on dry sunny rocky slopes in
the mountains, flowering in June–July. Plant
tufted. Basal leaves pinnate, with 5–9 leaflets.
Stems 8–50cm. Flowers with petals 8–14mm
long. Easily grown in well-drained soil in full
sun. A characteristic species of dry rocky slopes
in the foothills in Europe. Hardy to −25°C.

Acaena magellanica

Acaena 'Blue Haze'

Acaena microphylla at Wisley, Surrey

Sanguisorba tenuifolia var. *alba* in Hokkaido

Sanguisorba canadensis at Kew

Acaena magellanica Vahl syn. *A. glaucophylla* Bitter (*Rosaceae*)   Native of the Falkland Islands, South Georgia, Kerguelen Island, W Argentina and E Chile, north to 27°S, growing on sand and rocks near the sea, in scrub, open forest, moist grassland and bog at up to 1100m, flowering in November–March. Stems creeping and rooting. Leaf lamina 2–8cm long, with 5–8 pairs of leaflets. Flowering stems 7–14cm, with heads 1–3cm across, purplish when young with the unopened stamens; the spines in fruit 5–10mm long. 'Blue Haze' syn. 'Pewter' seems to be a very glaucous form. Hardy to −15°C.

Acaena microphylla Hook. fil. **Red Mountain Bidi-Bidi**   Native of New Zealand, on North and South Island (var. *robusta* Allan and var. *pallideoliracea* Bitter), growing in grassland and in riverbeds, at 0–1100m, flowering in December–February. Plant creeping. Leaves green, glabrous, to 3cm long. Flower heads 2.5cm in diameter. Easily grown in rather moist soil; good for ground cover between paving stones. Hardy to −10°C.

Sanguisorba alpina Bunge (*Rosaceae*)   Native of the Altai, in Siberia, Sinjiang and ?Mongolia, growing in alpine meadows, flowering in June–August. Plant forming spreading clumps of very glaucous leaves, with 15–19 ovate, cordate leaflets. Flower spikes elongated, 1–5cm long. Easily grown in rich, moist soil in full sun. Very similar to *S. armena* but smaller, with blunter, more curved teeth on the leaflets.

Sanguisorba armena Boiss.   Native of NE Turkey, especially around Erzurum, growing by mountain streams on treeless but grassy hills, flowering in July. Plant forming large clumps. Stems to 1.5m. Basal leaves with 15–19 ovate, cordate, strongly glaucous, leaflets. Flower spikes oblong, to 5.5cm long, erect or nodding, pinkish, with long stamens. Easily grown in rich, moist soil in full or light shade. This species has bold glaucous leaves when well grown, like a smaller version of *Melianthus major*. Hardy to −25°C.

Sanguisorba canadensis L.   Native of NE North America, from Newfoundland west to Michigan and south to Georgia, growing in wet meadows and swamps, flowering in July–October. Plant forming spreading clumps. Stems to 1m (or 2m!). Basal leaves green, with 7–15 ovate to oblong, cordate leaflets. Flower spikes elongated 2.5–15cm long, erect, the flowers at the base of the spike opening first. *S. stipulata* Raf. syn. *S. sitchensis* C. A. Mey from Japan is very similar, and also has narrow spikes of white flowers which open first at the base. It is a smaller plant, to 80cm, with shorter spikes 3–8cm long, usually white or greenish, rarely pinkish. Both are easily grown in good moist soil in sun or partial shade.

Sanguisorba hakusanensis Makino   Native of Honshu, with varieties in Korea, and on Hokkaido, growing in alpine meadows and in moist rock crevices, flowering in June–September. Plant forming clumps with flowering stems 40–80cm. Leaflets 9–13, on stalks 3–7mm long, ovate-oblong or ovate. Flower spikes 4–10cm long, nodding, with stamens 7–10mm long, usually deep pinkish purple. Easily grown in moist soil in a cool position. Hardy to −20°C.

Sanguisorba obtusa Maxim.   Native of Japan, on Mount Hayachine on Honshu, growing in

Sanguisorba hakusanensis at the Royal Botanic Garden, Edinburgh

Sanguisorba alpina

Sanguisorba officinalis

Sanguisorba obtusa

alpine meadows, flowering in August–September. Plant forming small clumps. Stems 30–50cm. Leaflets 13–17, crowded, nearly sessile. Flower spikes 4–7cm long, nodding, with stamens 8–10mm long, usually pink, white in 'Alba'. Easily grown in moist soil in sun or partial shade. Flowering in June–July in SE England. Hardy to −20°C.

Sanguisorba officinalis L. **Great Burnet**
Native of most of N Europe, south to Greece and Turkey, N Asia east to Japan, and North America (naturalized in Maine), growing in meadows and wet grassy places by streams, flowering in June–October. Plant forming large clumps, with stems to 1m. Basal leaves with 9–15 cordate, ovate to orbicular leaflets. Flower spikes erect, short, 1.2–2.5cm long, maroon,

blackish or flesh-red in var. *carnea* (Fisch.) Regel, from E Asia. Easily grown in moist, rich soil. Hardy to −25°C.

Sanguisorba tenuifolia Fisch. var. **alba** Trautv. & Meyer   Native of Japan, in all the islands, growing in meadows and damp places along streams, flowering in August–October. Plant forming small clumps, with stems 80–130cm. Leaflets 11–15, broadly linear to narrowly oblong, usually sessile. Flower spikes 2–7cm long, erect or nodding, narrow (6–7mm thick); flowers white with white stamens, or blood red in var. *purpurea* Trautv. & Meyer. Easily grown in moist soil in sun or partial shade. Var. *tenuifolia* grows in E Siberia, Heilonjiang (Manchuria), Korea and the north Pacific Islands. Hardy to −25°C.

Sanguisorba armena

Primula bhutanica 'Sherriff's Variety' at Sellindge, Kent

Primula bhutanica Fletcher **'Sherriff's Variety'** (s. *Petiolaris*) (*Primulaceae*)   Native of N Assam, E Bhutan and S Xizang, growing in coniferous and mixed forest, on damp mossy banks and under *Rhododendron* at 3000–4300m, flowering in May–June, and in February–March in England. Plant forming clusters of resting buds which open to reveal a mass of white farina-covered buds, then stemless flowers. Leaves, when mature, not floury, to 20cm long or more on well-grown specimens, oblanceolate, acute. Flowers pin-eyed in 'Sherriff's Variety', 2–3cm across, solitary or sometimes many on a short peduncle. This variety was collected by Ludlow & Sherriff in Bhutan and grown for many years in Mrs Sherriff's garden at Ascreavie, Angus; from here it was distributed to many gardens, and grows and increases easily, even in S England. Its main danger is dry heat in summer, and it should be planted so that the sun never shines directly on the leaves, e.g. on the north side of a high wall; frequent watering with a hose to wet the leaves will keep it alive during hot summers. Hardy to −25°C, but safer with snow cover.

Primula heucherifolia Franch. (s. *Cortusoides*) Native of W Sichuan, growing in shady places in bamboo forest, flowering in May–June. Plant stoloniferous with creeping rhizomes. Leaves with an orbicular blade, 7–11 lobed. Stem 15–30cm, with 3–10 nodding flowers. Flowers with a coloured ring in the throat, 1–2.5cm across. For a cool shady position in well-drained soil.

Primula kaufmanniana Regel (s. *Cortusoides*) Native of C Asia, in the Tien Shan and Pamir Alai at 1000–3700m, growing in shady rocky places, flowering May–June. Plant tufted. Leaves with blade 2–8cm long and broad, 9–11 lobed, softly hairy. Stems 8–22cm, with 3–6 flowers in 1 or 2 whorls. Differs from *P. cortusoides* L. in its rounder leaves, and usually smaller flowers. Hardy to −20°C or lower.

Primula kisoana Miq. (s. *Cortusoides*)   Native of C Honshu and Shikoku, growing in woods and shady places in the mountains, flowering in May, but in March–April in England. Plant stoloniferous, far-spreading. Stems 10–15cm, leaves 5–10cm across, softly hairy. Flowers 2–3cm across, with tube 15–20mm long. For semi-shade and leafy soil, in a cool, sheltered position. Hardy to −10°C.

Primula mollis Nutt. ex. Hook. syn. *P. sinomollis* Balf. fil. & Forrest (s. *Cortusoides*) Native of Bhutan, N Assam, N Burma and Yunnan, growing in shady places and scrub by streams at 2300–3300m, flowering in May–July. Plant forming rosettes of rather few softly hairy leaves, with kidney-shaped blades up to 12cm long and wide. Flowering stems to 60cm, with 2–10 whorls of 2–9 flowers. For a shady position in leafy soil. Hardy to −10°C.

Primula moupinensis Franch. (s. *Petiolaris*) Native of W Sichuan, especially above Wolong, Baoxing and Ya-an, growing in wet woods and in moss under shrubs at 2500–3000m, flowering in April–May. Similar to *P. sonchifolia*, but without scales around the resting bud, and with broader, obovate, very thin-textured leaves. Flowers lilac, *c.*1.5cm across.

Primula ovalifolia Franch. (s. *Petiolaris*) Native of NE Yunnan, W Hubei and W Sichuan, especially in the Wolong, Baoxing and Yan-an valleys, and on Omei Shan, growing on very shady or overhanging vertical banks and rocks, at 1200–1800m, flowering in April–May. Plants solitary, up to 20cm across, not forming resting buds; leaves 3–16cm long. Flowers reddish purple, 2–2.5cm across, 2–9 in an umbel, on a delicate stem to 15cm tall. Calyx loose, expanding after flowering. For a very shaded position, humid and warm in summer, dry in winter. Hardy to −10°C perhaps.

Primula polyneura Franch. (s. *Cortusoides*) Native of W China, in Kansu, Sichuan, Yunnan, SE Xizang, growing in woods and shady places at 2300–4300m, flowering in May–June. Plant stoloniferous, spreading. Stems 10–50cm. Flowers 1–2.5cm across with a yellow, greenish-yellow or orange eye, pale pink to crimson, purple or wine-red. Easily grown in moist, leafy soil in partial shade. Probably the hardiest of this group, to −20°C.

Primula sieboldii E. Morren (s. *Cortusoides*) Native of Japan, in S Hokkaido, Honshu and Kyushu, and in Korea, NE China and E Siberia, growing in moist, grassy places by rivers, flowering in April–May. Long cultivated in Japan, with numerous colours, the original wild form being pinkish-purple. Plant with creeping underground rhizomes. Leaves 4–10cm long. Stems 15–40cm with an umbel of 7–20 flowers, 2–3cm across in cultivated forms, 2–2.5cm in the wild. Easily grown in moist, leafy soil in cool sun or partial shade. Many named varieties are in cultivation, most of which were selected in Japan.

Primula sonchifolia Franch. (s. *Petiolaris*) Native of NE Burma and China in SE Xizang, W Sichuan and Yunnan, growing in wet mountain meadows and under *Rhododendron*, at 3300–4600m, flowering in May–July, but as early as February in cultivation in S England. Plant forming tight, pointed, resting buds which may be 5cm across, and covered with scales. Leaves covered with farina at flowering time, later naked, to 35cm when fully grown. Flowers 3–20 in an umbel, pale lavender, purplish, bright blue or 'intense indigo violet', 1.5–2.5cm across, often toothed around the edge. Requires similar conditions to *P. bhutanica*.

Primula sonchifolia from Cluny, Perthshire

Primula kaufmanniana at Ferghana, C Asia

Primula ovalifolia near Wolong, Sichuan

Primula kisoana at the Savill Gardens, Windsor

Primula moupinensis above Ya-an, Sichuan

Primula sieboldii, a white cultivar

Primula polyneura

Primula heucherifolia at Baoxing, Sichuan

Primula mollis

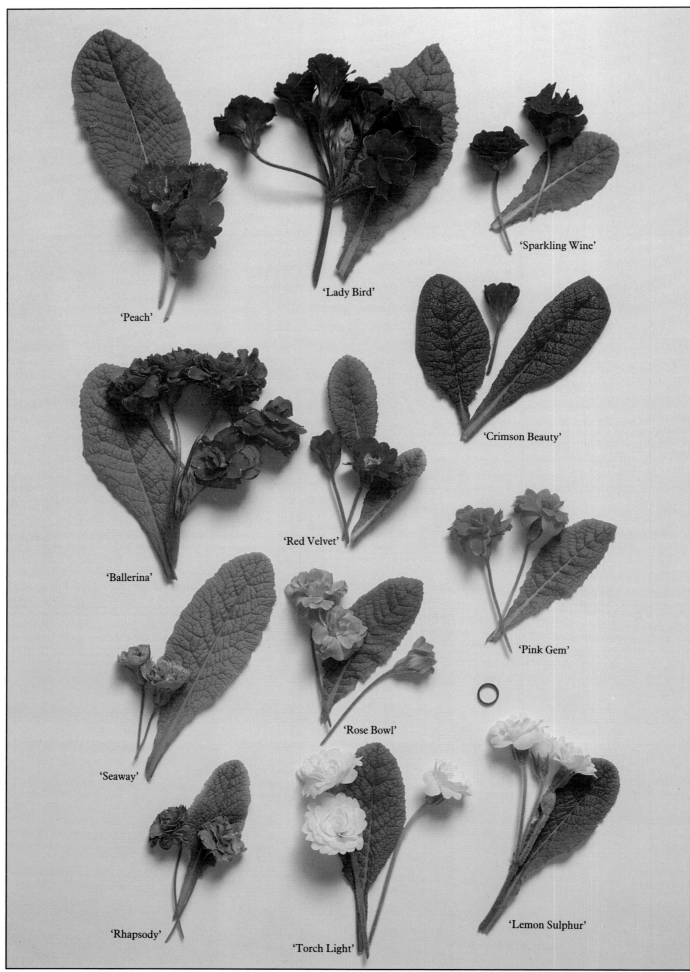

'Peach'

'Lady Bird'

'Sparkling Wine'

'Crimson Beauty'

'Ballerina'

'Red Velvet'

'Pink Gem'

'Seaway'

'Rose Bowl'

'Rhapsody'

'Torch Light'

'Lemon Sulphur'

Specimens from Hopley's Plants, 20 April. ½ life size

Double Primrose 'Fife Yellow'

Pale yellow and flesh pink primrose in an old garden in Kent

Primula vulgaris Huds. (*s. Vernalis*)
(*Primulaceae*) **Primrose**   The wild primrose of
Europe and Turkey is usually pale yellow in
colour but in many old gardens flesh-pink forms
interbreed with the yellow, and the pink form is
said to be common in Pembrokeshire. These are
not the same as the purplish-pink subsp.
sibthorpii from E Europe (see p.153). White
primroses are common in Mallorca (subsp.
balearica), on Andros (var. *pulchella*) and in
parts of the Atlas Mountains (var. *atlantica*), as
well as in cultivation. One good, neat, white
form is 'Gigha White' named after the island in
the inner Hebrides. Forma *viridiflora* Druce is
the name for the plant with a pale-green flower
of somewhat leaf-like texture. It appears
sporadically among populations of normal
primroses, being reported from Argyll and
Somerset, and may be due to infection with a
fungus-like mycoplasm. It remains green in
cultivation, and is not known to be particularly
infectious. Hardy to −25°C.

Double Primroses   Until recently these old-
fashioned double primroses were scarce and
expensive, being slow to propagate and often
poor growers because of virus infection; now
many are being propagated by tissue culture,
which produces healthy stocks at a reasonable
price. Some of the old varieties are shown here,
and some of the new ones, recently brought to
Europe from New Zealand by Dr Barker of
Hopley's Nursery and named in England by
him.
Old varieties
'Alba Plena'   An old double white.
'Double Red'   A large-flowered, double,
pinkish red.
'Fife Yellow'   An unusual brownish-yellow
double. 'Double Sulphur' is paler and even
more striking.
'Red Paddy' syn. 'Sanguinea Plena'   Semi-
double, white edge.
New varieties from Hopley's Plants, introduced
in 1989:
'Ballerina'   Flowers often several on a stout,
polyanthus-like stalk.
'Crimson Beauty'
'Lady Bird'   Flowers often several on a stout
polyanthus-like stalk.
'Lemon Sulphur'   Flowers often several on a
stout, polyanthus-like stalk.
The following have solitary, primrose-type
flowers in various colours: **'Peach'**, **'Pink Gem'**,
'Red Velvet', **'Rhapsody'**, **'Rose Bowl'**,
'Seaway', **'Sparkling Wine'**, **'Torch Light'**.

Double Primrose 'Red Paddy'

Double Primrose 'Double Red'

Primula vulgaris 'Gigha White'

Double Primrose 'Alba Plena'

Primula vulgaris f. *viridiflora*

Primula veris subsp. *macrocalyx* in NW China

Primula veris on chalk downland, Buckinghamshire

Primula megaseaefolia

Primula vulgaris subsp. *sibthorpii* at Wisley

Primula veris at Wye, Kent

Primula vulgaris

Primula luteola at Edinburgh

Primula elatior subsp. *pallasii*

Primula elatior subsp. *meyeri*

Primula elatior subsp. *elatior*

Primula juliae

Primula elatior (L.) Hill subsp. *elatior* Oxlip (s. *Vernalis*) (*Primulaceae*) Native of N Europe, from SE England to Finland and Russia, growing in woods and meadows, flowering in April–June, according to latitude. In England it is characteristic of coppiced woods on glacial clays between London and Cambridge and into E Norfolk, growing in huge numbers in some ancient woods, replacing the common primrose. It has pale-yellow flowers on a stem to 10–30cm. Leaves 10–20cm long, with sparse, curled hairs beneath; flowers 15–25mm across, up to 20 in a 1-sided umbel. Easily grown in shade or partial shade in heavy rich and chalky soil, moist in summer. Hardy to −25°C.

Primula elatior (L.) Hill subsp. *meyeri* (Rupr.) Valentine & Lamond syn. *P. amoena* M. Bieb. Native of the Caucasus, Georgia and NE Turkey, growing on rocks, cliff ledges, on stony, peaty, alpine meadows, on screes and in *Rhododendron* scrub at 1820–4000m, flowering in May–July. Plant forming small clumps of few rosettes. Leaves, when fully grown, 5–15cm long, usually white-woolly beneath. Flowering stem 5–15cm with up to 10 flowers of deep purple, violet-blue or pale lavender, 1.5–2.5cm across. This subspecies is rare in cultivation, but important as the parent of many of the *P.* × *pruhonicensis* hybrids. It needs careful cultivation in well-drained but moist, peaty soil, in sun or partial shade. Hardy to −20°C or less.

Primula elatior (L.) Hill subsp. *pallasii* W. W. Sm. & Forrest   Native of the Urals east to the Altai in C Asia and south to Transcaucasia and Turkey, growing in moist alpine meadows and grassy scrub, at 1900–3200m in Turkey, flowering in May–July. Leaves glabrous or nearly glabrous beneath. Flowers pale yellow, 3–6 in an umbel, similar in general appearance to subsp. *elatior*. Easily grown in heavy soil in partial or deciduous shade.

Primula juliae Kusn. (s. *Vernalis*)   Native of SE Caucasus near Lagodeki, growing in moist shady places by waterfalls, flowering in April–May. Plant forming mats of rounded leaves by its thin, creeping rhizome. Leaves 2–10cm long, the blade usually *c*.3cm across. Flowers pinkish with a yellow tube 2–3cm across. This dwarf and attractive species requires moist, leafy soil and a cool, shady position. It has been the parent of many hybrids (see p.154), of which *P.* 'Wanda' is probably the most familiar. *P. juliae* is named after its discoverer, Mme Julia Ludovikovna Mlokosewitsch, who also found, in the same locality, the familiar yellow paeony which bears her husband's surname.

Primula luteola Rupr. (s. *Farinosae*)   Native of E Caucasus, especially around Tuschetien, growing in moist meadows or by streams at 1400–3000m, flowering in May–June. Plant forming small clumps of a few rosettes,. Leaves 10–30cm, with fine, sharp teeth. Flowering stem 15–35cm, farinose at the apex, with a rather tight umbel of 10–25 flowers. Flowers *c*.1–5cm across with deeply notched lobes. For moist, but well-drained soil in sun or partial shade and a cool summer climate. Hardy to −20°C or less. Related to *P. auriculata* but with a more attractive habit, and always yellow flowers.

Primula megaseifolia Boiss. & Bal. ex Boiss. Native of NE Turkey from Trabzon eastwards to SW Georgia, growing in woods, damp gorges and on shady banks at up to 1100m, flowering in March-April, though often earlier in gardens. Plants forming small clumps. Leaves stalked, the blade cordate at the base, to 15cm long, with reddish-hairy petioles. Flowers to 9 in an umbel, pinkish, with a tube *c*.20mm long. For moist leafy soil in shade. This species should be heat tolerant, provided it is damp and shaded.

Primula veris L. subsp. *macrocalyx* (Bunge) Ludi   Native of S Russia and the Crimea, eastwards to Chinese Turkestan and south to N Iran and Turkey, growing in scrub by streams, in mountain meadows and among rocks, flowering in May–June. Like a rather large Cowslip, but with leaves which narrow gradually into the petiole, a very large, loose, yellowish calyx, and a corolla 19–28mm across. For good soil in sun or partial shade. Very hardy, to −20°C and lower.

Primula veris L. subsp. *veris* (s. *Vernalis*) **Cowslip**   Native of N Europe, from Scotland, Ireland and Spain to W Russia, with other subspecies in the mountains of S Europe, the Caucasus, Italy and Turkey, C Asia as far east as the Altai (subsp. *macrocalyx*), flowering in April–June. Subsp. *veris* is characteristic of dry, grassy slopes on chalk and limestone, the other subspecies of grassy alpine or subalpine meadows and scrub. Stems 10–30cm. Flowers in a one-sided umbel, 8–15mm across; larger in the other subspecies. A popular plant for meadow gardens, but requires full sun and a well-drained alkaline soil to survive well. On cold clay soils, the primrose *P. vulgaris* is more likely to succeed. Plants with large orange or red flowers are common in cultivation and probably contain genes of red-flowered polyanthus. Hardy to −20°C.

Primula vulgaris Huds. subsp. *sibthorpii* (Hoffman.) W. W. Sm. and Forrest   Native of Greece south to Euboea and Ikaria, the Crimea, Bulgaria, Transcaucasia and N Turkey; in Greece and W Turkey grows below 850m in the Mediterranean zone, on shady banks and cliffs, flowering in March–April. In the east of Turkey and Caucasus it is found in hazel groves and meadows in the mountains, at 2200m near Artvin, flowering in May. Flowers usually purplish pink, sometimes red. Leaves often similar to subsp. *vulgaris*, but reported to be more abruptly narrowed to the stalk.

Primula vulgaris Huds. subsp. *vulgaris* (s. *Vernalis*) **Primrose**   Native of W Europe, from Ireland to E Denmark and in the south to the Ukraine, the Crimea and Transcaucasia; also found in Lebanon, Turkey and NW Africa (var. *atlantica* Maide, usually white), growing in woods, shady cliffs and alpine meadows, usually in rather heavy soil, at up to 2100m in Turkey, flowering in January–June. Stems 3–20cm with only one flower. Leaves 2–30cm long; small leaves present at flowering, larger ones produced in early summer. Flowers 2–4cm across, yellow, occasionally white or flesh-pink. Best grown in heavy soil, with shade and moisture in summer. Hardy to −20°C.

Large polyanthus at the Savill Gardens, Windsor

Primrose hybrids There are four main groups of Primrose hybrid cultivars, as follows:
Primula × variabilis (*P. veris × P. vulgaris*) Generally known as Polyanthus, derived from crosses between Primrose and Cowslip. These hybrids are common in the wild where the parents grow together, and have been bred for hundreds of years to give much larger flowers in a wide range of colours, from blue and red to white and yellow.
Primula × pruhonicensis (*P. juliae × (P. elatior × P. vulgaris)*) This cross produces smaller hybrids of more refined form, usually with an umbel of flowers. *P. juliae* was introduced in 1911; the name *pruhonicensis* comes from the village of Pruhonice near Prague, where Count Ernst Silva Tarouca made a fine garden between 1886 and 1937. A pink form, shown here, is often wrongly called *Primula vulgaris sibthorpii*.
Primula × juliana (*P. juliae × P. elatior*) cultivars are smaller than *P. pruhonicensis*, often with only one flower per stalk. 'Wanda' is an old and popular variety of this group.

Primula × pruhonicensis
'Craddock White' Creamy white, with flowers 2.5cm across.
'Enchantress' Flowers larger and more solid than 'Guinivere', *c.*3cm across.
'Guinevere' syn. 'Garryard Guinevere' Probably raised by Mrs Johnson, Kinlough, Co. Leitrim, in Ireland. The original Garryarde primrose, which was named 'Appleblossom', appears to be lost. Stems to 15cm. Leaves bronze. Flowers *c.*2–5cm across.
'Lady Greer' A delicate pale yellow, with flowers 2.5cm across.
'McWatts Claret' An unusual brownish red.
'Tawny Port' A rich dark red. Flowers 2cm across. Close to 'Wanda'.
'Tomato Red' A unique shade of orange-red. Flowers 2–5cm across.
'Wanda' One of the oldest hybrids. Flowers *c.*2cm across.
'Wanda hose-in-hose' A double 'Wanda' with one corolla inside the other.

Primula × polyanthus
'Crescendo Blue' A large-flowered mid-blue, with pale-green leaves. Usually sold as F1 hybrid seed in mixed colours.
'Duckyls Red' Raised by Mrs Hazel Taylor at Duckyls, East Sussex. Fairly similar in habit to 'Cowichan Blue', with rather dark leaves and a small 'eye'.
'Cowichan Blue' With medium-sized flowers, and a small 'eye' to the flower. A fine deep blue, and purple stems; the dark leaves showing the influence of *P. × pruhonicensis*. Raised by Florence Bellis in Oregon, c. 1960, who also raised the Barnhaven strain. Height around 10cm.
'Pacific Giants Mixed' This is a well-known strain of large-flowered polyanthus, in a wide range of colours. 'Paradise' hybrids produce a more interesting selection of colours, including bicolours and semi-doubles.

Polyanthus 'Crescendo Blue'

Polyanthus 'Duckyls Red'

Polyanthus 'Cowichan Blue'

Primula × *pruhonicensis* 'Guinevere'

Primula × *pruhonicensis* (pink form)

'Wanda'

'Enchantress'

'McWatts Claret'

'Wanda hose-in-hose'

'Tomato Red'

'Tawny Port'

'Craddock White'

'Lady Greer'

Primula denticulata subsp. *alta* above Wolong, Sichuan

Primula waltonii at Branklyn, Perth

Primula sikkimensis

Primula alpicola var. *alba*

Primula alpicola var. *violacea*

Primula alpicola

Primula secundiflora at the Cruickshank Botanic Garden, Aberdeen

Primula florindae at Stancombe Park, Gloucestershire

Primula ioessa at the Savill Gardens, Windsor

Primula ioessa

Primula alpicola (W. W. Sm.) Stapf. (s. *Sikkimensis*) (*Primulaceae*)   Native of E Xizang in the Tsangpo valley and of Bhutan, near Thimpu, growing in shady bogs and moist alpine meadows at 3700–4600m, flowering in May. The flower colour is variable in the wild and the three main colours have been given variety names: var. *violacea* (Stapf.) W. W. Sm., flowers purplish; var. *alba* W. W. Sm., flowers white; and var. *luna* Stapf., yellow. Leaves with elliptic to oblong-elliptic blade, 2–8cm across rounded at the base, with a long stalk. Stem 15–90cm, farinose at apex with 1–4 whorls of flowers. Pedicels 1–8cm. Flowers 1.5–2.5cm long, nodding, up to 3cm across, scented. For wet, peaty soil. Hardy to −25°C.

Primula denticulata Smith (s. *Denticulata*) Native of Afghanistan to Bhutan and SE Xizang, growing in scrub, and open grassy slopes, not always by water, at 1500–4500m, flowering in April–June. Stems 3–15cm, elongating during flowering. Flowers 1–2cm across. Leaves to 30cm after flowering. Commonly cultivated and now available in reds, magenta and pink to white, as well as the original mauvish blue. For moist soil in sun or partial shade. Hardy to −25°C. *P. denticulata* subsp. *alta* (Balf. fil. & Forrest) W. W. Sm. & Fletcher, from Burma, east to Yunnan and W Sichuan, differs merely in its usually taller stem at flowering time, as shown here.

Primula florindae Ward (s. *Sikkimensis*) Native of SE Xizang in the Tsangpo basin at *c*.4000m, growing in shady bogs by running water and in streams, flowering in June–August in gardens. One of the largest *Primula* species with leaf blades 4–20cm × 4–15cm, cordate at

the base with long stalks to 30cm; stem 30–120cm with usually 1 umbel of flowers; these are up to 80, yellow or in some areas reddish or amber-orange, with a spicy scent, 1.5–2.5cm long and 1–2cm across. Easily grown in wet soil in shade or partial shade. Hardy to −25°C.

Primula ioessa W. W. Sm. from SE Xizang is similar, but differs in its more deeply toothed leaves, with the blade alternate at the base, and often shorter flowering stems. Its flowers are pinkish, mauve or white.

Primula secundiflora Franch. (s. *Sikkimensis*) Native of Yunnan, notably in the Lijiang mountains, especially in the north and SW Sichuan and E Xizang at 3500–4000m, growing in moist meadows, flowering in June–July. Leaves 3–30cm long; blade 1–4cm broad, oblong to obovate or oblanceolate, tapering into the very short, winged stalk. Stem 10–90cm, with farina towards the apex, with 1 or rarely 2 umbels of 5–20 flowers; these are 1.5–2.5cm long, reddish purple, bell-shaped, nodding. Similar in flower to *P. waltoni*, but distinct in leaf. Hardy to −25°C.

Primula sikkimensis Hook. (s. *Sikkimensis*) Native of Nepal, Sikkim, Bhutan and SE Xizang, east to Yunnan and S Sichuan, growing in wet bogs and by streams at 3300–4400m, flowering in May–July, often covering large areas with a yellow carpet. Leaves with elliptic to oblanceolate blade, 2–7cm across, longer than broad, attenuate at base to a short stalk. Stem 15–90cm, farinose at apex, with 1, rarely 2, whorls of flowers. Pedicels 2–10cm. Flowers 2–3cm long, 1.5–3cm across, yellow, bell-shaped, or more tubular and creamy white in

var. *hopeana* (Balf. fil. & Cooper) from Bhutan and Xizang at 4500–5000m. For wet, peaty soil. Hardy to −25°C.

Primula waltonii Watt (s. *Sikkimensis*)   Native of SE Xizang in the region south of Lhasa and Bhutan, in alpine meadows at up to 5800m, flowering in May–August. Leaves serrate with elliptic-oblong to oblanceolate blade, 2–7cm broad, long cuneate at the base, with a stalk shorter than or equalling the blade. Stem 20–70cm, with one umbel of flowers; these are 1.5–3cm long, 0.5–2cm across, pink to dark lilac or claret purple, funnel-shaped, powdered with farina inside, with a red eye. For moist but well-drained soil in a cool position in full light or partial shade. Hardy to −25°C.

Primula forrestii in the Lijiang mountains, N Yunnan

Primula nivalis near Alma Ata, in the Tien Shan

Primula nivalis

Primula capitata subsp. *sphaerocephala*

Primula capitata Hook. (s. *Capitatae*)
(*Primulaceae*)   Native of Sikkim, S Xizang,
Bhutan, NW Burma and Yunnan, growing in
scrub and grassy places, at 2900–5000m,
flowering in July–September. Leaves to 13 ×
2cm, rugose, denticulate, usually with farina
beneath. Stems 10–45cm, farinose, with a dense
head of flowers 7–10mm across. Subsp.
mooreana W. W. Sm. & Forrest is a large form
from Sikkim, commonly cultivated. Easily
grown in moist, well-drained soil. Remarkable
for its late flowering, often into August in
gardens. Subsp. *sphaerocephala* (Balf. fil. &
Forrest) W. W. Sm. & Forrest is the form from
Yunnan and SE Xizang; it has leaves without
farina and a globular head of more tubular
flowers. Hardy to −25°C.

Primula chionantha Balf. fil. & Forrest (s.
Nivales)   Native of NW Yunnan, especially on
the Chungtien plateau, in alpine meadows at
4000m. Leaves with blade 15–20cm long,
elongating after flowering, usually with yellow
farina. Stem 35–70cm with 1–4 umbels of
flowers. Close to *P. sinopurpurea*, but always
with white flowers. The easiest of the *Nivales*
section to grow, in moist peaty soil in sun or
partial shade. Hardy to −20°C.

Primula flaccida Balakrishnan syn. *P. nutans*
Delavay ex Franch. non Georgi (s.
Soldanelloideae)   Native of W & E Yunnan and
SW Sichuan, especially on the mountains above
Dali, growing in open pine forest and rocky
pastures at 3500m, flowering in June–July.
Leaves to 20 × 5cm, narrowly elliptic, softly
hairy. Stems to 50cm, farinose, with a dense
head of flowers to 5cm long. Largest flowers
2.5cm long and across, spicily scented. The
easiest and one of the largest of the section
Soldanelloideae, easily grown in partially
shaded, moist but well-drained soil. Short-
lived, but easily raised from seed.

Primula forrestii Balf. fil. (s. *Bullatae*)   Native
of Yunnan, mainly on the east side of the
Lijiang range, but also to the west in the
Lankong area, growing on dry limestone rocks
and cliffs in sun or partial shade, at *c*.3000m,
flowering in May. Plants tufted, often forming a
long-lived clump of rosettes. Leaves 6–20cm
long, rather sticky, hairy and aromatic, with the
blade rounded to cordate at the base. Flowers in
an umbel of 10–25, on a stem 15–90cm tall.
P. bullata Franch. is very similar, but has a
farinose calyx and the leaf blade tapering into
the stalk. For a vertical rock or wall face, with
some overhead protection in winter. Hardy to
−15°C, perhaps less if dry.

Primula nivalis Pallas (s. *Nivales*)   Native of C
Asia and S Siberia in the Tein Shan, Alatau and
the Altai; also in NW China and Mongolia, by
streams and on wet scree at 2500m and above,
flowering in May–July. Leaf blade to 16cm
long, oblong, elliptic or oblong lanceolate,
usually with white farina, serrate. Stems to
40cm. Flowers purple, 1.5–2.5cm across.
Difficult to grow, requiring well-drained soil,
wet in summer, dry in winter. Hardy to −25°C.

Primula vialii at Wisley

Primula tsariensis f. *alba*

Primula sinopurpurea Balf. fil. (s. *Nivales*)
Native of SW Xizang and W Yunnan where it is
widespread, and SW Sichuan, growing in moist
alpine meadows at 3000–4000m. Stems usually
c.25cm, but to 75cm in fruit. Leaves 5–35cm
long, 1.5–5cm across, with yellow farina.
Flowers purplish with a white or grey eye, 2.5–
3.5cm across. Not an easy species; best in wet
but well-drained, peaty sandy soil in full sun.

Primula tsariensis W. W. Sm. f. *alba* (s.
Petiolares)   Native of S Xizang and C Bhutan,
growing on damp mountainsides, by streams
and on the edge of bamboo forest, at 3500–
5000m, flowering in May–June. Plant tufted,
with leaves elliptic to ovate-lanceolate, dark
green, shining, without farina. Flowering stem
2–12cm, with 1–8 flowers. Corolla usually deep
purplish, rarely white in f. *alba*, 1.5–3cm
across. For moist, peaty soil in a cool position.
Hardy to −20°C or so.

Primula vialii Delavay ex Franch. (s.
Muscarioides) syn. *P. littoniana* Forrest   Native
of NW Yunnan and SW Sichuan, growing in
marshy fields at up to 2800m, flowering in July–
August. Leaves 20–30cm long, 4–7cm broad,
softly hairy. Stems 30–60cm tall; the
inflorescence usually *c*.8cm long. For moist, but
well-drained soil in a cool position. Hardy to
−20°C.

Primula chionantha

Primula flaccida

Primula sinopurpurea

Primula × chunglenta 'Lillemor'

Primula prolifera

Primula helodoxa

Primula japonica 'Miller's Crimson' (p. 162)

Primula japonica 'Postford White' (p. 162)

Primula japonica (p. 162)

Primula × chunglenta

Primula chungensis

Primula pulverulenta (p. 163)

Specimens from Sandling Park, Kent, 10 May. Life size

Primula 'Inverewe' at Sandling Park, Kent

Primula helodoxa at Sandling Park, Kent

Primula 'Red Hugh'

Primula cockburniana

Primula bulleyana

Primula bulleyana Forrest (*Primulaceae*)
Native of Yunnan, especially the Lijiang range,
growing by streams in wet mountain meadows at
3000–3200m, flowering in June–July. Leaves
12–35cm × 3–10cm with red petioles. Stem to
70cm, with 5–7 whorls of flowers, farinose at the
nodes and on the pedicels. Calyx lobes very
narrow, acute. Flowers orange; red in bud. For
wet, peaty soil. Hardy to −20°C. *P. aurantiaca*
W. W. Sm. & Forrest is from the edges of
streams at *c*.3500m in W Yunnan. It differs in
having less farina, stems to 30cm, and broader,
acute or obtuse calyx lobes.

Primula chungensis Balf. fil. & Forrest Native
of Yunnan, Sichuan and on the borders of Assam
and Bhutan, growing in marshes and in forest at
3000–3200m, flowering in May–June. Leaves
elliptic to oblong or oblong-ovate, shallowly
lobed 10–30cm × 3–10cm, without farina. Stem
to 80cm, farinose at the nodes, with 2–5 whorls of
up to 10 flowers. Pedicels 2cm. Flowers pale
orange 1.5–2cm across, monomorphic or
dimorphic. Early flowering in gardens, and best in
sun or part shade and moist peaty and sandy soil.
Hardy to −15°C. The closely related *P.
cockburniana* has dark-orange flowers, corolla tube
at most twice as long as the calyx, leaves with a
distinct petiole, and flowers always monomorphic.

Primula cockburniana Hemsl. Native of SW
Sichuan, especially around Kangding
(Tatsienlu), growing in marshy alpine meadows
at 2900–3200m, flowering in June–July. Leaves
to 15 × 4cm, with a definite stalk and regularly
finely toothed. Stem slender, to 40cm, farinose at
the nodes with 2–3 whorls of flowers. Flowers
monomorphic, 1.5cm across, with tube 1cm

long. For well-drained but moist soil in partial
shade, usually monocarpic, so must be raised to
seed regularly. Hardy to −20°C.

Primula helodoxa Balf. fil. Native of W
Yunnan, around Tengchung (Tengyueh) and in
NW Burma, growing by streams, in wet
meadows and in heavy clay soil at 2000m,
flowering in June. Leaves to 35 × 7cm, more or
less evergreen. Stem to 120cm with 4–8 whorls of
flowers, with farina at the nodes and on the
pedicels which hang slightly in bud. Flowers
c.2.5cm across, with a tube about 1.5cm long. A
good perennial. Easily grown in moist soil in sun
or partial shade, and can tolerate certain
competition, which makes it one of the best
species in cultivation. Now sometimes
considered conspecific with *P. prolifera* and *P.
smithiana* Craib.

Primula prolifera Wall. Native of the Khasia
hills in Assam. Plant without farina; leaves
evergreen 30 × 60cm; stem to 60cm; with around
4 whorls of flowers; flowers about 2cm in
diameter, produced about 2 weeks earlier than
P. helodoxa.

Candelabra Primula hybrids Many of the
species of the *Candelabra* section can cross freely,
and different colour forms have been raised in
shades of salmon, pale pink and scarlet. Among
the earliest were those raised at Lissadell, then
the garden of Sir Jocelyn Gore-Booth, in Co.
Sligo, by crossing *P. pulverulenta* with *P.
cockburniana*. One of these, 'Red Hugh'
(O'Donnell, brother-in-law of the O'Neill), is
still grown, and comes true from seed.
'Inverewe', also called 'Ravenglass Vermilion', is

Primula bulleyana (Brickell & Leslie 12320)

another bright red, raised from *P. pulverulenta*.
It is very robust, but is sterile and has to be
propagated by division. Beautiful soft colours
appear from the cross between *P. beesiana* and *P.
bulleyana*, including mauve, salmon pink and
creamy yellow. All these hybrid primulas are
easily grown in wet, peaty soil, and flower in
June. *P.* × *chunglenta*, a hybrid of *P. chungensis*
and *P. pulverulenta*, was raised at Wisley in 1929;
its flowers are red, fading to pink. All are hardy
to −20°C.

Primula pulverulenta and 'Bartley Strain' at Littlewood Park, Aberdeenshire

Primula pulverulenta at Sandling Park, Kent

Primula pulverulenta 'Lady Thursby'

Primula beesiana (*Primulaceae*) Forrest
Native of Yunnan, especially the Lijiang
mountains and SW Sichuan, growing in wet
mountain meadows and by streams at *c*.2600m,
flowering in July–August. Leaves to 22 × 6cm at
flowering; in fruit to 40cm. Stems to 75cm, with
2–8 whorls of flowers, farinose at the nodes.
Pedicels 1–3cm, not or slightly farinose. Flowers
with orange tube and 'rose-carmine' petals with
yellow eye, *c*.2cm across, deeply emarginate.
Differs from *P. pulverulenta* in having leaves
ovate-lanceolate, broadest near the middle, and
yellow- not red-eyed flowers. Hardy to −20°C.

Primula burmanica Balf. fil. & Ward   Native of
NE upper Burma and NW Yunnan, growing in
meadows and wet forests at rather low altitudes,
flowering in July–August. Leaves oblanceolate,
to 30 × 8cm. Stems to 60cm, without farina, with
up to 6 whorls of 10–18 flowers, on pedicels
c.2cm. Flowers purplish with a yellow eye,
dimorphic. Close to *P. beesiana* but differs by
being without farina except on the inside of the
calyx. A good plant for a wet position in shade or
partial shade. Hardy to −15°C.

Primula ianthina Balf. fil. & Cave   Native of
the Himalayas in Sikkim, growing in damp
meadows and scrub at *c*.3200m, flowering in
June–August. Plant forming rosettes of
oblanceolate leaves up to 25cm long, usually
c.15cm. Flowering stem to 60cm, powdered at
the nodes with yellowish farina, with 1–3 whorls
of up to 12 violet or pinkish flowers, 1.5–2cm
across, with wide corolla lobes. Less easy to
grow than others of the group. For moist soil,
preferably by a stream on a slope. Hardy to
−20°C or so.

Primula japonica A. Gray. (s. *Candelabra*)
Native of Japan on all the islands and in
Taiwan, growing along streams in the
mountains, flowering in June–July. Plant
without farina, except on the inside of the calyx.
Leaves to 25 × 8cm, obovate-oblong to broadly
spathulate. Stems to 50cm, with up to 6 whorls
of flowers; flowers monomorphic, 2cm across,
usually purplish red, but white in the form
'Postford White', the seed of which comes true.
'Miller's Crimson' is a good red, with less
magenta in it than the usual form (p. 160). A
good perennial, easily grown in partial shade, in
rich heavy soil; in sun the flowers tend to bleach
in an ugly way. Hardy to −20°C.

Primula ianthina

Primula beesiana

Primula wilsonii at the Royal Botanic Garden, Edinburgh

Primula japonica 'Miller's Crimson'

Primula poissonii (Brickell & Leslie 12307)

Primula japonica 'Postford White'

Primula poissonii Franch.   Native of Yunnan, where it is common especially above Dali and in Sichuan, growing by streams and springs at 2000–3000m, flowering in May–July. Similar to *P. anisodora*, but plant not scented, without farina. Leaves silvery, evergreen, oblong-obovate to 18cm × 4cm. Stem to 45cm with 2–6 whorls of flowers. Flowers purplish to crimson, with a yellow eye, flat, 2–3cm across. Calyx with red lines, and lobed to ⅓ to ½, with large teeth. For moist soil in full sun or partial shade, and wet but well-drained soil. Hardy to −20°C.

Primula pulverulenta Duthie   Native of W Sichuan near Kanding (Tatsienlu), growing in wet places and by streams, flowering in June–July. Leaves to 30 × 10cm obovate or oblanceolate, dentate. Stem to 100cm, covered with farina, as are the pedicels and calyx, with *c.*10 whorls of flowers. Flowers 2–3cm across, dimorphic, red with a dark eye, or pink in 'Bartley Strain'. 'Lady Thursby' is a good, pale selection of the 'Bartley Strain'. For wet, peaty soil. Hardy to −25°C.

Primula wilsonii Dunn syn. *P. poissonii* subsp. *wilsonii* (Dunn) W. W. Sm. & Forrest   Native of Yunnan and W Sichuan especially around Kanding, in wet places in the mountains. Plant aromatic, less silvery than *P. poissonii*. Leaves evergreen, oblanceolate up to 20 × 5cm, rounded at apex. Stem to 90cm, with 3–6 whorls of flowers, which are up to 1.5cm across, with short calyx teeth. For moist but well-drained soil. Hardy to −25°C.

Primula burmanica at Sandling Park, Kent

Armeria pseudarmeria

Armeria alliacea at Edington, Wiltshire

Anagallis monellii in SW Spain

Cortusa matthioli

Anagallis monellii L. syn. *A. linifolia* L.
(*Primulaceae*)   Native of Portugal and S, SE &
C Spain, growing in open pine woods, vineyards
and waste places, or as here on sand dunes,
flowering in March–May, but in July–
September in gardens. Stems 10–50cm long,
sprawling; flowers 1–2cm across, usually blue
with a reddish eye, or brilliant red in 'Sunrise'.
For well-drained soil, in a warm, dry position,
probably hardy only to − 10°C and best raised
from cuttings taken in late summer and
wintered under cover.

Armeria alliacea (Cav.) Hoffman. & Link syn.
A. plantaginea Willd. (*Plumbaginaceae*)
Native of W Europe, from Jersey, France and
Germany, south to Spain, Portugal and Italy,
growing in dry meadows, often in the
mountains, flowering in June–September.
Plant forming small clumps of narrowly
oblanceolate or linear spathulate leaves 50–
130mm long, 3–14mm wide. Flower stems 20–
50cm, with heads 1–2cm across, with brownish
or reddish bracts. Petals purplish, reddish,
pink or white. Easily grown in well-drained soil
in full sun. Hardy to − 20°C. The varieties of *A.
maritima* (Mill.) Willd., the common thrift, are
more suitable for the rock garden, and always
have narrow leaves to 2.5mm wide.

Armeria pseudarmeria (Murray) Mansfield
syn. *A. latifolia* Willd.   Native of C Portugal,
on the Cabo da Roca, growing on grassy granite
slopes near the sea, flowering in May–June.
Plant with stout, branched stems from the base,
forming dense clumps. Leaves 10–20cm long,
15–20mm wide, flat. Flowering stems 25–
50cm, with flower heads 3–4cm across. Flowers
usually white, also pink in cultivation. Hardy to
− 15°C perhaps.

Cortusa matthioli L. syn. *C. altaica* A. Los.
(*Primulaceae*)   Native of Europe, from the SW
Alps in France, east to Bulgaria, the Urals and
across Siberia to the Altai in Mongolia and N
China (Sinjiang) with var. *yezoensis* in Japan,
growing in shady places and rocky woods in the
mountains, usually on limestone, flowering in
April–June. Plant forming small clumps of
rounded leaves to 25cm tall; blade up to 12cm
across. Flowers 5–20 in an umbel, *c.* 1cm long.
For moist, very loose leafy soil in partial shade.
Hardy to − 20°C or less.

Dodecatheon clevelandii Greene
(*Primulaceae*)   Native of W California, from
San Francisco south to N Baja California,
growing in grassy places below 600m, flowering
in January–April. Roots white, without bulbils.

Leaves 5–11cm long, oblanceolate, toothed and
with wavy margins. Stems 18–40cm, with an
umbel of 5–16 flowers. Petals 10–20mm long. An
early flowering species for heavy soil, moist in
spring, dry in summer. Hardy to − 10°C.

Dodecatheon meadia L. **Shooting Star**
Native of E North America, from Pennsylvania
west to Manitoba, and south to Georgia and
Texas, growing in prairies and on moist cliffs,
flowering in April–May. Plant with white roots,
forming small clumps of stems 20–60cm tall.
Leaves oblong to ovate, 7.5–30cm long. Flowers
1.8–3cm long, pale pink, purplish or white in f.
album Macbride, shown here. For rich, moist
soil in sun or partial shade, kept moist in
summer. Hardy to −20°C or less.

Dodecatheon pulchellum (Raf.) Merr. syn. *D.
radicatum* Greene   Native of W North America,
from Alaska south to Wisconsin, in the Rockies,
and to N Mexico and in the E Sierra Nevada,
growing in marshes and wet meadows and open
woods at up to 3000m, flowering in April–May.
Plant with white roots, forming clumps of
upright stems to 50cm. Leaves 4–25cm long,
oblanceolate to ovate. Umbel with 2–25 flowers,
the petals 9–20mm long, magenta to pale purple.
For well-drained or moist soil in sun. Hardy to
−20°C.

Fauria crista-galli (Menzies ex Hook.) Mak.
syn. *Nephrophyllidium crista-galli* (Menzies ex
Hook.) Gilg. (*Menyanthaceae*)   Native of Japan
in Hokkaido and Honshu, of the Kurile Islands
and NW North America, on the Olympic
peninsula, growing in damp meadows, flowering
in June–August. Plant forming dense mats of
rather fleshy leaves to 30cm tall, but usually
*c.*20cm. Blade 4–10cm across. Flowering stem is
15–40cm, with a rounded head of flowers
*c.*12mm across without the ciliate petals of
Menyanthes. For moist, peaty soil in a cool
position or partial shade. Hardy to −20°C or less.

Hottonia palustris L. (*Primulaceae*) **Water
Violet**   Native of most of Europe, from
Scotland and Sweden east to Siberia, south to C
Italy, Romania and NW Turkey, growing in
fresh water, in ponds (sometimes seasonal) and
ditches, flowering in April–June. Submerged
leaves soft, in whorls, deeply pinnately divided
into linear lobes, to 10cm long. Flowering stems
emerging from the water, to 40cm long. Flowers
2–2.5cm across, in 3–9 whorls. A beautiful plant
for a small pond requiring pure, more or less
neutral water, unshaded, becoming rare in the
wild because of pollution and the draining of
ponds. It can tolerate partial drying out in

Hottonia palustris

Hottonia palustris near Wye, Kent

Dodecatheon clevelandii

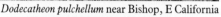

Dodecatheon pulchellum near Bishop, E California

Menyanthes trifoliata

summer, when it forms tight rosettes of bright green feathery leaves, on wet mud.

Menyanthes trifoliata L. (*Menyanthaceae*) **Bogbean** or **Buckbean**   Native to the whole of the Northern Hemisphere, from Ireland and most of Europe to Japan, and in North America from Alaska to Greenland, south to California in the Sierra Nevada, to Nebraska and to Long Island, growing in bogs and on the margins of lakes, ponds and canals, flowering in April–July, and sometimes later. Plant wide spreading by long–creeping, thick, surface rhizomes. Leaves 3-foliate, bean-like, fleshy, to 4–8cm long. Flowering stems to 40cm. Flowers *c*.15mm across, pink in bud, white when open, with long-ciliate petals. Easily grown in wet, peaty soil or shallow water. Hardy to −25°C.

Fauria crista-galli at Wisley

Dodecatheon meadia f. *album*

165

Polemonium caeruleum at Sellindge, Kent

Polemonium caeruleum subsp. *himalayanum* at Gadsar, Kashmir

Polemonium acutiflorum Willd. var.
nipponicum (Kit.) Ohwi (*Polemoniaceae*)
Native of Norway eastwards to N Russia,
Siberia and the Kurile Islands, with var.
nipponicum in the mountains of Honshu,
growing in damp scrub, by rivers and meadows,
flowering in July–August, earlier in cultivation.
Plant forming tufts of basal leaves, with leafy
stems 40–80cm, usually with not more than 8
pairs of leaflets. Flowers stalked, rather few in a
loose head, 18–22mm long. For moist peaty soil
and a cool position in sun or partial shade.
Hardy to −20°C.

Polemonium caeruleum L.   Native of N & C
Europe from Scotland and France eastwards
across Siberia, to the Himalayas and of W North
America from Alaska to the Sierra Nevada in
California, and in the Rockies (subsp.
amygdalinum), flowering in May–August. Very
variable, but with usually rather few stems to
120cm from a tufted rootstock. Stems usually
glandular above, and leafy. Flowers rotate,
8–15mm long, usually blue, lobes ovate, usually
rounded. Easily grown in a good moist soil in
full sun or partial shade. Hardy to −20°C and
below. Easily raised from seed, and sometimes
said to become a pest through self-seeding. This
should also be a good plant for the wild garden
as it survives in lush grass. Several subspecies or
closely related species are cultivated: subsp.
himalayanum (Baker) Hara is a delicate plant,
found in damp places among rocks from
Pakistan to W Nepal, at 2400–3700m. Stems
30–100cm. Flowers to 2cm long. Like *P.
acutiflorum*, but with more leaflets.

Polemonium carneum A. Gray   Native of
California, around San Francisco north to
Washington, growing in scrub and grassy
places, near the coast and in the hills up to
1800m, flowering in April–August. Plant
forming slowly spreading mats, with glandular-
pubescent flowering stems 40–80cm tall, usually
less in cultivation. Leaves with the 3 terminal
leaflets often joined at the base. Flowers
1–2.5cm across, purplish to pink. For a sunny
position and well-drained, leafy soil; tolerant of
summer drought. Hardy to −10°C, perhaps
lower. Crossed with *P. reptans* this has
produced the very pretty 'Lambrook Manor'.

Polemonium foliosissimum A. Gray   Native
of Colorado, Utah, New Mexico and Arizona,
growing in moist places by streams in the
mountains, flowering in July. Stems few from a
tufted rootstock up to 100cm tall, pubescent.
Leaflets elliptic to oblong-ovate. Flowers
purplish, 12–15mm long, the petals obtuse or
mucronate. Easily grown in a good garden soil.
Hardy to −20°C or below.

Polemonium pauciflorum S. Wats.   Native of
SE Arizona and N Mexico, growing along
streams in the mountains at 2000–3000m,
flowering in June–August. Plant with few
stems, 30–45cm from a thin rootstock. Leaflets
lanceolate; flowers 4cm long, with a long,
narrow tube, pale yellow. For rather moist, but
well-drained soil in sun or partial shade. Hardy
to −20°C or so. An elegant, quiet plant with its
hanging tubular flowers. *P. flavum* Green, also
from Arizona, has brighter-yellow flowers,
without a long tube, and acuminate lobes.

Polemonium reptans L. **Greek Valerian**
Native of E North America, from New York to
Minnesota, south to Kansas and Georgia,
growing in woods, flowering in April–May.

Polemonium acutiflorum var. *nipponicum*

Polemonium × richardsonii at Alford, Aberdeenshire

Polemonium pauciflorum

Polemonium carneum

Polemonium foliosissimum

Plant with a short rootstock and spreading usually glabrous stems up to 30cm. Leaflets oblong, ovate-oblong or lanceolate-oblong. Flowers 10–16mm across, blue. For leafy soil in sun or partial shade. Hardy to −20°C. There are several named cultivars of this species, such as 'Sapphire', 'Pink Beauty' and 'Blue Pearl'.

Polemonium × richardsonii Graham   The hybrid between *P. caeruleum* and *P. reptans*, forming clumps of shortly creeping rhizomes, and with numerous glandular-pubescent stems to 25cm. Flowers *c*.2.5cm across, pale blue or white in 'Album'. For good soil in sun or partial shade, moist in summer and probably best split and replanted every 3 years or so. Hardy to −20°C.

Polemonium reptans 'Sapphire'

Polemonium reptans

Hackelia setosa near Silver Lake, California

Borago pygmaea

Hackelia uncinata in Kashmir

Myosotis sylvatica

Myosotis scorpioides

Borago pygmaea (DC.) Chater & W. Greuter, syn. *B. laxiflora* Poiret (*Boraginaceae*) Native of Corsica, Sardinia and the island of Capraia (NE of Elba), growing in shady, rocky places, especially rampant after forest fires, flowering in May–July. Plant with a rosette of obovate, bristly leaves and several branched creeping and ascending stems to 60cm. Flowers pale blue, nodding, 5–8mm long. For a warm but partially shaded position, moist in summer. Hardy to −10°C, but often self-seeding if killed by frost. The unfortunate change of name is caused by Poiret's oversight of De Candolle's *Campanula pygmaea*, which was really this borage!

Hackelia setosa (Piper) Jtn. (*Boraginaceae*) Native of California, in the coast ranges from Lake Co. northwards, and in the Sierra Nevada, from Sierra Co. north to Oregon, growing in open grassy places in the conifer forest zone at 300–1800m, flowering in June–July. Plant forming dense clumps of upright stems to 50cm. Basal leaves bristly-hairy, linear-oblanceolate, blunt, upright, 5–10cm long. Flowers blue, 10–15mm across. For well-drained, sandy soil in sun or partial shade. Hardy to −15°C perhaps.

Hackelia uncinata (Royle ex Benth.) C. Fisher Native of the Himalayas from Pakistan to SW China, growing in open places in forest and in scrub, at 2700–4200m, flowering in June–August. Perennial with few upright stems from a stout rootstock. Basal leaves long-stalked, ovate, acuminate, with a cordate base. Stems 30–60cm, branched. Flowers to 1.3cm across, pale blue. Fruits hooked, with bristles. For a rather dry position in leafy soil and partial shade. Hardy to −20°C or less?

Myosotis scorpioides L. (*Boraginaceae*) **Water Forget-me-not** Native of most of N Europe, south to Romania and the Crimea, east across Siberia to N India, and as an escape from cultivation in E North America south to New York, Pennsylvania and Tennessee, in California, and in Japan. It grows in streams, by rivers and lakes and in marshes, flowering in May–September. Plant forming mats of creeping and rooting stems in shallow water or on wet soil, with yellowish-green, rather fleshy leaves. Flowering stems up to 100cm, usually *c.*30cm. Flowers 5–10mm across, bright blue. A beautiful and long-lived perennial with a long flowering season, growing by water or in moist borders, and easily propagated by planting rooted shoots. Hardy to −20°C or less.

Myosotis sylvatica Hoffm. **Forget-me-not** Native of most of Europe and SW Asia eastwards to the Himalayas and Japan, growing in open woods, flowering in May–June. Plant tufted with several ascending stems to 45cm from a central rootstock, usually short-lived, often biennial. Plant rather bristly-hairy, with dark-green leaves. Flowers up to 8mm across, pale blue or rarely white, and often pink if the plants are moved while in flower. For any moist soil in sun or partial shade; often disfigured by powdery mildew in dry conditions. Hardy to −20°C. Self-seeds freely.

Omphalodes cappadocica 'Cherry Ingram' at Washfield Nurseries, Kent

Omphalodes cappadocica (Willd.) DC.
(*Boraginaceae*)   Native of Soviet Georgia and
NE Turkey west to Ordu, growing on shady
rocks and cliffs and by streams in forests of
chestnut, hazel or other deciduous trees, at up
to 1000m, flowering March–May. Vegetative
stems, produced in summer, shortly creeping;
flowering stems 10–15cm. Leaves ovate,
cordate; blade 4.5–9cm, to 5cm wide. Flowers
4–8mm across. A delicate and beautiful plant;
evergreen, but with leaves killed by hard frosts.
Two slightly hardier clones have been selected:
'Anthea Bloom' survives well in the open in
England.
'Cherry Ingram' with narrower leaves than
usual and good large flowers. A typical large leaf
can have a lanceolate blade 17 × 4.8cm, long-
acuminate and barely cordate. All forms,
however, are best in a sheltered position in
partial shade, with protection from frost.

Omphalodes moupinense Franch.   Native of
W China, especially Sichuan, growing in scrub
and damp shady places, at *c*.2000m, flowering
in May. Plant with a few broadly heart-shaped
basal leaves and trailing flowering stems to
20cm. Flowers *c*.8mm across, pale blue. For
moist, leafy soil in shade and shelter. Hardy to
−15°C.

Omphalodes verna Moench.   Native of the SE
Alps, south to the Apennines in C Italy, and C
Romania, but often naturalized elsewhere in W
& C Europe, growing in damp mountain woods,
flowering in March–May. Vegetative stems
long-creeping. Leaves with ovate to cordate
blade, 5–20cm × 2–6cm, mucronate or
acuminate. Flowering stems 5–20cm. Flowers
8–10mm across. Requires a moist shady
position: because of its creeping stems and
usually smaller flowers, this is less showy than
O. cappadocica. A white-flowered form is
known in cultivation. Hardy to −15°C.

Omphalodes moupinense at Wolong, Sichuan

Omphalodes verna at Wisley, Surrey

Echium russicum with *Stipa* on the Steppes near Stavropol, S Russia

Echium russicum J. F. Gmelin syn. *E. rubrum* Jacq. (*Boraginaceae*)   Native of E Europe, from Austria southwards to Bulgaria and NW Turkey, and eastwards to Russia, the Caucasus and NE Turkey, growing on grassy steppes, open pine forest and rocky hills, at up to 2200m in Turkey, flowering in June–July. Plant with several stems to 60cm, but usually *c.*30cm, from a deep rootstock. Leaves lanceolate to narrowly elliptical. Flowers 9–12mm long, dark red with 4–5 exserted stamens. Although this is usually described as a biennial, it has proved reliably perennial at Edington, Wilts., and flowered for several years, planted in well-drained sandy soil in full sun. Hardy to −20°C or less.

Symphytum asperum Lepechin syn. *S. orientale* L. p.p. (*Boraginaceae*)   Native of NE Turkey, the Caucasus, N & NW Iran, growing in spruce forests, meadows, by streams and in scrub, at up to 2200m in Turkey, flowering in May–August. Plant with upright stems to 1.2m, from a deep rootstock. Lower leaves cordate or rounded at the base. Flowers at first pink, later blue or purplish, 12–15mm long. For moist, deep, rich soil in sun or partial shade. Hardy to −20°C.

Symphytum caucasicum M. Bieb.   Native of the Caucasus, growing in waste places, by streams, in scrub and on grassy roadsides, flowering in April– July. A very invasive plant, spreading by slender underground rhizomes, producing rosettes of leaves and upright, then sprawling, stems to 1m. Flowers pure blue, to 12mm long. For any good soil in sun or partial shade. This plant will smother anything but the largest perennials, but is very pretty for a long season, flowering again in late summer if the old stems are cut down.

Symphytum ibericum Stev. syn. *S. grandiflorum* auct. non DC.   Native of NE Turkey and Soviet Georgia, growing on shady banks and in *Rhododendron* scrub at up to 1350m in Turkey, flowering in March–July. Plant with creeping stolons forming extensive patches. Stems 15–40cm. Leaves ovate to ovate-lanceolate, sub-cordate or rounded at the base, stalked. Flowers cream, 14–16mm long, rarely pinkish, with a small calyx 3–6mm long. 'Hidcote Pink' is a form with good pink flowers, possibly a hybrid. 'Variegatum' has leaves very irregularly marked with cream. For moist or shady places; hardy to −20°C or so. The true *S. grandiflorum* DC., from the Caucasus, has large flowers, the calyx 6–8mm, the corolla 20–24mm long.

Symphytum orientale L.   Native of S Russia and the Caucasus, west to Istanbul and NW Turkey, growing on shady stream banks in pine

Symphytum × uplandicum 'Variegatum'

forest at up to 1500m in Turkey, flowering in April–June. Stems upright to 70cm. Leaves ovate or oblong-ovate, shortly hairy, not bristly. Calyx 6–9mm, divided to ⅓ or ½. Corolla 15–17mm long, pure white. *S. kurdicum* Boiss. & Hausskn. from SE Turkey, N Iraq and W Iran has white flowers 16–19mm long, but thinner, more bristly leaves. It is similar in habit. Both are attractive early-flowering species, tolerant of dry shade. Hardy to −15°C, perhaps less.

Symphytum 'Rubrum'   This is possibly a hybrid between *S. ibericum* and *S. officinale* and has rather small flowers of a good red, on upright stems.

Symphytum tuberosum L.   Native of Europe, from Scotland, where it is common in the east, south to France and Spain, and east to Russia and Turkey, growing in woods, scrub and by rivers, flowering in May–June. Plant creeping to form extensive patches, with a tuberous rhizome. Stems arching 15–40cm, little branched. Flowers pale yellow, 15–20mm long, the scales not exserted, as they are in *S. bulbosum* C. Schimper. Easily grown in shade or a cool position in sun. Early flowering, and dormant in summer. Hardy to −20°C or so.

Symphytum × uplandicum Nyman **'Variegatum'**   *S. × uplandicum* is the hybrid between *S. asperum* and *S. officinale*. It is naturalized over much of N Europe, and is usually found by roadsides and in waste places in damp soil. The flowers are usually pinkish, becoming purple or blue as they mature, and 12–18mm long. The variegated form is especially beautiful in autumn and spring, when the basal leaves are fresh, as shown here. Hardy to −20°C or less.

Symphytum orientale

Symphytum caucasicum at Sellindge, Kent

Symphytum tuberosum at Alford, Aberdeenshire

Symphytum asperum

Symphytum 'Hidcote Pink'

Symphytum ibericum

Symphytum 'Rubrum'

Anchusa azurea 'Opal'

Anchusa azurea near Ronda, S Spain

Anchusa azurea 'Opal' (foreground) and 'Loddon Royalist' (background)

Lithodora diffusa in S Spain

Cynoglossum nervosum at Dali, Yunnan

Alkanna tinctoria in S France

Alkanna tinctoria (L.) Tausch (*Boraginaceae*)
Native of S Europe, from Spain and France
eastwards to Romania, Turkey, Syria and North
Africa, growing in rocky places, open woods,
scrub, steppes and sand dunes at up to 1300m,
flowering in April–July. Plant with several
spreading or creeping stems to 30cm long, from
a central rootstock which exudes deep-reddish
juice when bruised. Leaves greenish or greyish,
1–7cm long. Flowers blue, 4–10mm across. For
well-drained sandy soil in a hot dry position.
Hardy to −10°C, perhaps less.

Anchusa azurea Mill. syn. *A. italica* Retz
(*Boraginaceae*)   Native of Europe, from
France, Spain and Portugal eastwards, North
Africa and Turkey, eastwards to Iran and
Arabia and into C Asia, growing on the edges of
arable fields, by roadsides, and on steppes and
stony hills, up to 2500m, flowering in May–
July. A common and conspicuous plant of
roadsides throughout the Mediterranean region
and C Asia. Plant with upright stems to 1.5m,
from a stout rootstock. Leaves 10–30cm long.
Flowers purplish or deep blue, 10–15mm
across. There are many named cultivars,
propagated by root cuttings: 'Loddon Royalist'
is a good deep blue, and 'Opal' is rather shorter
and paler. 'Little John' is only 45cm tall. All are
short-lived perennials requiring deep but well-
drained soil, and tolerant of drought. Hardy to
−15°C, perhaps lower.

Cynoglossum nervosum Benth. & Hook.
(*Boraginaceae*)   Native of the Himalayas from
Kumaon to Yunnan, growing on grassy banks,
and by rice fields, flowering in April–August.
Stems several to 60cm, from a stout rootstock.
Basal leaves narrowly lanceolate to 30cm long.
Flowers *c.*10mm across. For well-drained soil in
full sun. Graham Thomas recommends not too
good soil for this, or the stems will flop, and I
have found it tricky and short-lived in heavy
soil. Hardy to −15°C, possibly less. *C. amabile*
Stapf. & Drummond from Yunnan and
Sichuan, is closely related, but is usually
biennial, with larger, paler-blue flowers.

Lindelofia longiflora (Benth.) Baillon
(*Boraginaceae*)   Native of the Himalayas, from
Pakistan to W Nepal, and common in Kashmir,
growing on open, grassy slopes, at 3000–3600m,
flowering in June–August. Plant forming
patches of upright stems to 60cm or more from a
rhizome. Basal leaves long-stalked, lanceolate.
Stem leaves narrowly lanceolate, clasping the
stem at the base. Flowers deep blue to purple,
up to 1.5cm across. For well-drained, rich and
moist soil in full sun. Hardy to −20°C, possibly
less.
L. anchusoides (Lindl.) Lehm. has upper leaves
narrowed to the base, not clasping, and bright-
blue flowers.

Lithodora diffusa (Lagasca) Johnson syn.
Lithospermum diffusum Lagasca (*Boraginaceae*)
Native of W France, Spain and Portugal,
growing in pine woods, heathery scrub, and
sand dunes, flowering in March–June. Plant
sprawling to 1m or more, with creeping and
rooting stems, subshrubby at the base. Leaves
linear to oblong or elliptical. Flowers up to
20mm long. This species is commonly grown as
a rock garden plant, but is happiest on a heathy
bank in acid soil or sprawling among low shrubs
or heather. The commonest cultivar is 'Heavenly
Blue', with deep-blue flowers. 'Cambridge Blue'
is a very pale-blue form; there is also a rare white,
'Alba'. 'Grace Ward', an old variety, is said to
be lime-tolerant, unlike the other varieties,
which prefer acid soil. Hardy to −20°C.

Lindelofia longiflora near Vishensar, Kashmir

Lithospermum purpureocaeruleum

Lithospermum purpureocaeruleum L. syn.
Buglossoides purpureocaerulea (L.) Johnston
(*Boraginaceae*)   Native of most of Europe, from
England where it is rare and found on limestone
only in S Wales, N Somerset and S Devon, to
Spain and east to Russia and Turkey, the
Caucasus and N Iran, growing in scrub and
maquis, and on the edges of woods, flowering in
March–June. Plant forming spreading colonies
from a creeping rhizome, with ascending
flowering stems to 60cm, and long, spreading
sterile shoots. Leaves 3.5–8cm long. Flowers
14–20mm long, opening purple, becoming deep
blue. For dry soil in a warm position in partial
shade. Hardy to −20°C or less.

Lithodora 'Heavenly Blue'

Antirrhinum australe on a road cutting near Ronda, S Spain

Antirrhinum 'Black Prince'

Scrophularia auriculata 'Variegata'

Asarina procumbens

Scrophularia sambucifolia among limestone rocks in S Spain

Synthyris missurica

Mimulus ringens at Beth Chatto's garden

Parahebe perfoliata

Antirrhinum australe Rothm.
(*Scrophulariaceae*) Native of S & SE Spain,
growing on limestone rocks and walls, flowering
in April–June. Plant with several upright stems
to 120cm. Leaves opposite or in whorls of 3.
Flowers 40–45mm long, usually pinkish purple,
with pedicels shorter than the bracts. Although
they are usually grown as annuals, most
Antirrhinum species are perennial, and of the 17
or so species, 16 are found in Spain. *A. majus* L.,
from which the cultivated forms have been
bred, is found in S Europe, from Spain and
North Africa to Italy: it usually has pinkish-
purple flowers.
'Black Prince', shown here, is an old perennial
cultivar which flowers throughout the summer.
It has dark-purple leaves, and forms a low bush
about 30cm in diameter. *A. graniticum* Rothm.
usually has white flowers on pedicels longer
than the bracts, and is found in Spain and
Portugal on acid rocks. In cultivation the
perennials require very well-drained, poor soil.
Hardy to −10°C, perhaps less if kept dry.

Asarina procumbens Mill. syn. *Antirrhinum
asarina* L. (*Scrophulariaceae*) Native of S
France and NE Spain, growing on shady acid
rocks in the mountains, flowering in June–
September. Plant with trailing stems to 30cm or
more. Leaves *c*.5 × 6cm, softly sticky-hairy.
Flowers 30–35mm long. Easily grown in rather
dry, shady places, in sandy soil. Hardy to
−10°C, possibly less, i.e. it survives outdoors in
S England, with overhead protection.

Mimulus ringens L. (*Scrophulariaceae*) **Square-
stemmed Monkey-flower** Native of E North
America, from Nova Scotia south to Virginia and
west to Manitoba, Nebraska and Texas, growing
in wet places and along streams, flowering in
June–September. Stems upright to 1m, from a
tufted rootstock. Leaves sessile, auriculate at the
base, to 10cm long. Flowers pale purplish blue,
rarely white, *c*.2.5cm long and wide. For good
wet soil in sun or partial shade. Hardy to −20°C
or less. Other species of *Mimulus* are shown in
vol. 2, pp. 116–7.

Parahebe perfoliata (R. Br.) B. G. Briggs syn.
Veronica perfoliata R. Br. (*Scrophulariaceae*)
Native of SE Australia, especially on Mount
Victoria and on the Blue Mountains, flowering in
early summer. Plant with a subshrubby base and
trailing, sparingly branched stems to 75cm.
Leaves *c*.5cm across. Flowers 6mm across. For a
warm, sheltered position in full sun, looking best
sprawling through low shrubs. Hardy to −10°C.

Scrophularia auriculata L. '**Variegata**' syn. *S.
aquatica* auct. (*Scrophulariaceae*) Native of
most of Europe and North Africa eastwards to
Crete, growing in damp places, usually by
streams and rivers, flowering in June–
September. Plant with several upright, 4-winged
stems to 100cm. Leaves simple or with 1 or 2
pairs of small lobes. Flowers 7–9mm long,
brownish and much visited by wasps. The
variegated leaves are very beautiful from spring
onwards.

Scrophularia sambucifolia L.   Native of S
Spain and C & S Portugal and North Africa,
growing in damp places and among rocks at
c.1800m, flowering in April–June. Plant with
several stems to 80cm. Leaves lyrate,
pinnatisect. Flowers 12–20mm long. This
species has the largest flowers of any of the
European figworts, but is not often cultivated.
It should succeed in any good soil. Hardy to
−15°C, perhaps less.

Synthyris missurica (Raf.) Penn. syn. *S.
stellata* Penn. (*Scrophulariaceae*)   Native of W
North America, in Idaho, Washington, Oregon
and N California, growing in moist places in the
mountains and foothills, flowering in April–
July. Plant tufted, with stems to 60cm. Leaf
blades with blunt or sharp teeth, 2.5–8cm
across. Flowers 4–7mm long, in a loose spike-
like inflorescence, with large or small bracts
below the flowers. *S. reniformis* (Dougl.) Benth.
is smaller, to 15cm high, with curving stems not
exceeding the leaves, found in coniferous forests
south to San Francisco Bay. *S. schizandra* Piper
has stems to 30cm, with 2 leafy bracts and
fimbriate petals. It is found in moist, shady
habitats in Washington and Oregon. *S.
pinnatifida* Wats. is found from Washington east
to Idaho, Wyoming and Montana, growing in
rocky places in the mountains. It has pinnate
leaves and stems to 20cm. All species need moist
soil in a cool position, with *S. schizandra* and *S.
reniformis* needing more shade. Hardy to −20°C
perhaps.

Veronica spicata subsp. *incana*

Veronica spicata 'Heidikind'

Veronica exaltata

Veronica spicata subsp. *spicata*

Veronica gentianoides

Veronica filiformis

Veronica austriaca 'Shirley Blue' at the Royal Botanic Garden, Edinburgh

Veronica austriaca 'Crater Lake Blue'

Veronica austriaca L. subsp. ***teucrium*** (L.)
D. A. Webb (*Scrophulariaceae*)   Native of most
of Europe, the Crimea, the Caucasus (?) and
NW Turkey, growing in open woods and stony
meadows and hills, flowering in April–July.
Plant with numerous upright or ascending
stems to 1m. Leaves 2–7cm long, more or less
amplexicaul, crenate or serrate. Flowers 10–
14mm across, bright blue. For any good soil in
sun or partial shade. Hardy to −20°C or less.
There are several cultivars of this species.
'Crater Lake Blue'   Tall, to 45cm, upright
with deep-blue flowers.
'Shirley Blue'   Shorter, to 20cm, with
creeping, then ascending stems. There is also a
pink form.

Veronica exaltata Maund   Said to be native of
Siberia, flowering in gardens in June–August.
Plant with several upright stems to 120cm.
Leaves 15cm long. Flowers pale blue, *c.*8mm
across. For any good soil in full sun. Hardy to
−20°C and below.

Veronica filiformis J. E. Smith   Native of the
Caucasus, the Crimea, N Iran and N Turkey,
along the Black Sea coast growing in damp
meadows, grassy places in the forest, by streams
and on disturbed ground at up to 2200m,
flowering in March–August. Naturalized also in
much of Europe, especially on riverbanks and in
short grass and lawns. Plant creeping, soon
covering many square metres, with flowering
stems up to 15cm. Leaves more or less round,
5–13mm across. Flowers 8–14mm across,
usually pale sky blue in cultivation, but in the
wild often white or deeper mauve-blue. Easily
grown in any moist soil. Hardy to −15°C.

Veronica gentianoides Vahl   Native of the
Caucasus, the Crimea and N & C Turkey,
growing in mountain meadows and open woods,
at 1000–3600m, flowering in May–August.
Plant forming mats of gentian-like leaves,
2–6cm long, with upright flowering stems
5–60cm tall. Flowers 8–16mm across, usually
pale blue, but in Turkey sometimes dark blue,
rarely white. For moist but well-drained soil in
full sun. Hardy to −20°C or less.

Veronica spicata L. subsp. ***incana*** (L.)
Walters   Native of E Europe, east to Siberia
and NW China, growing in dry meadows and
steppes, flowering in June–July. Plant with
upright stems to 30cm, the whole plant silvery-
hairy. Flowers 4–6mm across, bright blue. For
well-drained rather dry soil in full sun. Hardy to
−20°C or less. Hybrids between subsp. *spicata*
and subsp. *incana* are frequently cultivated, and
combine the tall stems of *spicata* (especially the
form *V. hybrida* L.) with the grey leaves of
subsp. *incana*. 'Heidikind', with deep-pink
flowers, is one of these; it has stems to 30cm.
'Wendy' is a taller, pinkish cultivar.

Veronica spicata L. subsp. ***spicata*** (including
V. hybrida L.)   Native of Europe, from
England, where it is very rare, to Russia, Siberia
and NW China, growing in grassland and on
rocky hills, usually on limestone, flowering in
June–September. Plant with upright stems to
60cm. Leaves linear-lanceolate to ovate, almost
sessile, opposite, 2–8cm long. Flowers 4–6mm
across, usually bright blue. For well-drained
soil in full sun. Hardy to −20°C or less.

Veronicastrum sibiricum at Wisley, Surrey

Veronicastrum sibiricum (L.) Pennell
(*Scrophulariaceae*)   Native of Japan in all the
islands, Korea, N China, Sakhalin and E
Siberia, growing in grassy places in the
mountains and plains, flowering in July–
September. Plant with several upright stems to
1.8m. Leaves in whorls of 4–6, broadly
lanceolate, 10–15cm long, to 5cm wide. Flowers
tubular with corolla lobes shorter than the tube.
For any good soil in full sun or partial shade.
Hardy to −20°C or less.

Veronicastrum virginicum (L.) Farwell syn.
Veronica virginica L. **Beaumont's Root**   Native
of E North America, from Ontario to Manitoba
south to Massachusetts, Alabama and Texas,
growing in meadows, woods and scrub,
flowering in June–September. Stems several,
upright to 2m tall. Leaves in whorls of 3–9,
lanceolate or oblong-lanceolate. Flowers tubular
4mm long with short lobes, white or bluish. For
any good moist soil. Hardy to −20°C or less.

Veronicastrum virginicum

Incarvillea emodi in Pakistan

Incarvillea mairei at Inshriach, Aviemore, Scotland

Incarvillea mairei near Lijiang, Yunnan

Incarvillea delavayi

Incarvillea arguta Royle (Royle) syn.
Amphicome arguta Royle (*Bignoniaceae*)   Native
of the Himalayas, from NW India to Nepal, SE
Xizang, and SW China in Yunnan and Sichuan,
growing in dry valleys on rocky slopes and
cliffs, often limestone, at 1800–3500m,
flowering in May–August. Plant with many
rather weak stems from a subshrubby base.
Leaves with 5–9 leaflets, the terminal *c*.5cm
long. Flowers 2.5–3.8cm, pale pink. For very
well-drained soil or a crevice in a wall. Hardy to
−15°C, perhaps lower if in a very dry position.

Incarvillea delavayi Bur. & Franch.   Native of
SW China, in Yunnan, growing in grassy places
and scrub at *c*.2000m, flowering in May–July.
Plant with deep fleshy roots and a rosette of
pinnate leaves to 20cm long. Stems to 60cm,
with rather few, large flowers, *c*.8cm across.
Easily grown in deep, sandy but rich soil in full
sun, the crown protected in winter from slugs
and extreme cold. Hardy to −15°C, less with
protection.

Incarvillea emodi (Wallich ex Royle)
Chatterjee   Native of Afghanistan to W Nepal,
growing on cliffs and rocks, at 600–2500m,
flowering in March–April. Plant with a woody
rootstock. Leaves pinnate, with 9–11 leaflets
1–4cm long, ovate; mostly at the base of the
stem. Flowering stems to 50cm, not branched,
with 1-sided clusters of flowers 3.5–5.8cm long.
Capsule thin, to 18cm long. For a dry position
on a wall or raised bed. Hardy to −15°C,
perhaps. Photographed by Andrew Paterson in
N Pakistan.

Incarvillea mairei (Léveillé) Grierson   Native
of the Himalayas from W Nepal to Xizang and
SW China in Yunnan, growing on stony slopes,
often on limestone, in dry valleys, flowering in
May–June. Plant with deep, fleshy root and a
rosette of pinnate leaves, with a large terminal
lobe. Flowers 4–6cm long, often stemless when
first open, the stems elongating to *c*.50cm in
fruit. Clones in cultivation include 'Frank
Ludlow', with large, very deep-pinkish-crimson
flowers, from Bhutan, and pink forms with
paler flowers such as 'Bees' Pink'. For very

Niedzwedzkia semiretschenskia in Tashkent Botanic Garden

Ourisia 'Loch Ewe'

Ourisia coccinea at Washfield Nurseries, Kent

Ourisia macrophylla at Inshriach, Aviemore, Scotland

well-drained deep, sandy soil in full sun, with protection from slugs. Hardy to −20°C or less.

Niedzwedzkia semiretschenskia B. Fedtsch. syn. *Incarvillea semiretschenskia* (B. Fed.) Grierson (*Bignoniaceae*) Native of C Asia, growing on dry rocky hillsides, flowering in May–June. Plant with numerous wiry, upright stems to 45cm from a subshrubby base. Leaves deeply dissected with linear lobes. Flowers *c*.6cm long, 4cm across. Fruits *c*.5cm long, with *c*.6 very wavy wings. For very well-drained, dry soil in a warm position in full sun. Hardy to −15°C, perhaps less.

Ourisia coccinea Pers. (*Scrophulariaceae*) Native of S Chile, growing in valleys in the mountains, flowering in June in northern gardens. Plant with fleshy creeping rhizomes, forming mats of coarsely toothed, ovate leaves, with blades *c*.5cm long. Flowering stems to 18cm. Flowers *c*.3cm long. An elegant plant for moist, cool peaty soil in partial shade. Hardy to −15°C, less with snow cover.

***Ourisia* 'Loch Ewe'** A hybrid between *O. macrophylla* and *O. coccinea*, forming mats of coarsely crenate leaves, and whorls of 2–4 flowers on upright stems to 30cm. For moist peaty soil in partial shade. Hardy to −20°C, or less with snow cover.

Ourisia macrophylla Hook. **New Zealand Mountain Foxglove** Native of New Zealand, on North Island on Mount Egmont, and from East Cape southwards at up to 1500m, growing in damp shady places, flowering in October–January, or in June in the north. Plant with creeping rhizomes forming spreading mats of leathery, shallowly crenate, ovate leaves. Pedicels glandular. Flowers 12–18mm across, in 3–7 whorls, on upright stems to 60cm. *O. macrocarpa* Hook. fil., from South Island, has fewer larger flowers to 2.5cm across, on longer glabrous pedicels, with broader calyx lobes, and leaves up to 15cm long. It grows in damp places (and along streams) in scrub and herbfields. Both require peaty, moist soil in partial shade and a cool position. Hardy to −20°C.

Incarvillea arguta near Dali, Yunnan

Aster falconeri at Gadsar, Kashmir

Aster tongolensis

Celmisia spectabilis

Bellis sylvestris in S Spain

Celmisia coriacea

Anthemis cretica L. subsp. **cupaniana**
(Nyman) Trehane syn. *A. cupaniana* Tod. ex
Nyman (*Compositae*)   Native of Sicily, growing
on cliffs and rocky places, flowering in April–
June. Plant with ascending stems to 60cm from
a subshrubby base. Leaves almost glabrous, or
white and silky in the commonly cultivated
clones, pinnatisect with thin segments. Flowers
up to 6cm across, with a hemispherical-conical
disc. *A. cupaniana* is now included in *A. cretica*,
a very variable plant with 5 subspecies in
Europe, and 11 different ones in Turkey. A
valuable, early-flowering daisy for a warm, dry
and sunny position. Hardy to −10°C perhaps.

Aster falconeri (C. B. Clarke) Hutch.
(*Compositae*)   Native of the Himalayas, from N
Pakistan to W Nepal, growing in alpine
meadows at 3000–4200m, flowering in June–
August. Plant with few rosettes of oblong-
lanceolate basal leaves to 15cm long and
upright densely-leafy flowering stems to 15–35cm tall.
Flowers solitary to 8cm across, the rays with a
white base and a 3-lobed apex. For moist, well-
drained soil in full sun. Hardy to −15°C or less.

Aster tongolensis Franch.   Native of W
China, growing in stony alpine meadows at
c.3500m, flowering in June. Plant forming
spreading mats of hairy, dark-green leaves, with
numerous, almost leafless, flowering stems to
c.45cm. Flowers *c*.6cm across. There are now
several named clones of this species, such as
'Napsbury' and 'Lavender Star'. For well-
drained soil in full sun. Hardy to −20°C. *Aster
forrestii* Stapf. is very similar, but has broader
basal leaves and leafier stalks.

Bellis sylvestris Cyr. (*Compositae*)   Native of S
Europe, from Spain and France to Bulgaria,
Mediterranean Turkey and North Africa,
growing in grassy places and ditches, moist in
winter and spring, flowering in October–March.
Plant forming rosettes of leaves to 18cm long,
2.5cm across, with 3 veins; flower stalks 10–
45cm. Flowers 2–4cm across, often pinkish.
Differs from the common daisy *B. perennis* in its
larger flowers and 3-veined leaves. For any good
soil. Hardy to −10°C perhaps. Winter
flowering. *B. perennis* L., the Common Daisy,
has been long cultivated, as well as being a
common lawn weed. Large, pinkish and
double-flowered forms are often grown as
annuals, though they are good perennials and
very pretty in wild grass. Hardy to −20°C.

Celmisia coriacea (Forster fil.) Hook. fil.
(*Compositae*)   Native of New Zealand,
throughout South Island, growing in alpine and
subalpine herbfields and grassland, flowering in
December–February, or May–June in the
north. Plant forming single rosettes of leaves or
loose clumps. Leaves 20–60cm long, silky-
silvery above and beneath. Flower stems to
60cm. Flowers 5–12cm across. For moist but
well-drained, peaty, sandy soil in full sun, but a
cool position. These New Zealand alpine daisies
are easy to grow in cool climates such as
Scotland, where *C. coriacea* is often seen in
cottage gardens, but are more difficult to grow
in the south of England, as they dislike summer
heat. Hardy to −15°C.

Erigeron karvinskianus

Erigeron karvinskianus on the walls of Flora's garden in the Villa Torrigiani, near Lucca, Italy

Celmisia spectabilis Hook. fil.   Native of New Zealand, in South Island, from Mount Kikurangi southwards, growing in subalpine or alpine herbfields or tussock grassland, flowering in December–February. Plant forming single rosettes, or loose clumps. Leaves very tough and leathery, often shining green above, or hairy, densely woolly beneath, to 15cm long, 5cm across. Flowers to 5cm across, smaller than *C. coriacea*. For well-drained but peaty, sandy soil in full sun but a cool position. Hardy to −15°C or less.

Corethrogyne californica DC. (*Compositae*) Native of California, from San Francisco to Monterey (with var. *obovata* (Benth.) O. Kuntze north to Oregon), growing on grassy slopes near the coast, often on serpentine, flowering in April–July. Plant with spreading rootstock and leafy decumbent stems to 40cm from a woody base. Leaves 2–4cm long, linear or oblanceolate, greyish-hairy. Flowers purple to pinkish, with 30–40 rays, to 3cm across. For a dry position in full sun. Hardy to −5°C, perhaps less.

Erigeron karvinskianus DC. syn. *E. mucronatus* DC. (*Compositae*)   Native of Mexico, and often naturalized in S Europe, growing on rocks and in crevices in walls, flowering throughout the summer. Plant forming delicate clumps of slender stems to 50cm from a woody rootstock. Flowers *c.*2cm across, pinkish. An attractive plant for warm, dry places, which will seed itself freely in old walls. Hardy to −10°C, but often regenerating by seed if the parent plants are killed by frost.

Leucanthemum vulgare L. syn. *Chrysanthemum leucanthemum* L. (*Compositae*) **Ox-eye Daisy**   Native of most of Europe except the Azores, the Balearics, Crete and Spitsbergen, and of N Turkey, east to China, and naturalized in North America, growing in hay fields, old grassland and roadside banks, flowering in April–June. Plant with a creeping rootstock and upright flowering stems to 1m, usually *c.*40cm. Flowers 2.5–5cm across, solitary. For any soil in full sun. Hardy to −20°C or less. A very good plant for long grass, to flower after daffodils have finished, nor to be entirely neglected for the herbaceous border as an earlier and more refined version of the common *L. × superbum*.

Leucanthemum vulgare with *Phaiophleps nigricans* (vol. 2, p. 195), at Symnel Cottage, Kent

Anthemis cretica subsp. *cupaniana*

Corethrogyne californica

Convallaria majalis
'Prolificans'

Convallaria majalis
var. *rosea*

Convallaria majalis
'Fortin's Giant'

Convallaria majalis
(tall form)

Speirantha convallarioides

Maianthemum
bifolium

Smilacina stellata

Specimens from Wisley, 15 May. ½ life size

Convallaria majalis

Smilacina stellata in California

Convallaria majalis var. *rosea*

Smilacina racemosa at Wisley

Convallaria majalis L. (*Liliaceae-Convallariaceae*) **Lily of the Valley** Native of Europe, from N England south to the Caucasus and NE Turkey, and eastwards to Japan, and in North America in the Appalachians in Virginia, North and South Carolina, growing in woods, in scrub, on limestone pavement and meadows in the mountains, flowering in May–June. Plant forming spreading mats by rhizomes which creep on the soil surface, beneath the leaf layer. Stems with 1–4 leaves, 3–20cm long, 0.5–10cm wide. Inflorescence arising from the lower sheaths, to 20cm tall, with 5–13 wonderfully scented flowers. Several varieties are found in the wild, and other variants are cultivated. Shown here are var. *rosea* Reichb., which is common in parts of C and E Europe, and has small pinkish flowers; 'Prolificans', with numerous small flowers on a branched inflorescence, and 'Fortin's Giant', a large clone. Double-flowered white and pink clones and a clone with white striped leaves, 'Variegata', are also grown.

Maianthemum bifolium (L.) F. W. Schmidt (*Liliaceae-Convallariaceae*) Native of Europe, from England and Norway eastwards, to N Japan, usually growing in coniferous woods on acid soils, flowering in April–July according to altitude and latitude. Plant forming spreading mats by creeping underground rhizomes. Flowering stems hairy above, 5–25cm tall, usually around 15cm, usually with 2 cordate leaves. Petals 2–3mm. Berries red. A delicate, if invasive, plant, useful for groundcover in cool shady places. *M. canadense* Desf., from E North America, differs in its narrower, shorter-stalked, shallowly cordate leaves and often glabrous stems.

Smilacina purpurea Wallich Native of the Himalayas from NW India to SW China, growing in forests at 2400–4200m, flowering in April–June. Plant with creeping rhizome. Stems 20–40cm; leaves 3–9. Flowers in narrow spikes,

sometimes branched at the base; usually dark purplish, sometimes white. Easily grown in a moist, shady position and leafy soil. Hardy to −15°C, perhaps less (Grey-Wilson 150).

Smilacina racemosa (L.) Desf. syn. *Maianthemum racemosum* (L.) Link (*Liliaceae-Convallariaceae*) Native of North America, from British Columbia east to Nova Scotia, Georgia and Missouri, with var. *amplexicaulis* (Nutt.) Wats. in California to the Rockies, growing in damp coniferous and deciduous woods, flowering in March–July, according to latitude and altitude. Plant with a tufted rhizome, forming dense clumps of stems 30–90cm tall. Leaves rounded at the base, or clasping in var. *amplexicaulis*, pubescent beneath. Flowers with petals 1–2mm long. Berries red, spotted with purple.

Smilacina stellata (L.) Desf. syn. *Maian themum stellatum* (L.) Link Native of California north to British Columbia, and eastwards to Newfoundland, Virginia and Kansas, in wet places in woods and scrub, flowering in April–June. Plant with a creeping rhizome, forming extensive patches. Stems 30–60cm tall. Flowers 3–15 in a loose raceme; petals 5–7mm long. Berries reddish purple, becoming black. *Smilacina trifolia* Desf., from N North America and Siberia, usually has only 3 narrowly ovate leaves, and dark-red berries. Easily grown in moist, leafy soil. Hardy to −25°C.

Speirantha convallarioides Baker syn. *S. gardenii* Baillon (*Liliaceae-Convallariaceae*) Native of SE China, in Jiangxi (Kiangsi) growing in woods, flowering in ?April–May. Plant with thick rhizomes, spreading by stolons. Leaves evergreen to 15cm long. Flowering stems to 15cm. Flowers scented; petals 4–6mm long. For leafy soil in shade. Hardy to −10°C perhaps.

Smilacina purpurea at Kew

Smilacina racemosa in fruit

Polygonatum odoratum
'Flore Pleno'

Polygonatum odoratum

Disporum sessile 'Variegatum'

Polygonatum falcatum
'Pumilum'

Polygonatum multiflorum

Polygonatum falcatum
'Variegatum'

Polygonatum humile

Polygonatum × hybridum

Specimens from Kew and Wisley, 14 May. ⅓ life size

Disporopsis pernyi (Hua) Diels syn.
Polygonatum cyrtonema hort. (*Liliaceae-Convallariaceae*)   Native of China, in Yunnan, Guangxi and Gizhou, in forests at 1800–7500m, flowering in June. Plant evergreen, with stiff stems to 20cm from a shortly creeping rhizome, forming dense patches. Flowers solitary or in pairs, with petals diverging and almost reflexed in the lower part when open. For leafy soil in shade or partial shade. Hardy to −10°C, perhaps less.

Disporum sessile (Thunb.) D. Don (*Liliaceae-Convallariaceae*)   Native throughout Japan and in Sakhalin, growing in woods in the hills, flowering in April–May. Plant forming colonies from underground creeping rhizomes. Stems 30–60cm. Flowers 1–3, greenish white, about 3cm long. Berries blue-black.
'**Variegatum**'   A clone with white-striped leaves, shown here, is frequent in gardens. For other *Disporum* species see vol. 2, pp.82–3.

Polygonatum biflorum (Walt.) Ell. (*Liliaceae-Convallariaceae*)   Native of North America, from New Brunswick west to Michigan, south to Tennessee, West Virginia and Florida, growing in deciduous woods and scrub, flowering in April–July. Stems up to 90cm. Leaves 5–10cm long, pubescent, especially the veins beneath. Flowers usually in pairs, 8–12mm long, greenish. Filaments papillose. The smaller of the two North American species, usually found in dryish places in woods.
P. canaliculatum Pursh (syn. *P. commutatum* (Schult.) Dietr.), usually found in damp places can reach 2.5m high and is totally glabrous.

Polygonatum curvistylum Hua   Native of Sichuan and Yunnan, growing in stony places as scrub on limestone at *c.*3000m, flowering in June. Rhizome shortly creeping. Stems dark purple to 80cm. Flowers pinkish, purple inside, narrowest at the throat.

Polygonatum falcatum A. Gray   Native of most of Japan and Korea, growing in woods in the hills, flowering in May–June. Rhizomes short, creeping, so the plant forms clumps of stems 50–85cm tall. Leaves 8–20cm long, 1.8–2.5cm wide, usually rough on the veins beneath. Flowers 1.1–2.2cm, in groups of 2–5. Berries small, 3–4mm across. 'Variegatum' is the clone commonest in cultivation, an attractive plant with reddish stems and a white edge to the leaf. *P. humile* (q.v.) is often wrongly called *P. falcatum*, and *P.* 'Pumilum', shown here, is a small form of *P. falcatum*.

Polygonatum humile Fisch.   Native of N China (Heilongjiang), E Siberia, Korea and Japan, in Hokkaido, N Honshu and Kyushu, growing in meadows and open woods at low altitudes, flowering in June–July. Rhizomes slender, creeping, forming spreading colonies of angled, upright stems 15–30cm tall; leaves 4–7cm long, hairy on the veins beneath. Flowers solitary or in pairs. Usually a dwarf plant with upright stems. Hardy to −20°C.

Polygonatum × hybridum Brugger   A hybrid between *P. multiflorum* and *P. odoratum*, common in gardens and sometimes naturalized in N & W Europe. Rhizomes stout, shortly creeping, especially above. Stems to 90cm, scarcely angled. Leaves glabrous beneath, up to 20 × 8cm; flowers mostly in groups of 4 in the axils of all except the uppermost 2 or 3 leaves. Filaments papillose. Seldom sets more than 1 or 2 berries. Easily grown and elegant with its

Polygonatum odoratum (Furse & Synge 435) at Kew

Polygonatum severtzovii near Tashkent

Polygonatum biflorum in New Jersey

arching stems. The leaves are often stripped by the grey larvae of a sawfly.

Polygonatum multiflorum (L.) All.   Native of Europe, from W England eastwards to Turkey and European Russia, and W Siberia, growing in woods, usually on limestone, flowering in May–June. Rhizome stout, short, creeping; stems 30–90cm, not angled. Leaves 5–15cm, glabrous beneath. Flowers 9–20mm long, in groups of 2–6, usually confined to the lower half of the stem.

Polygonatum odoratum (Miller) Druce
Angular Solomon's Seal   Native of most of Europe, including W England, eastwards to the Caucasus, N Iran, Siberia and Japan, growing in woods, usually on limestone, flowering in April–June. Rhizome long, creeping, forming colonies. Stems 30–85cm, angled, leaves 3–15cm; flowers solitary or in groups of 2–4. 'Flore Pleno' has attractive double flowers, and white-striped and -edged forms are also cultivated. Hardy to −25°C.

Polygonatum severtzovii Regel   Native of C Asia, in the Tien Shan, Pamir Alai and Kopet Dağ, growing in scrub and among shady rocks, flowering in April–June. Rhizome shortly creeping. Stems 20–100cm. Leaves whorled, the upper with curled tips. Flowers 15–20mm long. Berries first red, later purple. *P. verticillatum* (L.) All., from Europe and N Turkey to W Siberia and the Himalayas, is similar, but has flowers only 8–10mm long and leaves not curled at the tips. *P. sibiricum* Delaroche, from N China, Mongolia and E Siberia, has stems to 3m, climbing through the scrub and flowers in groups of up to 30.

Disporopsis pernyi at Harry Hay's, Surrey

Polygonatum curvistylum at Harry Hay's

The habitat of *Iris japonica* in low hills near Baoxing, Sichuan, W China

Iris confusa Sealy (s. *Lophiris* (Evansia))
Native of W China, in Yunnan and W Sichuan, growing on steep rocky slopes among rocks and scrub, flowering in May. Like *I. japonica*, but with the fan of leaves on a stiff, bamboo-like stem up to 60cm high. Leaves *c*. 5cm wide. Flowers 4–5cm across, normally white, with yellow and purple spotting. For a sheltered and warm position in partial shade; hardy to $-5°C$ perhaps, and only really satisfactory outdoors in warm parts of the USA such as S California. Brian Mathew recommends planting it in a tub which can be brought indoors during cold spells in winter.

Iris cristata Solander (s. *Lophiris*)   Native of Maryland west to S Ohio, and Indiana south to Georgia, Tennessee and Missouri in the Appalachians and Ozark mountains, growing in moist oak woods and along streams, flowering in April–May. Rhizomes creeping on the surface and branching freely to make a radiating mat. Stems, including the flower, to 7cm. Leaves soft, glabrous, bright green, 10–20cm tall. Flowers 3–4cm across, usually bluish, rarely pink or white. Easily grown in leafy soil in partial shade, but requires protection from slugs, frequent division, and replanting every other year if it is to thrive and persist. Hardy to $-20°C$. *Iris lacustris* Nutt. is an even dwarfer plant from the shores of Lakes Huron, Michigan and Superior; its floral tube is shorter than the bracts.

Iris japonica Thunb. (s. *Lophiris*)   Native of Japan (except Hokkaido) and China westwards to Sichuan, on grassy and rocky slopes, in woods in the hills, and among rocks by streams, flowering in April–May. Plant with a creeping aerial rhizome, rooting at intervals. Leaves 30–80cm long, 2.5–5cm wide, evergreen, shining green in a broad fan; stems 30–80cm, branched; the flowers opening in succession, white, pale to mid-blue or purplish, 5–6cm across. 'Ledger's Variety' seems to be the common one in cultivation in Europe. It is triploid, and another in cultivation, the 'Capri form', which has crests with paler-orange markings, is possibly of hybrid origin and is highly sterile. The robust variety 'Born Graceful', raised in 1966, is a cross between these two. It has stems to 120cm and flowers 6–7.5cm across. The darker-flowered form shown here was growing in W Sichuan, at Baoxing, where the species is very common, with flowers of all shades of colour. Easily grown in a sheltered warm site in sun or partial shade. The flowers are susceptible to damage by late spring frosts and the plant will fail to flower after an exceptionally cold winter.

Iris lazica Albov (s. *Unguiculares*)   Native of NE Turkey and Georgia, from Giresun eastwards, growing on sandy shady banks, beneath bracken or in scrub at near sea level to 250m, flowering in February–April. Plant forming a slowly spreading clump. Leaves evergreen, dark green, 15–32cm long, 8–15mm wide. Flowers deep purplish blue, to 8cm across, 2–4 on a short branching inflorescence *c*. 5cm long, with overlapping spathe-like bracts. Capsules on a *c*. 6cm stalk. For a warm, sunny or partially shaded position on well-drained, but leafy soil. Related to *I. unguicularis*, but the area where this grows is very warm, wet and cloudy in summer. It flowers best in a warm position in England. Hardy to $-15°C$ or so: the leaves are killed at $-10°C$.

Iris japonica (dark form)

Iris japonica (white form)

Iris lazica from the Black Sea coast, near Of, NE Turkey

Iris unguicularis 'Walter Butt' at Washfield Nurseries. Kent

Iris tectorum in Sichuan

Iris unguicularis (Algerian form)

Iris unguicularis (white form)

Iris tectorum

Iris unguicularis subsp. *carica* var. *angustifolia*
from Greece

Iris cristata in Virginia

Iris confusa

Iris tectorum Maxim. (s. *Lophiris*) Native of
Burma and SW & C China, and naturalized in
Japan, though commonly cultivated throughout
this area, on the roofs of thatched houses, the
tops of old walls, and found also in shady rocky
slopes and in scrub, flowering in May. Stems to
50cm, usually *c.*30cm tall, with few branches,
each with 2–3 flowers. Leaves semi-evergreen,
30–60cm long, 2.5–5cm wide. Flowers 8–10cm
across, purplish blue or white. Although seldom
seen in gardens in Europe, *I. tectorum* is not
difficult, though I have not found it grows or
flowers as prolifically as in its native habitat.
There it would have dry, cold winters and
warm, wet summers, with perfect drainage;
loose, leafy soil in a warm but partially shaded
position should suit it best.

Iris unguicularis Poiret syns. *I. stylosa* Desf.,
I. cretensis Janka Native of Algeria, Tunisia,
S & W Turkey and W Syria, Greece and Crete,
growing in rocky places and woods usually of
pine at up to 1000m, flowering in March–April,
but often as early as December in cultivation.
Plant forming dense clumps. Leaves greyish
green, to 75cm long, and 1.8cm across (the
Algerian subsp.); the Greek subsp. to 7mm
across. Flowers pale to deep bluish mauve,
rarely white; to 8cm long, stemless, on a tube
9–28cm long. Capsules hidden among the
leaves. The Cretan subspecies, subsp. *cretensis*,
is very dwarf, with leaves less than 3mm across,
and often less than 15cm long: the flowers may
be pale bluish, with narrow falls and standards.
Narrow-leaved forms are found in the

Peloponnese and on the south coast of Turkey,
called subsp. *carica* (W. Schultz) A. Davis &
Jury, but have larger flowers. The North
African plants, which have the largest flowers,
are the ones generally cultivated. Easily grown
in a dry, sunny position, and requiring a warm
place, with rich, well-drained soil to flower
freely. Hardy to −15°C.
'Mary Barnard' A good deep purplish blue,
said to be from Algeria, of the same colour as is
commonest in the Peloponnese. Free-flowering.
'Walter Butt' A most beautiful pale lavender
blue, with a large flower. Free-flowering. White
forms are also in cultivation, but the commonest
has narrow-petalled flowers, and is always
infected with virus.

Iris scariosa near Karamay, NW China

Iris scariosa

Iris lutescens from S France, near St Tropez

Iris attica from Parnassos Oros, Greece

Iris aphylla L. (s. *Iris* – pogon) Native of C & E Europe, from SE France to S Poland and the N Caucasus, growing on rocky slopes, flowering in May. Plant deciduous; stems 15–30cm; leaves to 2cm wide. Flowering stems branched at or below the middle, often near the base. Flowers 1–5, purple or violet, 6–7cm across. Bracts green. The form shown here is from the westernmost locality of the species, in the Alpes Maritimes, where it has been called *I. perrieri* Simonet ex P. Fournier.

Iris attica Boiss. & Held. syn. *I. pumila* subsp. *attica* (Boiss. & Held.) Hayek Native of S Yugoslavia, Greece and NW Turkey, growing in rocky places usually on limestone, flowering in April–May. Plant deciduous in winter, forming small but spreading mats; stems very short; height 5–10cm, including the flowers, the recurved leaves 4–7mm wide. Flowers solitary, 3.5–4.5cm across, varying in colour, even in the same population, from purple to yellow and reddish with various bicolours, as shown here. Easily grown in a bulb frame, but not reliably hardy outside in N Europe or NE North America.

Iris lutescens Lam. syn. *I. chamaeiris* Bertol. Native of NE Spain, S France and Italy, growing on bare rocky or sandy hills, often on granite, or in open pine woods, flowering in March–April. Plant evergreen, forming dense mats. Stems 5–20cm; leaves 0.5–2.5cm wide. Flowers 1 or 2 per stem, 6–7cm across, often with standards rather larger than the falls, yellow, dark purple or bicoloured, with a yellow beard. Easily grown in a bulb frame or well-drained soil in a warm sheltered place. Hardy to −15°C perhaps. Plants shown here from SW France, west of St Tropez.

Iris pseudopumila Tineo Native of SE Italy, W Yugoslavia and Sicily, growing on rocky hills and in dry scrub, flowering in March–April. Plant evergreen, forming small mats. Stems c.3cm, including the flowers, to 25cm. Leaves 1–1.5cm wide, slightly curved. Flowers yellow, purplish, white or bicoloured, 6–8cm across. Beard white with yellow tips. Probably best in a bulb frame or very sheltered sunny position. Hardy to −10°C perhaps.

Iris scariosa Willd. ex Link Native of Asia, from the Urals eastwards to the Tien Shan in NW China, growing on rocky hillsides or steppes, sometimes in nearly desert or saline conditions, up to 3000m, flowering in May–June. Plant deciduous (?), forming dense mats. Stems 5–30cm; leaves greyish, recurved,

Iris subbiflora

Iris, unnamed hybrid

Iris shachtii near Malatya, C Turkey

1–2.5cm wide. Flowers 2 per stem, 4–5cm across, with loose, rather thin-textured bracts, usually bluish or purplish, with white or yellow forms rarer. In NW China the flowers were always purplish and it was very dwarf, but a striking sight on bare and apparently totally dry hills, taller and lusher on rocky hillsides with paeonies (p.96), tulips and fritillaries. Beard white. Probably easily grown in dry soil, with most water in spring. Should be very tolerant of dry cold.

Iris schachtii Markgraf   Native of C Turkey, especially on the Anatolian plateau east of Ankara and between Kayseri and Malatya, growing on rocky hillsides and open steppes, at up to 1800m, flowering in May. Plant deciduous, forming small clumps. Height 10–30cm, stem usually branched; leaves up to 1.5cm wide. Flowers 1–3, 5–6cm across, usually yellowish, though often purple, with green purple-tinted bracts which are transparent on the margins. Beard yellow. This species requires good soil and full sun, dry in summer if it is to flower freely. Hardy to −20°C perhaps.

Iris subbiflora Brot. syn. *I. lutescens* subsp. *subbiflora* (Brot.) Webb & Chater   Native of C & NE Portugal and SW Spain, with one locality near Antequera, growing on rocky hills and open scrub often on limestone, flowering in April. Plant evergreen, forming dense clumps. Stems 20–40cm. Leaves 0.5–2.5cm wide, upright. Flowers 7–8cm across, usually purple. Beard white or purple. An attractive plant which grows and flowers regularly in S England in well-drained, sandy soil. Hardy to −15°C.

Iris taochia Woron. ex Grossh.   Native of NE Turkey, growing on rocky screes at 1500–1700m, flowering in May–June. Plant deciduous, forming dense clumps. Stems 25–35cm tall, with 1–3 branches. Leaves 1.5–2.5cm wide, upright. Flowers 5–7cm across, purple, yellow or brownish-red in the same population. Beard yellowish or white, tipped yellow. This requires bulb-frame treatment to flower in S England, but would grow outside in hotter, drier parts of Europe and the USA. Hardy to −20°C. This species appears to be confined to the environs of Tortum: I have seen it making large dense clumps on otherwise barren, steep volcanic screes.

Iris hybrid   This old garden variety is probably a hybrid between *I. lutescens* and *I. germanica*, and is a forerunner of the intermediate bearded irises. It has 1–2 flowers on a stem.

Iris aphylla (*I. perrieri*)

Iris pseudopumila near Brindisi

Iris taochia from near Tortum

Iris taochia near Tortum, NE Turkey

Iris albertii near Medeo, Alma Ata

Iris pallida at Sellindge, Kent

Iris albertii Regel (s. *Iris* – pogon)   Native of C Asia, in the Tien Shan and Pamir Alai, at 1700–2000m, growing on rocky hillsides and grassy mountain steppes, flowering in May. Plant forming spreading clumps. Stems up to 1m in cultivation, to 70cm in the wild, widely branched. Leaves 2–3cm across; bracts green with papery edges. Beard white tipped yellow. Flowers 6–8cm across, purplish blue. Easily grown, especially in a bulb frame, for protection from winter wet, requiring full sun to flower well. The widely branching stems are typical.

Iris albicans Lange   Native of Saudi Arabia and the Yemen, growing in dry, rocky places at up to 2200m, flowering in February–May. This iris was brought northwards by the Arabs and planted on their cemeteries, and is now found more or less wild, often still on abandoned cemeteries in much of the S Mediterranean, especially in Turkey, S Spain and Crete. Plant forming spreading clumps. Stems 30–60cm with, at most, 1 very short branch and usually 2 terminal flowers. Leaves very glaucous, incurved at the tips. Bracts broad, blunt, green or purplish below, papery on the margins. Flowers usually white, sometimes pale blue, sweetly scented. Easily grown in full sun and dry, well-drained soil. Source: S Arabia, John Marr 147. *I.* 'Florentina' (see p.196) differs in its bracts, which are all papery at flowering, its stalked lateral branches, and slightly blue-flushed flowers.

Iris germanica L. **'Nepalensis'** syns. 'Purple King', 'Atropurpurea'   This is one of the many named clones of *I. germanica*. It is distinct in its

entirely red-purple flowers, with the hairs of the beard white towards the apex, yellow tipped towards the base of the falls. Introduced in the 19th century from Katmandu. Early flowering in gardens.

Iris imbricata Lindl.   Native of Soviet Azerbaijan and N Iran in the Talysh and Elburz mountains, growing on grassy alpine slopes, screes and in damp rocky places at 1400–3000m, flowering in May–June. Plant forming dense clumps. Stems 30–60cm, branched, with 2 or 3 flowers. Leaves flat, upright, grey-green, 2–3cm wide. Bracts inflated, pale green, transparent only at the tip. Beard dark yellow. Flowers 7–9cm across, pale yellowish. This species is beautifully illustrated in Brian Mathew's *The Iris*, growing with scarlet Oriental poppies in the alpine meadows of the high Elburz.

Iris pallida Lam. subsp. *pallida*   Native of W Yugoslavia, growing on rocky limestone hillsides and the sides of gorges leading down to the Adriatic, flowering in May. Plant forming spreading clumps. Stems up to 1.2m, much branched. Leaves very glaucous, 1–4cm or more wide, up to 60cm high. Bracts entirely silvery and papery at flowering. Flowers 3–6, pale lilac blue, 9–11cm across. Easily cultivated in ordinary garden soil in a sunny position, and very free flowering. This species is beautiful not only for its flowers but also for its very pale glaucous leaves which remain healthy through the whole summer. Source: S Yugoslavia near Titograd (Podgorica).
I. pallida 'Variegata' is an excellent garden plant, with the advantage of the variegated

leaves when the flowers have finished; there are said to be 2 forms, 'Argentea', with white stripes on the leaf edges, and 'Aurea', with golden stripes. In practice, one tends to see a whitish-yellow form.
Subsp. *cengialtii* (Ambr.) Foster, from NE Italy, has stems only to 45cm, browner bracts, and greener leaves. The darker purple flowers have a white or orange-tipped beard. Photographed by Brian Mathew.

Iris purpureobractea Mathew & T. Baytop   Native of NW & C Turkey, notably on Honaz Dağ, growing in dry rocky places, in cedar or pine forest at 60–1600m, flowering in April–May. Plant forming clumps. Stems 20–50cm. Leaves 1.5–2.5cm wide. Bracts purplish. Flowers pale yellow veined with greenish brown, or pale-blue veined darker blue, 10–12cm from top to bottom. For well-drained soil in full sun. Hardy to −15°C perhaps.

Iris variegata L.   Native of C & E Europe, from S Germany and Austria, eastwards to the W Ukraine and south to S Yugoslavia and Bulgaria, growing in open woods, scrub and rocky places, flowering in May–June. Plant forming dense clumps. Stems 15–40cm, branched towards the top. Leaves dark green, to 30cm tall and 3cm wide, distinctly ribbed. Bracts green or purplish. Flowers 3–6, 5–7cm across, with pale-yellow standards, and nearly horizontal red- or purple-striped falls. Beard yellow. Easily grown in ordinary garden soil and more shade-tolerant than most species of this group. This is a parent of many of the bicoloured bearded irises.

Iris pallida subsp. *cengialtii*

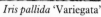
Iris pallida 'Variegata'

Iris purpureobractea at Brian Mathew's

Iris albicans from Arabia, at Kew

Iris germanica 'Nepalensis'

Iris imbricata at Kew

Iris variegata

Iris 'Bromyard'

'Summer Nights'

'Sarah Taylor'

'Saltwood'

'Darkover'

'Sunny Smile'

'Truly'

'Bibury'

'Low'

'Double Lament'

'Royal Emblem'

Specimens from Wisley, 14 May. ½ life size

Iris 'Smarty Pants'

Iris 'Arctic Fancy'

Iris 'Partridge'

Iris 'Double Lament'

Iris 'Bibury'

'Arctic Fancy' (intermediate, bearded)
Registered by A. Brown 1964. Parents: 'Dale Dennis' × 'Rococo'. Plicata, standards white, stitched violet; falls white, stitched violet; beard pale violet with yellow tips. Height 50cm. Early season.

'Bibury' (standard dwarf, bearded)   Registered by J. D. Taylor 1975. Parents: 'Saltwood' × seedling. Standards white; falls white with pale yellow hafts; beard orangy. Height 30cm. Early season.

'Bromyard' (standard dwarf, bearded)
Registered by J. D. Taylor 1979. Parents: 'Saltwood' × seedling. Standards blue-grey; falls blended, maroon with yellow centres; beard golden. Height 28cm. Early season.

'Darkover' (standard dwarf, bearded)
Registered by N. K. Stopes 1983. Parents: 74/73 (35/71m ('Blueberry Muffin' × 36/69m) × 'Gingerman') × unknown. Deep maroon self with bluish beard. Height 25cm. Early season.

'Double Lament' (standard dwarf, bearded)
Registered by J. D. Taylor 1969. Parents: ('Green Spot' × *pumila*) × 'Velvet Caper'. Violet self with dark flush on the falls; beard pale tipped orange. Height 30cm. Mid-season.

'Low' (standard dwarf, bearded)   Registered by A. Brown 1969. Parents: (sibling of 'Sunny Heart' and 'Cartwheel') × 'Lilli-Var'. Standards bright chrome-yellow; falls deep oxblood-red with a narrow margin of chrome yellow about 4mm, is solid and smooth; beard bright orange. Height 30cm. Early season.

'Partridge' (intermediate, bearded)
Registered by J. D. Taylor 1973. Parents: seedling C43 × ('Staten Island' × 'Dandy'). Standards gold; falls maroon. Height 60cm. Late season.

'Royal Emblem' (standard dwarf, bearded)
Registered by L. W. Brummitt 1978. Parents: 'Blueberry Muffin' × 'Purple Landscape'. Standards red-purple; falls red-purple (velvety); beard more violet. Height 30cm. Early to mid-season.

'Saltwood' (standard dwarf, bearded)
Registered by J. D. Taylor 1971. Parents: 'Sunny Heart' × Taylor seedling J42/1. Standards lemon; falls yellow with lemon ring round. Height 33cm. Early season.

'Sarah Taylor' (standard dwarf, bearded)
Registered by J. D. Taylor 1979. Parents: Jones M212/3 × 'Stockholm'. Standards cream; falls

pale primrose; beard blue. Height 30cm. Early season.

'Smarty Pants' (low border, bearded)
Registered by A. White. Parents: 'Sans Souci' × unknown. Reddish toned. Mid-season.

'Summer Nights' (standard dwarf, bearded)
Registered by L. Boushay 1979. Parents: ('Honey Talk' × 'Grace Note') × 'Stockholm'. Ruffled blend of bluebird-blue and olive self, bluer at the base; beard the same colour. Height 29cm. Early to mid-season.

'Sunny Smile' (standard dwarf, bearded)
Registered by N. K. Scopes 1977. Parents: ('Eye Shadow' × 'Lenna M.') × 'Sapphire Heart'. Standards pale golden yellow; falls slightly deeper colour; beard white. Height 30cm. Early season.

'Truly' (standard dwarf, bearded)   Registered by B. Warburton 1977. Parents: 'Daughter' × 'Dear Love'. Very pale-blue self with darker veining; beard white-cream. Height 30cm. Early season.

Iris 'Happy Mood'

'Devilry'

'Anne Elizabeth'

'Amphora'

'Downland'

'Sky Caper'

'Austrian Sky'

'Little Suki'

'Langport Carnival'

Iris germanica (p. 196)

Specimens from Wisley, 14 May. ⅔ life size

Modern bearded irises

Iris 'Small Wonder'

Iris 'Owlet'

Iris 'Jeremy Brian'

'Amphora' (standard dwarf, bearded)
Registered by J. D. Taylor 1972. Parents:
'Sunny Heart' × seedling 242. Standards white;
falls white with clear yellow spot; beard yellow.
Height 30cm. Mid-season.

'Anne Elizabeth' (standard dwarf, bearded)
Registered by J. D. Taylor 1973. Parents:
'Circlette' × 'Plicatree'. Plicata white with blue-
violet edges and veining; beard white. Height
28cm. Early to mid-season.

'Austrian Sky' (dwarf, bearded)   Registered by
G. W. Darby 1957. Parents: (seedling ×
'Welch') × 'Blue Ensign'. Blue self with darker
blue thumbprint and veins on falls and sky blue
standards. Height 30cm. Mid-season.

'Devilry' (standard dwarf, bearded)
Registered by J. D. Taylor 1969. Parents:
seedling E96/10 × 'Lemanis'. Purple self with
brown beard. Height 33cm. Mid-season.

'Downland' (intermediate)   Registered by R.
Usher 1969. Parents: 'Little Rosy Wings' ×

'Captain Gallant'. Standards plum red; falls
burgundy-red, edge plum-red; beard bronze.
Height 48cm. Mid-season.

'Happy Mood' (intermediate, bearded)
Registered by A. Brown 1967. Parents: 'Knotty
Pine' × 'Rococo'. Standards white with light-
blue markings; falls white with a band of blue
markings; beard ivory, tipped orchid. Height
56cm. Early season.

'Jeremy Brian' (standard dwarf, bearded)
Registered by B. Price 1975. Parents: 'Blue
Denim' × 'Sparkling Champagne'. Pale silver-
blue self; beard yellow tipped. Height 25cm.
Early to mid-season.

'Langport Carnival' (intermediate, bearded)
Introduced by Kelway & Son prior to 1940;
parents not known. Smoky violet with a distinct
large brown patch on the falls; beard violet with
orange tips. Height 56cm. Early season.

'Little Suki' (standard dwarf, bearded)
Registered by N. K. Scopes 1970. Parents:

'Robert Melrose' × 'Velvet Capers'. Standards
creamy tan with purple shadows at base; falls
deeper tan. Height 30cm. Early season.

'Little Vanessa' (standard dwarf, bearded)
Registered by J. D. Taylor 1968. Parents:
(Langdale seedling × seedling) × 'Red Dandy'.
Standards magenta; falls magenta, with white
beard. Height 30cm. Mid-season.

'Owlet' (standard dwarf, bearded)   Registered
by J. D. Taylor 1976. Parents: 'Jane Taylor' ×
seedling. Standards lavender; falls lavender
with darker spot. Height 33cm. Early season.

'Sky Caper' (miniature dwarf, bearded)
Registered by Warburton 1962. Parents: 'Fairy
Flax' × AM-5 (blue *pumila*). Pale purplish-blue
self; beard white. Height 15cm. Early season.

'Small Wonder' (semi-dwarf, bearded)
Registered by G. Douglas 1953. Parents: 'Helen
McGregor' × *pumila* blue. Medium-French-
blue self; beard yellow. Height 28cm. Early to
mid-season.

'Green Spot'

'Canary Bird'

'Langport Wren'

'Langport Honey'

'Amethyst Flame'

'Florentina'

Langport Chief'

'Langport Finch'

'Langport Chapter'

'Blue Pansy'

Iris germanica

Iris germanica 'Nepalensis'

Specimens from Eccleston Square, 20 May. ⅕ life size

'Amethyst Flame'

Iris germanica

Iris germanica L. (*Iridaceae*)   Origin unknown, probably of hybrid origin, but perhaps native in the E Mediterranean. Widely cultivated as an old garden plant and also for the perfume extracted from its rhizome. Commonly naturalized in dry, rocky places. Flower stems stout and well branched, 40–90cm, branches to 5cm. Leaves 30–70cm × 20–35mm, somewhat glaucous, straight. Flowers with lavender-purple standards 55–90mm × 40–60mm; falls deep velvety purple with distinct white haft-markings, 55–90 × 40–60mm; the beard white or whitish. An excellent plant for dry town gardens, where it will flower happily in light deciduous shade in March–May. Scented.

Iris germanica 'Florentina' syn. *Iris florentina* auct. vix L. **Orris Root**   Flowers white,

flushed with very pale blue, with distinct haft markings and a yellow beard, fragrant. The bracts are almost wholly brown and papery at flowering time. Now considered to be a form of *I. germanica*. Cultivated in Italy especially in the area around Florence for perfume. Early-flowering, and easily grown in ordinary garden soil and full sun. The root must be dried before the scent, which resembles violets, is released.

Iris germanica 'Nepalensis' syn. *I. germanica* 'Atropurpurea'   An ancient variety that crops up in old gardens and can be found naturalized; it has deep-purple-violet standards and falls with a white beard. Scented. (See also p.190.)

'Amethyst Flame' (tall, bearded)   Registered by B. R. Schreiner 1957. Parents: 'Crispette' ×

('Lavandesque' × 'Pathfinder'). Amethyst-violet self; beard pale yellowish. Height 97cm. Mid-season.

'Blue Pansy' (tall, bearded)   Kelway & Son 1966. 'Black Hills' × 'Knight Valiant'. Deep-violet-blue self with golden beard. Height 102cm. Mid-season.

'Canary Bird' (tall, bearded)   Kelway & Son 1957. 'Berkeley Gold' seedling. Lemon-yellow. Height 97cm. Early to mid-season.

'Green Spot' (intermediate, bearded) Registered by P. H. R. Cook 1951. Parents: seedling × yellow *pumila*. Whitish self with green spot on falls; yellow beard and markings. Height 25cm. Very early in season.

Irises at Claude Monet's garden at Giverny in late May

'Langport Chapter' (intermediate, bearded)
Medium blue with purple markings; beard
purplish. Height 45cm. Early season.

'Langport Chief' (intermediate, bearded)
Introduced by Kelway & Son prior to 1940.
Parents not known. Purplish-blue with darker
markings on the falls; beard tipped gold. Height
40cm. Early season.

'Langport Finch' (intermediate, bearded)
Introduced by Kelway & Son prior to 1940.
Light-blue self with darker veining on the falls;
beard whitish with yellow tips. Height 45cm.
Early season.

'Langport Honey' (intermediate, bearded)
Introduced by Kelway & Son prior to 1940.
Parents not known. Orange-yellow with strong
purple-brown markings on the falls; beard gold.
Height 66cm. Early season.

'Langport Wren' (intermediate, bearded)
Introduced by Kelway & Son prior to 1940.
Parents not known. Deep magenta-brown with
black veining on falls and standards; beard
yellow. Height 66cm. Early season.

'Plicata'   Is extremely similar to *I. pallida*
(p.190), the difference being that it is a semi-
albino form with purple colour on the veins at
the edges of the standards and falls. The beard
is yellow.

'White May' (intermediate, bearded)
Introduced by P. B. J. Murrell 1939. Parents:
'Orange Queen' × 'Senlac'. Standards pure
white. Early season.

Iris 'Plicata' at Myddelton House

Iris 'White May'

'Brown Trout'

'Spring Festival'

'Big Day'

'Dante'

'Headlines'

'Helen McGregor'

'Gold Flake'

'Golden Planet'

'Argus Pheasant'

Specimens from Eccleston Square, 6 June. ½ life size

'Argus Pheasant' (tall, bearded) Registered by N. De Forest 1947. Parents: 'Casa Morena' × 'Tobacco Road'. Golden-brown self; beard deep yellow. Height 100cm. Mid-season.

'Big Day' (tall, bearded) Introduced by Kelway & Son prior to 1940. Parents not known. Medium blue with white haft markings; beard white. Height 90cm. Mid-season.

'Brown Trout' (tall, bearded) Registered by Kelway & Son 1959. Parents: 'Magic Carpet' × 'Ranger'. Standards copper; falls deep red. Height 90cm. Mid-season.

'Bruno' (tall, bearded) Introduced by A. J. Biss 1922. Parents: 'Dominian' × unknown. Dark-yellow blended bicolour. Fragrance grape-like. Height over 76cm. Mid- to late season.

'Dante' (tall, bearded) Registered by R. Kelway 1958. Parents: 'Mexico' × unknown. Standards golden bronze; falls blood-red with bronze edge. Height 76cm. Mid-season.

'Gold Flake' (tall, bearded) Registered by O. D. N. and P. B. J. Murrell 1933. Parents: 'W. R. Dykes' × unknown. Ruffled golden bronzy-yellow with a cream patch and bronze veining on the falls. Height 102cm. Mid-season.

'Golden Planet' (tall, bearded) Registered by Kelway & Son 1956. Parents: 'Desert Song' × unknown. Yellow self with deep-gold haft markings; beard yellow. Height 86cm. Early to mid-season.

'Gracious Living' (tall, bearded) Registered by L. W. Brummitt 1966. Parents: 'Melodrama' × 'Mary Randall'. Standards cream; shaded colour of the falls at base of midrib; falls imperial-purple-shaded lilac below beard; hafts sepia. Height 90cm.

'Headlines' (tall, bearded) Registered by L. Brummitt 1953. Parents: 'Extravaganza' × 'Louise Blake'. Standards pure white; falls velvety, deep purple, purple; beard yellow. Height 90cm. Late season.

'Helen McGregor' (tall, bearded) Registered by N. Graves 1943. Parents: 'Purissima' × 'Cloud Castle'. Clear, bright-pale-blue self; beard whitish or touched with yellow. Height 100cm. Mid-season.

'Lady Mohr' (tall, bearded – Arilbred) Registered by Salbach 1943. Parents: (seedling × 'William Mohr') × Ib–MAC. Standards pale violet with purple markings; falls cream with purple markings; beard brown. Height 90cm. Mid-season.

'Muriel Neville' (tall, bearded) Registered by H. Fothergill 1963. Parents: ('Queechee' × 'Great Day') × ('Sequatchie' × 'Blood Cornelian') × ('Mexican Magic' × 'Benton Mocha') × 'Ebony Echo'. Crimson. Height 107cm. Mid-season.

'Orange Dawn' (tall, bearded) Registered by S. Linnegar for A. Howe 1981. Parents: 'May Melody' × unknown. Standards buff-orange; falls apricot orange. Height 96cm. Mid- to late season.

'Spring Festival' (tall, bearded) Registered by D. Hall. Parents: seedling × 'Mary Hall'. Standards light pink; falls medium pink; beard red. Height 94cm. Mid-season.

'Staten Island' (tall, bearded) Registered by K. D. Smith 1947. Parents: 'The Red Admiral' × 'City of Lincoln'. Yellow with pink tones. Height 97cm. Mid-season.

'Wheatear' (tall, bearded) Registered by B. L. C. Dodsworth 1984. Parents: 'Ultrapoise' × 'Radiant Light'. Ruffled apricot self with tangerine beard. Height 97cm. Late season.

Iris 'Lady Mohr' (showing viral streaks)

Iris 'Wheatear'

Iris 'Muriel Neville'

Iris 'Staten Island'

Iris 'Bruno'

Iris 'Gracious Living'

Iris 'Orange Dawn'

'Passport'

'Out Yonder'

'Derwentwater'

'Lady Ilse'

'Fantasy Fair'

'Valimar'

'San Leandro'

'Mary Frances'

'Lovely Letty'

Specimens from Claire Austin, Albrighton, 20 June. ⅓ life size

'**Actress**' (tall, bearded) Registered by K. Keppel 1975. Parents: 'Ford Wish' × 69-41c: (('Marquesan Skies' × 'Babbling Brook') × 'Touche'). Wisteria-violet self; beard pale with a lavender-blue tip, throat Indian-orange. Height 90cm. Early to mid-season. Remontant.

'**Arcady**' (tall, bearded) Registered by H. Fothergill 1959. Parents: 'Jane Phillips' × 'Pegasus'. Standards pale blue; falls pale blue, slightly darker in the centre; beard white-tipped, pale yellow. Height 122cm. Mid- to late season.

'**Babbling Brook**' (tall, bearded) Registered by Keppel 1965. Parents: 'Galilee' × 'Symphony'. Light-blue self; beard white-touched yellow. Ruffled. Height 97cm. Mid-season.

'**Blue Rhythm**' (tall, bearded) Introduced by C. G. Whiting 1945. Parents: 'Annabel' × 'Blue Zenith'. Mid-blue-toned self. Height 100cm. Lemon scented. Mid-season.

'**Blue Sapphire**' (tall, bearded) Registered by B. Schreiner 1953. Parents: 'Snow Flurry' × 'Chivalry'. Light silvery-blue self; beard white. Height 102cm. Early season.

'**Derwentwater**' (tall, bearded) Registered by H. J. Randall 1953. Parents: 'Helen McGregor' × 'Cahokia'. Delicate-pale-blue self; beard creamy white. Height 86cm. Mid-season.

'**Fantasy Fair**' (tall, bearded) Registered by J. Nelson 1977. Parents: ('Flame and Sand' × 'Pink Taffeta') × 'Buffy'. Ruffled and heavily laced smoky-pink-orchid, blended a touch rosy-tan on the haft; beard red. Height 90cm. Mid-season.

'**Gilston Gwyneth**' (tall, bearded) Registered by H. Fletcher 1963. Parents: 'Pegasus' × ('Cascadian' × 'Keene Valley'). Standards mid-blue, ruffled; falls lighter blue. Height 86cm. Mid-season.

'**Jane Phillips**' (tall, bearded) Registered by N. Graves 1946. Parents: 'Helen McGregor' × ('Pale Moonlight' × 'Great Lakes'). Delicate-blue self; beard white. Height 102cm. Mid-season.

'**Lady Ilse**' (tall, bearded) Registered by K. Smith 1950. Parents: 'Jane Phillips' × 'Keene Valley'. Soft-blue-violet self with slight yellowish haft markings; beard creamy white. Height 104cm. Late mid-season.

'**Lovely Letty**' (tall, bearded) Registered by D. Hall 1960. Parents unknown. Pale-violet-blue self with a tangerine beard. Height 80cm. Mid-season.

'**Mary Frances**' (tall, bearded) Registered by L. Gaulter 1971. Parents: 'Town and Country' × ('Marie Phillips' × 'Sterling Silver'). Ruffled light-blue-orchid self; beard white with a hint of yellow. Height 98cm. Mid-season.

'**Out Yonder**' (tall, bearded) Registered by G. Wickersham 1969. Parents unknown. Standards very pale blue with a touch of darker veining; falls violet-indigo; beard white or a touch yellowish. Height 90cm. Mid-season.

'**Passport**' (intermediate, bearded) Registered by J. Ghio 1970. Parents: unknown × 'Oracle'. Lightly ruffled pale blue-purple white self with a darker area with dark-purplish-blue veins on the falls; beard white. Height 60cm. Early season.

'**San Leandro**' (tall, bearded) Registered by L. Gaulter 1968. Parents: [(['Fuchsia' × 'Party Dress'] × ['Frost and Flame' × sibling]) × ('Arctic Flame' × sibling)] × 'Rippling Waters'. Light-purple self; beard tangerine. Height 90cm. Mid-season.

'**Valimar**' (tall, bearded) Registered by J. R. Hamblen 1956. Parents: ('Helen McGregor' × 'Radiation') × 'Palomino'. Ruffled, standards pinky violet; falls the same with orange haft markings; beard orange-red. Height 90cm. Mid- to late season.

'Jane Phillips'

'Blue Rhythm'

'Blue Sapphire'

'Actress'

'Gilston Gwyneth'

'Babbling Brook'

'Arcady'

Part of the classic iris collection at Myddelton House, Middlesex

Iris 'Sign of Leo'

Iris 'Night Raider'

Iris 'Royal Touch'

Iris 'Magic Man'

'Annabel Jane' (tall, bearded)   Registered by B. Dodsworth 1973. Parents: 'Sterling Silver' × 'Champagne Music'. Standards pale lilac; falls medium lilac; beard white with yellow tips. Height 120cm. Mid-season.

'Black Swan' (tall, bearded)   Registered by Fay 1960. Parents: 'Sable Night' × 53-68. Reddish-black self; beard brown. Height 90cm. Mid-season.

'Brummitt's Mauve' (tall, bearded) Registration not found but presumed to be L. Brummitt. Parents not known. Violet-brown self, the edges of the falls brown and the centre vibrant violet, orangy markings on the haft; beard golden yellow. Height 97cm. Late season.

'Deep Pacific' (tall, bearded)   Registered by E. Burger 1975. Parents: 'Cup Race' × 'Royal Touch'. Navy-blue self with a medium-blue beard. Height 70cm. Mid- to late season.

'Los Angeles' (tall, bearded)   There is some confusion about this name. It is sometimes spelt 'Los Angelus'; also, as far as I can tell, it was registered by either W. J. Rudill 1926 or by S. B. Mitchell in 1927; these two registrations make it most confusing. My specimens have rich-violet-blue self, with browny-purple haft markings; beard white tipped yellow. Height 80cm. Mid-season.

'Magic Man' (tall, bearded)   Registered by B. Blyth 1979. Parents: [(['Fanfare Orchid' × ('Arctic Flame' × 'Morning Breeze')] × 'Latin Tempo')] × 'Cabaret Royale'. Standards light blue, with a deeper infusion of colour around the midrib; falls velvety purple with 3mm band of light blue around the edges; beard tangerine. Height 98cm. Mid- to late season.

'Night Raider' (tall, bearded)   Registered by C. Burrell 1976. Parents: ('Licorice Stick' × 'Rawlins' 68-17) × [('Dark Fury' × ('Black Hills' × 'Velvet Dusk')]. Velvety blue-black self, including the beard. Height 84cm. Early to mid-season.

'Ninevah' (tall, bearded)   Registered by Keppel 1965. Parents: 'Bang' × 'Capitola'. Standards purplish, flushed brown at base; falls red-violet washed warm brown; beard dark brown. Height 76cm. Early season.

'Raspberry Ripples' (tall, bearded) Introduced by O. D. Niswonger 1967. Parents: ('Pink Fulfilment' × 'Orchid Jewel') × 'Rippling Waters'. Frilly edged deep-rose-purple self with browny-orange beard. Height 90cm. Mid-season.

'Royal Ruffles' (tall, bearded)   Registered by E. Purviance 1962. Parents: 'Black Forest' × 'Chivalry'. Marine-blue self with a blue beard. Height 74cm. Early to mid-season.

'Royal Touch' (tall, bearded)   Registered by Schreiner's 1966. Parents: [J219-A 'Blue Ensign' × ('The Admiral' × 'Great Lakes')] × 'Randolph' × ['Pierre Menard' × ('Distance' × 'Sylvia Murray')]. Dark-marine, blue-violet self; beard navy-blue. Height 90cm. Late season.

'Sable' (tall, bearded)   Registered by P. H. Cook 1938. Parents: [{[('Innocenza' × 'Blue Boy') × 'Cinnabar'] × ['Cinnabar' × ('Innocenza' × 'Blue Boy')]} × 'Cinnabar'] × ('Seminole' × 'Cinnabar'). Standards dark purple-blue; falls darker velvety violet; beard orange and white. Height 84cm. Mid-season.

'Sign of Leo' (tall, bearded)   Registered by L. Zurbrigg 1976. Parents: 'Jet Black' × 'Lovely Again'. Standards violet with some red influence; falls violet with red influence and blackish overlay; beard bronze. Height 90cm. Early season, remontant in late summer.

'Ninevah'

'Raspberry Ripples'

'Los Angeles'

'Brummitt's Mauve'

'Royal Ruffles'

'Deep Pacific'

Specimens from Claire Austin, 12 June. ⅓ life size

Iris 'Black Swan'

Iris 'Sable'

Iris 'Annabel Jane'

Iris fields at Claire Austin, Abrighton

Iris 'Joyce Terry'

Iris 'Star Shine'

Iris 'Golden Encore'

Iris 'Debby Rairdon'

Iris 'Lime Crystal'

Iris 'Grace Abounding'

'Aunt Martha' (border, bearded) Registered by J. Allen 1970. Parents: ('Snow Goddess' × 'Limelight') × 'Yellow Dresden'. Heavily laced light-yellow self with a white area around the tip of the light-yellow beard. Height 60cm. Mid-season.

'Debby Rairdon' (tall, bearded) Registered Kuntz 1964. Parents not recorded. Standards subdued yellow with white on reverse side; falls pearly white with white on reverse, side edges yellowish; beard golden. Height 90cm. Mid- to late season.

'Frost and Flame' (tall, bearded) Registered by D. Hall 1956. Parents unknown. White self with a touch of purple, and yellow markings on the haft; beard red. Height 90cm. Early season.

'Gala Crown' (tall, bearded) Registered by P. E. Corey 1958. Parents: (('Bureau' × seedling) × 'Anthea') × 'Pink Tea'. Pale melon colour blended with a touch of pink; beard orange. Height 90cm. Mid-season.

'Gold Alps' (tall, bearded) Registered by L. Brummitt 1952. Parents: 'Admiration' × seedling. Standards creamy white with pale-yellow veining; falls deepish golden yellow, with darker veins at the haft; beard golden yellow. Height 90cm. Mid-season.

'Golden Encore' (tall, bearded, remontant) Registered by F. Jones 1972. Parents: (('Happy Birthday' × 'Fall Primrose') × 'Fall Primrose') × 'Renaissance'. Vivid-yellow self with a small white blaze on the falls; beard bright gold. Height 90cm. Early, and again in late summer.

Iris 'Spirit of Memphis'

Iris 'Lemon Brocade'

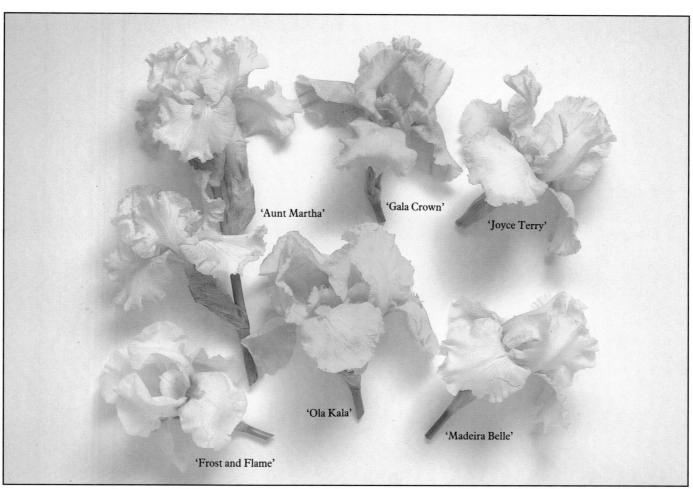

'Aunt Martha' 'Gala Crown' 'Joyce Terry'

'Ola Kala' 'Madeira Belle'

'Frost and Flame'

Specimens from Claire Austin, 15 June. ⅓ life size

Iris 'Pale Primrose' *Iris* 'Gold Alps'

'Grace Abounding' (tall, bearded) Pauline M. McCormick on behalf of H. Fothergill 1976. ('Cream Crest' × sibling of 'Gilded Minaret') × sibling. Lemon-yellow self, lightly ruffled; cinnamon hafts; brilliant-yellow beard. Height 98cm. Mid-season.

'Joyce Terry' (tall, bearded) T. Muhlestein 1974. 'Charmaine' × 'Launching Pad'. Lightly ruffled, standards yellow, paler in the centre; falls white with a yellow edge and deeper yellow haft markings; beard deeper yellow. Height 98cm. Mid- to late season.

'Lemon Brocade' (tall, bearded) N. Rudolph 1973. 'Cream Taffeta' × 67-54. Ruffled lemon-yellow self with whitish-green patches on the falls; beard white tipped yellow-orange. Height 86cm. Mid-season.

'Lime Crystal' (tall, bearded) B. Blyth 1975. Parents: 'Apropos' × 'Twist and Shout'. Standards lime-yellow; falls a shade darker; beard yellow. Height 86cm. Mid- to late season.

'Madeira Belle' (tall, bearded) Registration not found. Ruffled, white self, standards tinged with a hint of violet. Height 80cm. Late season.

'Ola Kala' (tall, bearded) Registered by J. N. Sass 1942. Parents: ('Prairie Sunset' × unknown) × ('Golden Age' × unknown). Rich deep-yellow self; beard deep yellow. Height 86cm. Late season.

'Pale Primrose' (tall, bearded) N. Whiting 1946. 'Happy Days' × 'Midwest Gem'. Pale yellow self with a small white patch on the falls and darker haft markings; beard golden yellow. Height 76cm. Late season.

'Spirit of Memphis' (tall, bearded, remontant) Registered by L. Zurbrigg 1976. Parents: ('Miss Illini' × 'Grand Baroque') × 'Halloween Party'. Medium-yellow self, ruffled and heavily laced; beard yellow. Height 90cm. Mid-season, and again in late summer.

'Star Shine' (tall, bearded) Registered by N. Wills 1947. Parents: ('Hermitage' × 'Hernani') × 'Song of Gold'. Standards pale yellow; falls white with yellow edges and veining; beard yellow. Height 90cm. Mid- to late season.

'Jungle Shadows'

'Autumn Leaves'

'Little Sheba'

'Flareup'

'Strawberry Sundae'

'Carnaby'

'Olympic Torch'

'Firecracker'

'Etched Apricot'

Specimens from Claire Austin, 12 June. ⅓ life size

'**Autumn Leaves**' (tall, bearded)   Registered by K. Keppel 1972. Parents: 'Vaudeville' × 'Radiant Apogee'. Standards blended pale brown; falls yellowish brown, strongly marked with red purple veining; beard orange-yellow. Height 86cm. Mid-season.

'**Carnaby**' (tall, bearded)   Registered by Schreiner's 1973. Parents: 'Wine and Roses' × Y 1307-A: (R 118–BX 'Rippling Waters'). Standards ruffled light wine-pink; falls deep rose-pink in the centre, edges light wine-pink; beard orange. Height 90cm. Mid- to late season.

'**Chartreuse Ruffles**' (tall, bearded)   Registered by N. Rudolph 1975. Parents: (seedling × Blocher 233) × 'Louise Watts'. Ruffled, standards pale lilac-pink with a deeper flush, chartreuse edge; falls greenish white with wide chartreuse edge; beard tipped yellow. Height 86cm. Mid-season.

'**Deputé Nomblot**' (tall, bearded)   Registered by Cayeaux et Le Clerc 1929. Parents not recorded. Standards pink; falls pink, darker veining over a lighter patch on the haft; beard golden yellow. Height 74cm. Late season.

'**Etched Apricot**' (tall, bearded)   J. Gibson 1967. 'Henna Stitches' × 'Wild Ginger'. Ruffled, standards brownish apricot; falls white ground etched apricot with a hint of purple; beard golden. Height 76cm. Mid-season.

'**Firecracker**' (tall, bearded)   Hall 1942. ('Morning Splendour' × 'Legend') × ('Dauntless' × 'Rameses'). Standards red-brown over a yellow ground; falls yellow with red-brown veining and etching, around the edge; beard deep golden. Height 74cm. Early to mid-season.

'**Flareup**' (tall, bearded)   J. Ghio 1977. 'Coffee House' sib × (('Ponderosa' × 'Travel On') × 'Ponderosa'). Ruffled, standards yellowy brown; falls same colour with yellow haft markings; beard yellowy brown. Height 97cm. Mid-season.

'**Jungle Shadows**' (intermediate, bearded)   E. Sass and H. Graham 1959. 'Black Delight' × seedling 54-95. Rich blended golden-brown self with a violet patch on the falls; beard golden orange. Height 66cm. Mid-season.

'**Lady River**' (tall, bearded)   Kelway 1966. 'Melody Fair' × 'Party Ruffles'. Apricot-pink self, ruffled with bronzy-violet veining on the haft; beard orangy-red. Height 75cm. Mid-season.

'**Little Sheba**' (tall, bearded)   T. M. Abell. 'Saffron Charm' × 'Arabi Pasha'. Small-flowered, pale-oyster self with greenish yellowish veining; beard pale with touches of cobalt violet. Height 74cm. Mid-season.

'**Olympic Torch**' (tall, bearded)   R. Schreiner 1956. 'Inca Chief' × (Schr. 49–46 × 'Watchfire'). Light golden-bronze self; beard bronze-yellow. Height 97cm. Mid-season.

'**Sabre Dance**' (tall, bearded)   Registered by O. Brown 1970. Parents: ('Grandiflora' × (pink seedling × 'Gypsy Lullaby' sibling)) × 'Barcelona' sibling. Standards touched light blue blending to flesh at outer edges; falls champagne-brushed lavender-rose deep on shoulders, with a copper lustre overall; beard red. Height 97cm. Mid-season.

'**Strawberry Sundae**' (tall, bearded)

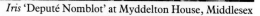

Iris 'Deputé Nomblot' at Myddelton House, Middlesex

Iris 'Sabre Dance'

Iris 'Chartreuse Ruffles'

Iris 'Witch of Endor'

Iris 'Lady River'

Registered by H. Schmelzer 1977. Parents: ('Harem Silk' × 'Wine and Roses') × 'Wine and Roses'. Standards creamy ruffled; falls strawberry–wine colour, edge creamy; beard red. Height 80cm. Mid-season.

'**Wild Ginger**' (tall, bearded)   Registered by J. Gibson 1960. Parents: 'Tohdah' × 'Floradora Flounce'. Plicata, standards burnt-umber-shaded orchid; falls white with golden-brown stitching-shaded-orchid at the edges. Height 90cm. Early to mid-season.

'**Witch of Endor**' (tall, bearded, remontant) B. Miller 1977. 'Rainbow Promised' × 'Cayenne Capers'. Black-crimson self with a white area with dark-crimson veining on the hafts; beard golden, ruffled. Height 97cm. Early to mid-season, and again in late summer.

Iris 'Wild Ginger'

Bearded irises in the garden at Eccleston Square, London

Iris 'Stepping Out'

Iris 'Lovely Again'

'Flaming Sword' or **'Flammenschwert'** (tall, bearded) Registered by Goos and Koenemann 1920. Parents not recorded. Standards yellow; falls dark purple-brown with very strong white veining on the hafts; beard yellow. Height 76cm. Mid-season.

'Lovely Again' (tall, bearded, remontant) Registered by R. G. Smith 1963. Parents not recorded. Lavender self with a yellow beard. Height 76cm. Mid-season, and again in late summer.

'Mary Vernon' (tall, bearded) Registered by N. McKee 1941. Parents: (No. 3814 × 'Janet Butler') × 'Chosen'. Standards good yellow; falls red-brown with creamy yellow edge and haft markings; beard yellow. Height 74cm. Mid-season.

'Melbreak' (tall, bearded) Registered by H. J. Randall 1957. Parents: ('Cherie' × 'Angela Borgia') × 'Mary Randall'. Ruffled; standards violet pink with deeper veining and a lighter orange patch at the haft; beard tangerine. Height 97cm. Mid- to late season.

'Needlecraft' (tall, bearded) Registered by L. Zurbrigg 1976. Parents: ('Ribbon Round' × R. G. Smith E5AR) × 'Cross Stitch'. White ground plicata. Height 86cm. Mid-season.

'Sea Venture' (tall, bearded) Registered by Bennett Jones 1971. Parents: 'Avis' × 'Eternal Love'. Ruffled; standards pale-blue-flushed, deep marine-blue at the base; falls pale blue; beard yellow. Height 86cm. Mid-season.

'Stepping Out' (tall, bearded) Registered by Schreiner's 1964. Parents not known. Plicata, with large white areas with sharply patterned edges of blue-black-violet. Height 97cm. Mid- to late season.

'Sultry Sky' (border, bearded) Registered by L. W. Neel 1952. Parents: 'Fair Elaine' × 'Wabash'. Standards pinky cream, yellowing at the base; falls straw-coloured ground with purple-brown centre; beard yellow. Height 97cm. Mid-season.

'Wabash' (tall, bearded) Registered by E. B. Williamson 1936. Parents: 'Dorothy Dietz' × 'Cantabile'. Bicolour, standards white; falls velvety purple with white veining at the haft; beard bright yellow. Height 86cm. Mid-season.

'Whoop 'em Up' (border, bearded) Registered by D. Brady 1973. Parents: ('Bang' × 'Plunder') × 'Extravaganza'. Standards golden yellow; falls maroon with golden yellow on reverse side extending to the top as an all-round edge; beard yellow. Height 68cm. Mid-season.

Iris 'Needlecraft'

Iris 'Mary Vernon'

Iris 'Whoop 'em Up'

Iris 'Sultry Sky'

Iris 'Wabash'

Iris 'Flaming Sword'

Iris 'Melbreak'

Iris 'Sea Venture'

'Tyrian Robe'

'Royal Trumpeter'

'Rose Violet'

'Foggy Dew'

'My Smoky'

'Royal Oak'

'Gracchus'

'Superstition'

'Frontier Marshall'

'Ultrapoise'

Specimens collected, 4 June. ⅓ life size

'**Blue Duchess**' syn. 'Crystal Blue' (tall, bearded)   Registered by Kelway & Son 1966. Parents: 'Jane Phillips' × 'Blue Cameo'. Light-blue self. Height 97cm.

'**Blue-Eyed Brunette**' (tall, bearded) Registered by C. C. Hall. Parents: 'Queechee' × 'Carnton'. Standards cigar-brown; falls brown with a blue spot. Height 90cm.

'**Dancer's Veil**' (tall, bearded)   Registered by P. Hutchinson 1959. Parents: (plicata seedling × 'Dancing Waters') × 'Rosy Veil'. White ground plicata etched blue-purple. Height 90cm. Mid- to late season.

'**Dovedale**' (tall, bearded)   Registered 1980 by B. L. C. Dodsworth. Parents: 'Raspberry Ripples' × 'San Leandro'. Mid pinkish-lilac self. Height 82cm. Late season.

'**Dusky Dancer**' (tall, bearded)   Registered by Watt Foulger in 1952 and released by W. Luihn in 1966. Parents: 'Dark Fury' × 'Black Swan'. Very dark violet-black self, ruffled; beard dark-blackish. Height 90cm. Mid- to late season.

'**Foggy Dew**' (tall, bearded)   Registered by Keppel 1968. Parents: 'Siva Siva' × 'Diplomacy'. Plicata, standards pastel blend of greyish cream and lavender; falls white ground with soft-violet border with darker markings; beard white, tipped yellow. Height 97cm. Mid-season.

'**Frontier Marshall**' (tall, bearded)   Registered by Schreiner's 1964. Parents: ('Trim' × 'Tall Chief') × 'Gypsy Jewels'. Uniform crimson lake, red self; beard with a bronzy cast. Height 90cm. Early to mid-season.

'**Gracchus**' (tall, bearded)   Introduced by T. S. Ware 1884. Parents unknown: probably a hybrid of *I. variegata*. Standards light yellow; falls strongly veined reddish. Height 74cm.

'**My Honeycomb**' (tall, bearded)   Registered by J. M. Gibson 1958. Parents: seedling of 'Taholah'. Standards light brown; falls brown with rich brown veining, white patch on centre; beard yellow. Height 89cm. Mid-season.

'**My Smoky**' (tall, bearded)   Registered by Kelway & Son 1956. Parent: 'Magic Carpet' seedling. Plicata, white with faint yellowish touches; falls edged rose-brown. Height 87cm. Mid-season.

'**Rose Violet**' (tall, bearded)   Introduced by J. H. Kirkland 1939. Parents not recorded. Red self. Mid-season.

'**Royal Oak**' (tall, bearded)   Registered by C. C. Hall 1962. Parents: 'Queechee' × 'Carnton'. Standards cigar brown; falls bluish-mauve, edge brown. Height 76cm. Mid-season.

'**Royal Trumpeter**' (tall, bearded)   Registered by C. Reynolds 1969. Parents: ((59-27('Savage') × Ib-Mac) × 'Red Slippers')) × L.P. 65-03 ('Barbizon' × 'Fire Ruby'). Red self; beard brown-red. Height 74cm. Late season.

'**Superstition**' (tall, bearded)   Registered by Schreiner's 1977. Parents: (v435-1 × 1560-15) × 'Navy Strut'. Ebony-hued self; beard blue-black. Height 90cm. Mid-season.

'**Tyrian Robe**' (tall, bearded)   Registered by C. C. Hall 1968. Parents: 'Redbourne' × seedling V178. Violet-purple self. Height 90cm. Mid-season.

'**Ultrapoise**' (tall, bearded, plicata)   Registered by Noyd 1961. Parents: ([(C. 'Honeyflow' × 'Tobacco Road') × 'Cliffdell'] × [('Salmon Shell' × Hall 44-09) × 'Pink Formal']) × 'Garden Gold'. Straw-yellow self with a pink flush in the standards; beard tangerine. Height 86cm. Mid-season.

Iris 'Gracchus'   *Iris* 'Blue Duchess'

Iris 'Dovedale'

Iris 'Blue-Eyed Brunette'

Iris 'Dusky Dancer'

Iris 'Dancer's Veil'

Iris 'My Honeycomb'

Part of the classic iris collection at Myddelton House, Middlesex

Iris 'Emerald Fountain'

Iris 'I Do'

Iris 'Dream Lover'

'Bewick Swan' (tall, bearded)   Registered by B. L. C. Dodsworth 1980. Parents: 'Crystal Blaze' × 'Rippling Waters'. White self, yellow hafts; red beard. Height 102cm. Mid-season.

'Brother Carl' (tall, bearded, remontant) Introduced by L. A. Zurbrigg 1983. Parents: 'Sister Helen' × 'I Do'. White self with delicate darker veining on the falls; beard white with yellow tip. Height 76cm. Mid-season.

'Christmas Angel' (tall, bearded)   Registered by R. De Forest 1959. Parents: 'Frances Kent' × 'Paradise Pink'. White self with bright-gold haft. Height 97cm. Mid-season.

'Cliffs of Dover' (tall, bearded)   Registered by O. W. Fay 1952. Parents: 'New Snow' × 'Cahokia'. Pure-white self; beard yellow. Height 90cm. Mid-season.

'Cup Race' (tall, bearded)   Registered by Buttrick 1962. Parents: ('Bluebird Blue' ×

'South Pacific') × 'Concord Town'. White self, ruffled, with mauve and yellowish tints. Height 90cm. Mid- to late season.

'Dream Lover' (tall, bearded)   Registered by E. Tams 1970. Parents: 'Miss Indiana' × ('Melodrama' × 'Rippling Waters'). Ruffled. Standards blue-white; falls dark bluish purple; beard blue. Height 91-97cm. Mid- to late season.

'Emerald Fountain' (tall, bearded)   Registered by D. Brown 1960. Parents: ['Blue Sapphire' × ('Hit Parade' × 'Pink Formal')] × ('Mary Randall' × 'Limelight'). Standards pale uranium-greenish with a blue infusion, ruffled; falls flax-blue, edges brushed uranium-green; beard yellow. Height 97cm. Mid- to late season.

'English Cottage' (tall, bearded, remontant) Registered by L. Zurbrigg 1976. Parents: [('Crinkled Ivory' × 'Autumn Sensation') × 'Grand Baroque'] × 'Cross Stitch'. Standards

white with some very pale plicating of violet; falls white with light-violet plicata markings at haft only; beard near white. Height 87cm. Early season, and again in late summer.

'Gudrun' (tall, bearded)   Registered by Mrs W. R. Dykes 1930. Parents not known. White self with yellow veining on the haft; beard orange-yellow. Height 100cm. Mid-season.

'I Do' (tall, bearded, remontant)   Registered by L. Zurbrigg 1973. Parents: 'Grand Baroque' × 'Amy'. Standards white with a slight cast of violet and greenish yellow, green at the midrib; falls white, with some green texture veining in the centre; beard white-tipped, pale yellow, ruffled. Height 81cm. Early to mid-season, and again in late summer.

'Vanity' (tall, bearded)   Registered by B. Y. Morrison 1928. Parents not recorded. Blended with pale-pink tones; falls lighter; beard red. Height 94cm. Mid-season.

Iris 'Gudrun'

Iris 'Christmas Angel'

Iris 'Cliffs of Dover'

Iris 'English Cottage'

Iris 'Cup Race'

Iris 'Brother Carl'

Iris 'Vanity'

Iris 'Bewick Swan'

'Banbury Welcome'

'Pacific Moon'

'Banbury Beauty'

'Banbury Fair'

'Banbury Gem'

'Phillida'

'Lavender Royal'

'Banbury Velvet'

Irises from Wisley, 21 May. ½ life size

Iris douglasiana Herbert (s. *Californicae*)
Native of the Pacific coast, from S California to
Oregon, growing on open, grassy slopes,
flowering in March–May. Plant forming loose
clumps. Leaves evergreen, dark green, ribbed,
to 2cm wide. Stems to 80cm tall, usually with
1–4 side branches, with 1–3 leaves. Flower
colour varying from pale cream to bluish or
deep reddish-purple. Flowers with tube 1.5–
2.8cm long; falls oblanceolate to obovate,
5–8.7cm long; standard oblanceolate 4–7cm
long, to 1.8cm wide. Style 1–2cm long, coarsely
toothed. Capsule sharply triangular in section.
This is the tallest of the Pacific coast irises and
the commonest species along the California
coast; it is easily grown in rather moist, peaty
and sandy soil. Hardy to −15°C perhaps.

Iris innominata Henderson (s. *Californicae*)
Native of NW California (in del Monte Co.) and
in SW Oregon, growing on sunny or partially
shaded hillsides, in mixed forest, on the inner
side of the coast ranges, flowering in May–June.
Plant forming loose clumps. Leaves dark-shiny-
green, paler beneath, 2–4mm wide. Stems to
20cm tall, with 2–4 leaves. Bracts opposite,
subequal, with scarious margin enclosing 2
flowers. Flower colour variable, from yellow to
pale bluish or deep purple. Flowers with tube
1.5–3cm long; falls 5–8.5cm long; standards
4.5–7cm long, oblanceolate; style crests 0.9–
1.4cm long, squarish, toothed. This and many
other species are variable in colour, and hybrids
are common in the wild, so the species of these
Pacific Coast irises are difficult to name with
confidence. They are all, however, easily grown
in well-drained, preferably acid, sandy soil in
sun or light shade.

Iris purdyi Eastw. (s. *Californicae*)   Native of
NW California, growing in Redwood forest and
mixed forest along the coast ranges, in open
woods and on roadside banks, flowering in
May–June. Plant forming loose clumps. Leaves
evergreen, dark green above, greyish beneath,
to 8mm wide. Stems to 35cm tall, unbranched,
with many short overlapping leaves. Bracts
opposite, inflated, enclosing 2 flowers. Flower
colour from creamy yellow to pale bluish,
variously veined. Flowers with tube 2.8.–4.8cm
long; falls 5.5–8.4cm long, oblanceolate;
standards 5–7cm × 0.9–2cm; style crests 0.9–
2.1cm long, narrowly ovate. Easily grown in
well-drained and rather dry sandy soil in partial
shade.

Iris tenuissima Dykes (s. *Californicae*)   Native
of N California from Butte to Siskiyou and
Humboldt counties, growing in clearings in dry
woods of oak, pine or mixed evergreens, often
on roadside banks, flowering in April–June.
Plant with a slender rhizome; leaves *c*.6mm
wide, often reddish at the base, to 40cm long.
Stems usually 2-flowered, around 20cm.
Flowers usually pale cream, with purplish or
brownish veins, but less veined in var.
purdyiformis R. C. Foster which is probably the
plant shown here. Falls 4.7–7.5cm, 1.1–1.8cm
wide, narrowly ovate. Standards 4.4–6.4cm
long, 0.6–1.4cm wide. Perianth tube slender
below, dilated above. Style crests 1.1–2.3cm
long, recurved. For well-drained soil in partial
shade, dry in summer. Hardy to −15°C,
perhaps less.

Pacific Coast Irises   This group is derived
from hybrids of the *Californicae* irises and all are

Iris tenuissima near Mount Shasta, California

Iris 'Restless Native'

Irises near Mount Shasta, California

Iris purdyi

Iris 'Purple Dream'

Iris 'Banbury Beauty'

rather similar in everything except flower colour, which varies from deep purple and yellow to cream, brown, pink and white. They form spreading clumps, with usually evergreen leaves up to *c*.20cm and large numbers of flowers on stems 30–50cm high. They prefer well-drained, acid, fertile sandy soil and a warm, sheltered position in sun or partial shade. Most are hardy to around −15°C and so require protection from hard winter frosts in continental climates.

'Banbury Beauty' (Pacific Coast)   Registered by M. Brummitt in 1960. Parents: *douglasiana* 'Amaguita' × (innominata × *douglasiana* seedling). Light lavender with a purple zone on the falls. Height 53cm.

'Banbury Fair' (Pacific Coast)   Raised by M. Brummitt in 1967.

'Banbury Gem' (Pacific Coast)   Raised by M. Brummitt in 1974.

'Banbury Velvet' (Pacific Coast)   Registered by M. Brummitt in 1969. Parents: seedling × seedling. Standards violet; falls deep violet, velvety. Height 30cm. Mid-season.

'Banbury Welcome' (Pacific Coast) Registered by M. Brummitt in 1964. Parents: *douglasiana* 'Amaguita' × 'Lenz'. Deep raspberry, with gold and buff at the throat. Height 46cm.

'Lavender Royal' (Pacific Coast)   Registered by M. Brummitt in 1982.

'Pacific Moon' (Pacific Coast)   Registered by B. Hager in 1973. Parents: 'Ojai' × 'Grubstake'. Standards cream with pale-lavender veining, falls cream with lavender veining. Height 38cm. Early season.

'Phillida' (Pacific Coast)   Raised by N. Scopes in 1985.

'Purple Dream' (Pacific Coast)   Raised by N. Scopes in 1983.

'Restless Native' (Pacific Coast)   This appears to be a perpetual-flowering cultivar, photographed here in the Santa Barbara Botanic Garden in February, long before the normal hybrids begin to flower.

Iris innominata (yellow form)

Iris douglasiana at Salt Point, California

Iris innominata (pale blue form)

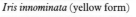

Iris 'Lavender Royal'

Iris kerneriana (B. Mathew 9001) at Kew

Iris masia near Gaziantep, SE Turkey

Iris masia

mid-winter, a deceitful invitation to birds which may think they are edible, like holly. A white-seeded form, which must be very beautiful, is in cultivation, but is very rare; a yellow-seeded form is also rumoured to exist and there is a form with white-striped leaves. The evergreen leaves are not very hardy, being killed by cold winds around −15°C, even in S England in severe winters.

Iris halophila Pallas (s. *Spuriae*) syn. *I. spuria* subsp. *halophila* (Pall.) Mathew & Wendelbo Native of S Romania and the E Ukraine to Siberia and NW China and south to the N Caucasus, growing in wet places in the steppes and by rivers often in saline soils, flowering in June. Stems 40–90cm. Leaves 7–12mm wide. Flowers 6–7cm across, pale to deep yellow; probably one of the hardiest of the spurias, and easily grown in moist heavy soil in full sun. Hardy to −25°C.

Iris kerneriana Aschers. & Sint. ex Baker (s. *Spuriae*)   Native of N Turkey from Bolu east to Erzurum and south to Kaz Dağ and Ankara, growing in dry, grassy turf, oak scrub and open pine forest at 300–2300m, flowering in May–July. Stems 20–45cm, rarely to 50cm. Leaves 2–4mm wide, rarely to 1cm. Flower 7–10cm across. Bracts with wide transparent margins, scarious after anthesis. Easily grown in a sunny position, in good but well-drained soil. This species has often been confused with *I. halophila* Pallas (q.v.), which has wider leaves 7–12mm wide, and bracts which do not become scarious after anthesis. At flowering the tube of *I. kerneriana* extends at least 2cm beyond the spathe, but the spathe extends almost to the base of the segments in *I. halophila*.

Iris masia Stapf. ex Foster syn. *I. grant-duffii* Baker subsp. *masia* (Stapf.) Dykes (s. *Syriacae*)   Native of SE Turkey from Gaziantep to Diyabakir, and of N Syria and Iraq, growing in fields and on rocky basalt steppe, expecially on Mount Masia (today Karaça Da.), at up to 1050m, flowering in April–May. Plant tufted with sharp almost spiny fibres around the rhizome. Stems to 35–70cm. Leaves 3–6mm across, tough. Flowers always purplish. *I. grant-duffii*, with which this species has sometimes been confused, has greenish-yellow flowers and is found near the Mediterranean coast in Israel and Syria, in wet or marshy ground. Hardy to −15°C perhaps.

Iris milesii Foster (s. *Lophiris* ('evansia'))   Native of the Himalayas from Kashmir to Uttar Pradesh (west of Nepal), growing in conifer forests at 1600–2700m, flowering in June. Stems branched, 30–100cm. Rhizome short for the 'evansia' section, green. Leaves pale green, 30–60cm long, 4–7cm wide, with sterile fans produced in summer. Flowers 6–8cm across. Beautiful but rarely seen, though apparently not difficult in a sunny border in sandy, peaty soil. Hardy to −15°C, perhaps less for short periods.

Iris foetidissima L. (s. *Foetidissimae*) **Gladdon** or **Roast Beef Plant**   Native from S England to the Azores to Spain, Portugal and North Africa and the Canaries, east to Italy and Sicily, growing in open woods, scrub and sunny hedge banks, especially on chalk and limestone, flowering in May–July. Stems 30–90cm. Leaves evergreen, shining, pungent. Flowers normally purplish, but yellow forms are frequent, especially in cultivation. The main garden value of the Gladdon is in its beautiful orange-red seeds which remain attached in the open pods in

Iris sintenisii Janka (s. *Spuriae*)   Native of SE Europe, from S Italy and Yugoslavia to Greece and NW Turkey, east to Kutahya, growing in grassy places and scrub, at up to 1350m in Turkey, flowering in June–July. Stems 8–25cm. Leaves evergreen, dark green, tough, 1–5mm across and up to 50cm long. Flowers 5–6cm across, not scented. Easily grown in semi-shade, but can disappear if neglected. Hardy to −15°C. Subsp. *bradzae* (Prodan) D. A. Webb & Chater, grows in wet, saline soils in N and E Romania and Moldavia; it has narrow 1.5–3.5mm wide leaves and an inflated spathe.

Iris foetidissima (yellowish form)

Iris milesii at Kew

Iris foetidissima seeds in winter

Iris sintenisii near Bolu, NW Turkey

Iris halophila on the steppes near Stavropol, S Russia

Iris setosa

Iris setosa
(white form)

Iris chrysographes
(text p. 221)

Iris chrysographes
'Black Knight'

Iris pseudacorus
(pale form)

Iris graminea

Iris versicolor

Specimens from Beth Chatto, Unusual Plants, 9 June. ½ life size

Iris chrysographes Dykes (s. *Sibiricae*) See p.221.

Iris graminea L. var. ***pseudocyperus*** (Schur) Beck (s. *Spuriae*) Native of S Europe, from France and NE Spain east to Poland, Bulgaria and the N Caucasus, growing in grassy places in scrub and in open woods, flowering in May–June. Var. *pseudocyperus* is a larger plant with unscented flowers said to be from E Europe, but Brian Mathew records a similar variety from Spain. Stems 20–40cm; leaves 35–100cm long, to 1.5cm wide. Flower of the normal variety said to smell like plums, 7–8cm across; easily grown in leafy soil in partial shade. A larger, softer-leaved plant than *I. sintenisii* (p.217). Hardy to −20°C.

Iris hexagona Walt. (s. *Hexagonae*) Native of South Carolina and Georgia to Florida and Texas, growing in swamps, flowering in March–May. Stems 30–90cm. Leaves 1.2–3cm wide, bright green; flowers 10–12cm across, purplish with a yellow patch on the falls. Easily grown in wet soil; shown here by a small stream on the rock garden at Kew. Hardy to −15°C perhaps.

Iris pseudacorus (pale form) See p.229.

Iris setosa Pall. ex Link (s. *Tripetalae*) Native from Newfoundland to Ontario and Maine, then from Alaska west to E Siberia, NE China and Japan, in Hokkaido and Honshu, growing in wet peaty meadows, sometimes in brackish marshes in N Japan, by rivers and in open woods, flowering in June–August. Many varieties have been described, but all can be recognized by the very small, bristle-like standards. A beautiful white is frequent in cultivation. One of the tallest is subsp. *hondoensis* Honda, up to 75cm, with purple flowers. Stems normally 15–90cm; leaves 1–2.5cm wide. Flowers 6–9cm across. Capsule inflated, rounded at the apex. Easily grown in moist places by water or in a border in rich peaty soil. In my experience acid soil is not essential for the form from N Hokkaido. Hardy to −25°C.

Iris setosa Pall. ex Link subsp. ***canadensis*** (M. Foster) Hulten syn. *I. hookeri* Penny This is the subspecies from NE America, from Newfoundland and Labrador, to Quebec, Ontario and Maine, growing in grassy and rocky places on the sea coast, flowering in June–August. Stem usually short, but up to 60cm, unbranched, with 1–2 flowers. Petals bluish. Often a rather small plant, easily grown in moist soil.

Iris versicolor L. syn. *I. virginica* L. (s. *Laevigatae*) Native of Newfoundland, to Manitoba south to Florida and Arkansas, and naturalized in Europe, e.g. on Ullswater and in Perthshire, growing in swamps, wet meadows, scrub and by lakes and rivers, flowering in May–July. Stems 20–80cm; leaves 1–2.5cm wide; flowers 6–8cm across, usually bluish purple but reddish purple in var. *kermesina*. Easily grown in wet soil by water, or in a moist border in rich soil. Hardy to −25°C.

***Iris* 'Gerald Darby'** A form of *I. versicolor*, raised in the 1960s, with purple bases to the leaves and bluish-purple flowers of good shape. Leaves *c.*2cm wide. Easily grown on the edge of a shallow pond or a moist border, flowering in early summer.

Iris setosa at Beth Chatto

Iris setosa subsp. *canadensis*

Iris hexagona at Kew

Iris 'Gerald Darby'

Mixed irises by the waterside

Iris chrysographes (black form)

Iris chrysographes at the Royal Botanic Garden, Edinburgh

Iris delavayi on the rock garden at Kew

Iris aff. *delavayi* SBEC 1063

Iris 'Holden Clough'

Iris forrestii hybrid

Iris chrysographes Dykes (s. *Sibiricae*)
Native of NE Burma, Yunnan and Sichuan,
growing in wet meadows and marshes, at 1300–
4500m, flowering in June–September. Plant
forming spreading clumps. Leaves 35–45cm,
equalling the stems, 1–1.5cm wide. Stems
unbranched, with 2 flowers. Flowers reddish
purple to almost black, usually with yellowish
veining on the falls. Standards at an oblique
angle, not upright. Easily grown in rich, moist
peaty soil, in full sun or partial shade. Hardy to
−15°C. Shown here are the black form, possibly
the same as 'Black Knight' and 'Black Velvet',
and a rich purple form. All the dark forms look
especially beautiful with the morning sun
shining through the flowers. See also p.218.

Iris clarkei Baker ex Hook. fil. (s. *Sibiricae*)
Native of E Nepal, Sikkim, Bhutan, SE Xizang
(Tibet) and Manipur, growing on damp, grassy
hillsides and marshes, sometimes at the edge of
Rhododendron and *Abies* forest, often in great
quantity, at 2500–4300m, flowering in May–
July. Plant forming loose clumps. Stems 30–
60cm, sometimes with 1–3 branches, usually
with 2 flowers per branch. Leaves 1.3–2cm
wide. Flowers to 7.5cm across, bluish purple to
dark blue or reddish purple. Standards
horizontal, giving the flower a flat shape. Falls
with a pale patch shading from yellow or white.
An attractive plant, rare in cultivation, and
sometimes confused with dwarf forms of *I.
setosa* (q.v.). For a moist, peaty soil in sun or
light shade. Hardy to −15°C.

Iris delavayi Micheli (s. *Sibiricae*)   Native of
W Yunnan and SW Sichuan, growing in wet
meadows at 3000–4000m, flowering in July–
August (June in cultivation in S England). Plant
forming large clumps. Leaves to 90cm, shorter
than the stems. Stems up to 1.5m tall, with 1–3
branches; flowers 2 per branch, light to dark
purplish-blue, with a large white patch on the
blade of the falls. Standards at an oblique angle,
not upright. Easily grown in wet ground, and
handsome with its tall stems held well above the
leaves. Hardy to −15°C.

Iris forrestii Dykes (s. *Sibiricae*)   Native of W
Yunnan, NE Burma and S Sichuan, growing in
alpine meadows at 2900–4300m, flowering in
June. Plant forming dense clumps, with stems
usually 35–40cm tall. Leaves shorter than the
flowering stems, glossy on one side, greyish on
the other. Stems with 2 flowers, 5–6cm across,
yellow with brownish-purple lines. Standards
erect, soon becoming curled (as here). Pedicels
short, less than 7.5cm long in fruit, compared
with more than 10cm in *I. wilsonii*, the other
yellow-flowered species of this group. Easily
grown in moist peaty soil. This species
hybridizes in gardens with purple-flowered
species of the section, producing brownish or
greenish flowers with various combinations of
yellow and purple.
Iris 'Charm of Finches'   raised by Hansford
Morris is a selected form or hybrid of *I. forrestii*.

Iris 'Holden Clough'   A chance hybrid
between *I. chrysographes* and *I. pseudacorus*,
which arose among a batch of seedlings of *I.
chrysographes* in the Holden Clough nursery in
Yorkshire, England, in the 1960s. This unusual
parentage is confirmed by the chromosome
number of the plant. The leaves are about 65cm
high, usually longer than the flower stems. This
grows well in ordinary good garden soil, as well
as by water, flowering in June.

Iris clarkei (Chamberlain 1631)

Iris 'Splash Down'

Iris 'Splash Down'   Raised by Hansford in
1972. Stems c.120cm. Parentage: *I. sibirica* × *I.
bulleyana*.

Iris wilsonii C. H. Wright   Native of W
China, in W Hubei, W Yunnnan and probably
also in Sichuan and Shensi, growing by streams
and in wet meadows at 2300–4000m, flowering
in July. Plant forming dense clumps. Leaves
60–75cm, often rather floppy, greyish-green.
Stems little longer than the leaves, to 80cm tall,
unbranched with 2 yellow flowers, 6–8cm
across. Standards held at an oblique angle. Falls
pale yellow, veined and dotted with brown or
purple. Easily grown in moist peaty soil or by
water. Hardy to −15°C.

Iris wilsonii at Crathes Castle

Iris 'Charm of Finches'

Iris forrestii

'Royal Blue'

Iris sibirica 'Alba'

'Savoir Faire'

'Cambridge'

'Perry's Blue'

'Skywings'

'Ego'

Iris sibirica specimens from Beth Chatto, Unusual Plants, 9 June. ½ life size

Iris sibirica (wild form) with Primula japonica

Iris sibirica 'Silver Edge'

Iris sibirica 'Alba' at Beth Chatto's

Iris sibirica, like a white form of 'Flight of Butterflies'

Iris sibirica 'Ewen'

Iris sibirica 'Ruffled Velvet'

Iris sibirica 'Caesar'

Iris sibirica L. (s. *Sibiricae*)   Native of Europe, from W France (in one place only) and Switzerland, eastwards to Russia, Yugoslavia and Bulgaria, N Turkey and the Caucasus, east to Lake Baikal, growing in wet meadows, reed swamps by lakes, and by streams, flowering in May–June. Plant forming dense clumps of narrow, upright leaves. Stems 50–120cm. Leaves to 80cm tall, 1cm wide. Flowers 1–3, to *c.*9cm from top to bottom, bluish violet, rarely white (in f. *alba*). Easily grown in moist soil by water, or in a normal border in rich soil which does not dry out in summer. Hardy to −20°C and below.

Iris sibirica **cultivars**
'Caesar'   Registered by F. Cleveland Morgan in 1930.
'Cambridge'   Registered by M. Brummitt 1964.
'Ego'   Registered by McGarvey 1965.
'Ewen'   Registered by C. McEwen 1970.
'Flight of Butterflies'   Registered by J. Witt 1972, it has small blue flowers, like the white form shown here.
'Perry's Blue'   Raised by A. Perry.
'Royal Blue'   Registered by Taylor 1932.
'Ruffled Velvet'   Registered by C. McEwen 1973.

'Savoir Faire'   Registered by S. DuBose 1974.
'Silver Edge'   Registered by C. McEwen 1973.
'Sky Wings'   Registered by W. Peck 1971.

Iris orientalis 'Shelford Giant'

Iris orientalis

Iris crocea at Sissinghurst Castle, Kent

Iris spuria (English wild form)

Iris xanthospuria (Rix 1306) from Kalkan

Iris spuria 'A. W. Tait'

Iris spuria subsp. *musselmanica* at Erevan Botanic Garden, Armenia

Iris crocea Jacq. syn. *I. aurea* Lindl. (s. *Spuriae*)   Native distribution uncertain, but found, usually near cemeteries, in the Kashmir valley at 1600–2000m, flowering in June. Stems to 1.5m, or to 2m in gardens. Leaves 1.5–2cm wide. Similar to a yellow *I. orientalis* but with larger flowers, 12–18cm across. Easy to grow in good rich soil and full sun. Hardy to −20°C.

Iris lactea Pallas (s. *Ensatae*)   Native of C Asia, from Kazakstan eastwards to Korea, in N and W China and in Mongolia, extending southwards to the E Himalaya from Afghanistan to N India and Xizang, growing on banks by rivers, by roadsides, between irrigated fields and by sandy lake margins and dry river beds, at 800–3700m, flowering between May and July according to altitude. Plant forming dense clumps. Leaves greyish green, to 6mm wide, rather stiff. Stems 15–30cm, 1–2 flowered. Flowers usually pale bluish, sometimes white, 4–6cm across, scented. This rather modest species is likely to be exceptionally hardy, and easily grown in climates with warm summers, in moist, sandy soil.

Iris missouriensis Nutt. (s. *Longipetalae*)   Native of W North America, from Mexico northwards to British Columbia, eastwards to South Dakota and Alberta, and common in inland California, especially on the eastern side of the Sierra Nevada. It grows in wet meadows and marshes, pine woods or by streams, at up to 3000m, flowering in May–July, according to altitude, in areas wet until flowering, but often dry later. Plant forming extensive dense clumps, often covering large areas. Leaves grey-green, 3–6mm wide. Stems 20–50cm tall, branched, with pale-bluish or whitish flowers, solitary or in pairs; bracts transparent, papery, greenish at the base and on the keel. Falls to 6cm long, 2cm wide; standards *c.*1cm wide. Easily grown in a sunny position, kept wet in spring. Brian Mathew recommends transplanting this species in spring or early autumn, not in summer.

Iris orientalis Mill. syns. *I. ochroleuca* L., *I. spuria* L. subsp. *ochroleuca* (L.) Dykes   Native of NE Greece near Alexandropoulos and W Turkey, east to Kayseri, and on Lesbos and Samos, growing in damp meadows, marshes, and ditches up to 1400m, flowering in May–June. Stems 50–100cm. Basal leaves 1–2cm wide. Flowers 8–10cm across.
'Shelford Giant'   An extra large clone, originating near Ephesus, with stems to 2m. Easily grown in warm, heavy soil, but not always free-flowering in gardens. Like all the *spuria* irises, it takes some years to flower freely after being moved.

Iris spuria L. subsp. **musselmanica** (Fomin) Takht.   Native of N and NW Iran, the S Transcaucasus and Turkey westwards to Kayseri, growing in damp meadows, often in saline soil, on grassy plains by rivers, often in huge colonies, at 800–1900m, flowering in May–July. Stems 50–100cm. Leaves 8–17cm broad. Flowers *c.*10cm across, usually bluish, but white plants are common among the blue, with the haft of the falls equal to or little longer than the blade. Easily grown in warm, rich soil, but susceptible to slug damage, so less robust than *I. orientalis* or *I. xanthospuria*.

Iris spuria L. subsp. **spuria**   Native of Europe, from England, in Dorset and Lincolnshire, to S Sweden, and east to Hungary and Czechoslovakia, growing in wet meadows and saline marshes, flowering in June–July. Stems

Iris missouriensis in NE California in a marsh

Iris missouriensis

Iris missouriensis

30–80cm; flowers 6–8cm across, with the haft of the falls much longer than the blade. 'A. W. Tait' is an attractive form, more free-flowering in gardens than most, and easy in normal garden soil.

Iris xanthospuria B. Mathew & T. Baytop syn. 'Turkey Yellow'   Native of SW Turkey near the coast east of Muğla, and in Hatay, and possibly also near Ankara, growing in marshy fields, in *Eucalyptus* plantations and by streams, which may dry out in summer, flowering in April–May. Stems to 1m or even 2m in gardens. Leaves 1.5–2cm across. Flowers 9–11cm across. Easily grown in good, heavy garden soil in full sun. Hardy to −15°C at least.

Iris lactea

Iris 'Cambridge Blue' at Hidcote Manor, Gloucestershire

Iris 'Custom Design'

Iris monnieri

Iris monnieri DC. (*Iridaceae*) This is now considered by Brian Mathew to be an ancient hybrid between *I. orientalis* and *I. xanthospuria*, introduced to France and there known as 'Iris de Rhodes', when painted by Redouté in the early 19th century. The flowers are pale lemon yellow, but the plant is otherwise similar to *I. orientalis*. *Iris* 'Ochracea', the hybrid between *I. orientalis* and *I. crocea*, has deeper-yellow flowers, and tall stems to 1.5m.

Iris spuria cultivars These cultivars all form strong-growing upright plants around 2m tall, flowering mainly in June. They require good, rich, moist soil and full sun if they are to flower freely and do better in continental climates with hot summers. They require a year or two to settle down and flower freely after planting, but are then good perennials. Because of their hardiness and tolerance of heat, as well as saline or alkaline soils, *spuria* iris hybrids are popular in the inland parts of the United States. Most of the modern hybrids have been raised in America, and the colour range and flower shapes are continually being improved. The species from which these hybrids were derived are shown on the previous page. Numerous new cultivars have been named, including bicolours, and flowers which contain brown and red-purple shades. 'Adobe Sunset', 'Imperial Bronze', 'Red Clover' and 'Cherokee Chief' sum up the newer hybrids. Most of these plants were photographed at Wisley, where they may be seen growing in a trial.

'Cambridge Blue' Introduced by Barr and Sons in 1924. The original hybrid between *I. monnieri* and *I. spuria*, 'Monspur', was made by Sir Michael Forster, and from this cross, Thomas Barr bred 'Cambridge Blue', 'Premier', and 'A. J. Balfour'.

'Clarke Cosgrove' Raised by B. Hager in the USA in 1974.

'Custom Design' Raised by B. Hager.

'Dawn Candle' Raised by Ferguson in 1965.

'Media Luz' Raised by B. Hager in 1967.

'Norton Sunlight'

'Protégé' Raised by B. Hager in 1966.

Iris 'Cambridge Blue'

Iris 'Dawn Candle'

Iris 'Clarke Cosgrove'

Iris 'Norton Sunlight'

Iris 'Media Luz' in the Trial at Wisley

Iris 'Protégé'

Iris 'Sano-no-Yuki'

Iris ensata 'Rose Queen' at Beth Chatto's

Iris 'Shihainami'

Iris 'Mandarin'

Iris 'Haro-no-umi'

Iris 'Nari-hera'

Iris pseudacorus at Gibbon's Brook, Sellindge, Kent

Iris ensata Thunb. syn. *I. kaempferi* Siebold
(s. *Laevigatae*)   Native of NE Asia, in Japan,
Korea, NE China and E Siberia, growing in
marshes, ditches and wet, grassy places,
flowering in June–July. Plant forming dense
clumps of narrow, upright leaves to 60cm tall,
1.2cm wide, with a distinct thickened midrib.
Flowering stems 40–80cm, with few branches.
Flowers purple, *c*.10cm across, with small erect
standards. Hardy to −20°C or less. For wet soil
or shallow water, if possible rather drier in
winter. The wild form is sometimes called var.
spontanea (Mak.) Nakai; the plant shown here
was collected by Brian Halliwell (BH 407X),
and has typical reddish-purple flowers. Bluer-
flowered forms were photographed in the wild
by Roy Lancaster in N China.

'Kaempferi' Irises   These are the large-
flowered cultivated forms of *I. ensata*, some
possibly hybrids with *I. laevigata*, most of
which were bred in Japan. They generally have
larger, flatter flowers, often with both inner and
outer segments rounded and ruffled. Mauve-
blue is the commonest colour, but there are also
pinks, a near crimson, white, and a pale yellow,
'Aichi-no-Kagayaki', a hybrid with *I.
pseudacorus*, which, however, is rather a poor
grower with leaves golden in the spring. All the
cultivars require moist, peaty soil, preferably
with the rhizomes above the water level, but the
roots growing down into wet soil. They flower
in mid-summer. The following is a small
selection of the cultivars established in
cultivation in Europe:

'Haro-no-umi'   Red-purple with a pale edge.

'Mandarin'   Pinkish purple.

'Nari-hera'   Deep purplish blue, double.

'Rose Queen'   Pale pink, otherwise like the
wild type in size and shape.

'Sano-no-Yuki'   Double white.

'Shihainami'   Deep purple, double.

Iris laevigata Fischer (s. *Laevigatae*)   Native of
Japan, Korea, N China and Siberia from Lake
Baikal and the Altai eastwards, growing in
marshes, by lakes and rivers, flowering in May–
July, usually before *I. ensata*. Plant forming
loose clumps, with rather spreading rhizomes.
Leaves 40–60cm long, to 4cm wide, without a
distinct midrib. Stems 30–70cm, usually 3-
flowered. Flowers 8–10cm across, bluish, rarely
white. Easily grown in wet ground or shallow
water. The commoner clone in gardens, shown
here, often has flowers again in the autumn, and
there is also a striking variegated form. Hardy to
−20°C and below.

Iris pseudacorus L. (s. *Laevigatae*) **Yellow
Flag**   Native of Europe, from the Faeroes,
Ireland and Scotland, south to North Africa and
east to W Siberia, the Caucasus, Turkey, Iran
and Syria, naturalized in North America; it
grows in wet fields and marshes, and by rivers
and lakes, flowering April–August. Stems to
150cm. Leaves 1.5–3cm across. Flowers
7–10cm across. There is a pale-yellow-flowered
form, and var. *bastardii*, in which the flowers
lack the brownish markings. This has been
hybridized with *I. chrysographes* to give 'Holden
Clough' (see p.221), and with *I. ensata* (see
above). There is also a stripy-leaved form of *I.
pseudacorus*, 'Variegata', with leaves yellow-
centred with pale-green edges when they
emerge. Later the whole leaf becomes pale
greenish. A double-flowered form is also in
cultivation.

Iris laevigata

Iris ensata (wild form)

Glossary

* indicates a cross-reference

Acuminate gradually tapering to an elongated point

Acute sharply pointed, with an angle less than 90°

Amplexicaul with the base of the leaf encircling the stem

Anther the part of the *stamen which contains the pollen

Anthesis the time of opening of the flowers

Axil the angle between the leaf stalk and the stem

Bract a modified leaf below a flower

Bracteole a small *bract

Bulbil a small bulb, sometimes produced by a plant instead of a seed

Calyx the outer parts of a flower, usually green

Canaliculate with the sides turned upwards, channelled

Capsule a dry fruit containing seeds

Carpel the part of the flower which produces the seeds

Ciliate with a fringe of hairs on the margin

Clavate shaped like a club, narrow at the base, swelling towards the apex

Clone the vegetatively propagated progeny of a single plant

Cordate heart-shaped, with rounded lobes at the base

Corolla the inner parts of the flower, comprising the petals, usually used when the petals are united into a tube

Crenate with shallow, rounded teeth

Cultivar a cultivated variety, denoted by a fancy name in inverted commas, e.g. 'Loddon Pink'

Decumbent trailing loosely onto the ground

Dentate with sharp, regular teeth

Diploid containing twice the basic number of chromosomes (the usual complement)

Exserted sticking out, usually of the *style or *stamens from the flower

Filament that part of the *stamen which supports the *anther

Flexuous wavy, usually of a stem

Forma a minor variant, less different from the basic species than a *variety. Abbreviated to **f.** or **ff.** if plural

Genus a grouping of *species, such as *Iris* or *Paeonia*

Glabrous without hairs or glands

Glandular with glands, which are usually stalked, like hairs with a sticky blob on the apex

Glaucous with a greyish bloom, especially on the leaves

Globose more or less spherical

Hastate with a broad but pointed apex, and two diverging lobes at the base

Hyaline transparent, often soft or papery

Hybrid the progeny of two different species

Incised with deep cuts in the margin

Inflorescence the flowers and flower stalks, especially when grouped

Laciniate deeply and irregularly toothed and divided into narrow lobes

Lanceolate shaped like a spearhead, widest below the middle, with a tapering point

Leaflets the parts of a compound leaf

Linear long and narrow, with parallel sides

Lyrate with a broad, but pointed apex and lobes becoming smaller towards the leaf base

Monocarpic usually dying after flowering and fruiting

Nectary the part of the flower which produces nectar

Oblanceolate shaped like a spearhead, but widest above the middle

Obtuse bluntly pointed, with an angle greater than 90°

Orbicular almost round

Ovate almost round, but with a pointed apex, broader than lanceolate

Palmate with lobes or leaflets, spreading like the fingers of a hand

Panicle a branched *raceme

Pedicel the stalk of a flower

Peduncle the stalk of an *inflorescence

Peltate shaped like a round shield, with the stalk in the centre

Petal generally the coloured part of the flower

Pinnae leaflets of a *pinnate leaf

Pinnate with leaflets on either side of a central axis

Pinnatifid with lobes on either side of a central axis

Pinnule a small *pinna

Puberulent with a fine but rather sparse covering of hairs

Pubescent with a fine coating of hairs, denser than *puberulent

Raceme an *inflorescence with the flowers on a central stem, oldest at the base

Rhizome an underground modified stem, often swollen and fleshy

Rootstock the part of the plant from which the roots and the stems arise

Rosette an encircling ring of leaves

Scarious dry and papery, usually also transparent

Sepal the outer, usually green parts of the flower vs. petal

Serrate sharply and finely toothed

Sessile without a stalk

Spathulate with a broad, rounded apex and tapering into a narrow stalk

Species group of individuals, having common characteristics, distinct from other groups; the basic unit of plant classification. Abbreviated to **sp.** or **spp.** if plural

Stamen the pollen-bearing part of the flower, usually made up of *anther and *filament

Staminode a sterile *stamen, often a flattened *filament

Stigma the sticky part of the flower which receives the pollen

Stolon a creeping and rooting, usually underground stem which produces new plants

Style that part of the flower which carries the *stigma

Subcordate weakly heart-shaped at the base

Suborbicular almost round, but usually slightly narrower

Subspecies a division of a species, with minor and not complete differences from other subspecies, usually distinct either ecologically or geographically. Abbreviated to **subsp.** or **subspp.** if plural

Tetraploid with four times the basic number of chromosomes

Triploid with three times the basic number of chromosomes: these plants are usually sterile, but robust growers and good garden plants

Truncate ending abruptly, as if cut off at right angles

Umbel an *inflorescence in which the branches arise from a single point, usually forming a flat or gently rounded top

Undulate wavy, usually of the edges of a leaf

Variety a group of plants within a *species, usually differing in one or two minor characters. Generally referring to natural variations, the term *cultivar is used for man-made or chosen varieties. Adjective varietal, abbreviated to **var.** or **vars.** if plural

Index

INDEX

INDEX

INDEX

INDEX

INDEX

INDEX

INDEX